The Glamour System

The Glamour System

Stephen Gundle

and

Clino T. Castelli

First published in 2006 by
PALGRAVE MACMILLAN
Houndmills, Basingstoke, Hampshire RG21 6XS and
175 Fifth Avenue, New York, N.Y. 10010
Companies and representatives throughout the world.

PALGRAVE MACMILLAN is the global academic imprint of the Palgrave
Macmillan division of St. Martin's Press, LLC and of Palgrave Macmillan Ltd.
Macmillan® is a registered trademark in the United States, United Kingdom
and other countries. Palgrave is a registered trademark in the European
Union and other countries.

ISBN-13: 978–0–333–73380–6 hardback
ISBN-10: 0–333–73380–0 hardback

This book is printed on paper suitable for recycling and made from fully
managed and sustained forest sources.

A catalogue record for this book is available from the British Library.

Library of Congress Cataloging-in-Publication Data
Gundle, Stephen, 1956–
    The glamour system / Stephen Gundle and Clino Castelli.
        p. cm.
    Includes bibliographical references and index.
    ISBN 0–333–73380–0
        1. Lifestyles – History. 2. Fashion – History. 3. Beauty, Personal – History.
    4. Manners and customs – History. I. Trini Castelli, Clino, 1944– II. Title.

HQ2042G85 2006
306.0973—dc22   2005056373

10 9 8 7 6 5 4 3 2 1
15 14 13 12 11 10 09 08 07 06

Printed and bound in Great Britain by
Antony Rowe Ltd, Chippenham and Eastbourne

Contents

Acknowledgements

A variety of debts has been accumulated during the lengthy elaboration of this volume. Stephen Gundle, who has materially written the text, has discussed glamour with a great number of friends, colleagues, relatives and students. Their initial enthusiasm was replaced over time by a patience and forbearance for which he is grateful. In particular he would like to record his gratitude to Richard Barraclough, Guido Bonsaver, Rebecca Bonsaver, Luisa Bracchi, Stella Bruzzi, Martin Conway, Barbara Corsi, Denise Cripps, Rosalinda Dal Prà, David Ellwood, David Forgacs, Sophie Gilmartin, Robert Gordon, Athena Gourdoumbas, Caroline Hollinrake, Claire Honess, Jordan Lancaster, Giulio Lepschy, Robert Lumley, Louise Marsh, Franco Minganti, Penny Morris, Anne Mullen, Daniele Nannini, Ignazia Posadinu, Chris Rigden, Vanessa Roghi, Nina Rothenberg, Antonia Stables, Nicholas White, Nicola White, Nikola White and Susanna Zinato. Peter Kramer and Noelle Anne O'Sullivan kindly provided constructive comments on draft versions of some chapters. Thanks are due to the author's sister Alison Gundle, who provided important background references to Celtic and Arthurian mythology and some other mystical sources. Reka Buckley, who co-authored two earlier articles on glamour with Gundle, contributed significantly to the elaboration of the ideas presented here. She shared her own work with him, drew his attention to several sources and helped clarify key problems of interpretation. She also provided detailed commentary on several drafts of the text.

Acknowledgement is necessary of the important contribution of Nanni Strada to the initial elaboration of the material scenarios contained in Part II. Special thanks must also go to Sita Trini Castelli, who first introduced Gundle to her father, Clino Castelli, and therefore was pivotal in creating the collaboration that has resulted in this volume. Finally, Stephen Gundle would like to acknowledge the background influence on this work of his mother, Doreen Gundle, whose practical interests in fashion, design and textiles were a significant presence in his childhood. They have proved to have had a stronger impact on his intellectual concerns than until recently he would have acknowledged.

Introduction

In *The Stars*, the French sociologist Edgar Morin argued that, for the audience, Hollywood film stars were god-like figures, the worship of whom implied a process of spiritualisation. At the same time, however, the stars were manufactured commodities. 'The star is a total item of merchandise,' he wrote. 'There is not an inch of her body, not a shred of her soul, not a memory of her life that cannot be thrown on the market' (Morin 1960: 137). Of all the stars produced by Hollywood cinema, Marilyn Monroe was the most marketable. Originally a classically curvaceous pin-up, she was fashioned by the alchemists of 20th Century Fox into a stereotypical blonde, the dream of all returning soldiers, something that 'Michelangelo might have carved out of candy' (McCann 1988: 20). Although she was neither the first sex symbol nor the first dumb blonde, she became important because she was turned into an image of desirable female sexuality at the precise moment when this sort of appeal could be combined for the first time with wholesomeness and innocence. In films such as *All About Eve*, *Niagara*, *How to Marry a Millionaire*, *Gentlemen Prefer Blondes* and *The Seven Year Itch*, all made between 1950 and 1955, her sex appeal was normalised, even if it continued to be considered 'something to be possessed, like a mistress bought with diamonds' (Dyer 1988: 75).

Monroe's life appeared to be the epitome of glamour. An orphan from a difficult background, she managed to break into Hollywood. In 1953 she married the baseball hero Joe Di Maggio and became an American idol, half of a golden couple that captured the popular imagination. Everyone knew who she was, her picture was constantly on the covers of magazines and her every deed seemed to be covered in the press. With her repertoire of poses and trademark white, gold or red dresses, she drew the eye and confirmed her status as a star. According to custom, her private and family life was offered up for public consumption. As an object to be consumed, she lived the large-scale life that set the standard for the consumer society of the 1950s.

No star more than Marilyn Monroe represented the contradiction between the star as god and the star as commodity. In Morin's view, she was 'the last star of the past but the first star without the star system', a figure who in the eyes of posterity incarnated both the splendour of the golden age of Hollywood stardom and the human tragedies that sometimes were consumed in the shadow of the seductive mask of fame. The image of Monroe, an image that was carefully prepared, constructed and communicated during her life, and which lives on in the infinite variety of advertisements, posters, T-shirts and trinkets which continue – over forty years after her death – to bear her features, was above all a glamorous image. Typically, the image is glossy and perfect; it is standardised even though the viewer knows that behind the gloss the subject is Monroe. The dyed-blonde hair, the faultless white complexion, the dreamy eyes that look out directly at the spectator, the shiny red lips that – seductively half-open – reveal immaculate white teeth, and the celebrated beauty spot are all signs of the constructed personality. All elements of spontaneity, and most of those denoting individuality, have been eliminated. This is entirely in keeping with the process whereby Hollywood turned individuals into desirable icons for a mass audience (Ewen 1988: 89).

Like almost all stars, Monroe came from nowhere. She was neither a princess nor an heiress, but simply an ordinary girl whose success was due entirely to her looks, determination and luck. Even Graham McCann, the author of a sympathetic and non-exploitative study of the Monroe phenomenon, recognises that 'it is not clear why the tricks of tinsel town made Monroe into a star when so many other ambitious models were tried, tested and rejected (some of whom were more "typical" as the embodiments of conventional ideas of "beauty")' (1988: 21). The chance element introduces, on the one hand, an element of gratuitousness and disposability; on the other hand, a further possibility of collective identification. The glamour of Marilyn Monroe rests, in the end, on the fact that she was any girl; she was not a special being, but an envied and enviable projection of the dreams of the masses in the contemporary era.

Glamour is a term that is ubiquitous in contemporary culture yet its origins are obscure and its meanings varied. Many dictionaries date the term from the consolidation of the Hollywood studio system in the 1930s. The French *Le Robert*, identifying the term as signifying 'charme' in the realm of show business and fashion, refers to 'the tradition of Hollywood glamour', while the *Dictionary of American Slang* asserts tautologically that 'a glamour (or glamor) girl' is 'a professional beauty, a girl or woman known to the public as glamorous'. For *Webster's Third New International Dictionary* (1961), glamour is 'an elusive, mysteriously exciting and often illusory attractiveness that stirs the imagination and appeals to a taste for the unconventional, the unexpected, or the exotic'. In what is perhaps the most complete attempt at a definition offered by a dictionary, *Webster's* adds a number of secondary meanings: 'a strangely alluring atmosphere of romantic enchantment; bewitching, intangible, irresistibly magnetic charm ... personal charm and poise combined with unusual physical and sexual attractiveness'.

Etymological dictionaries trace the origins of the word glamour to sources much older than movie stardom and Hollywood in the studio era. According to *The New Fowler's Modern English Usage* (1996), glamour was originally a Scottish word. Etymologically, it was an alteration of the word grammar which retained the sense of the old word 'gramarye' ('occult learning, magic, necromancy'). When it passed into standard English around the 1830s, it did so with the meaning of a 'delusive or alluring charm'. A century later, in the 1930s, it was applied to the charm or physical allure of a person, especially a woman. After first being used in this sense in the United States, it spread to Britain and other countries. The *Oxford English Dictionary* (1989) also highlights its Scottish origins and derivation from grammar, although this is indicated to mean magic, enchantment and spells rather than necromancy and the occult. *The Oxford Dictionary of English Etymology* (1974) also makes reference to 'magic spell' and 'magic beauty' (although the meaning of the latter term is opaque). Walter Skeat, in his *Etymological Dictionary of the English Language* (1924), indicated that the term 'glamer' was used in Low Scotch from around 1700. He suggested in addition a possible connection with the Icelandic 'glàmr', which carries lunar connotations implying a lack of seriousness. *A Dictionary of the Older Scottish Tongue* (1938) reports that glamner, glaumin and glamour were all in use as well as glamer, and suggests that possibly the word derived not from grammar but rather from clamour.

The most exhaustive treatment of the term's Scottish origins is to be found in an 1879 *Etymological Dictionary of the Scottish Language*. For the volume's author, glamer or glamour was 'the supposed influence of a charm on the eye, causing it to see objects differently from what they really are. Hence to cast glamer o'er one, to cause deception of sight'. However, he does not trace it to either grammar or clamour but to splendour (glimbr in Scottish). He also makes reference to the Icelandic glàmr ('a poetical name for the moon'), but concludes that more significant than this is the term 'glam-skygn', meaning squint-eyed. In Iceland, he asserts, this affliction was sometimes seen as the effect of witchcraft or enchantment. 'Glam-sight' became illusion or moonshine in Scottish.

There are two basic roots to the word glamour, which cannot be entirely separated. On the one hand there is the strain which refers to grammar. This is not only Scottish; as Anna Laura and Giulio Lepschy point out, the old French 'gramaire' meant 'book of spells' while 'grimoire' referred to an 'obscure, incomprehensible discourse' (Lepschy and Lepschy 1992: 290–1). This is because grammarians were regarded as the possessors of a secret knowledge by those who were unable to read or write. Their books contained knowledge to which few had access and which therefore were held to be magical. The *Dictionnnaire historique de la langue française* suggests that 'grimoire' was used in the Middle Ages to refer to grammars in Latin which were incomprehensible to most people. In consequence a 'grimoire' became a book of magic. This put grammarians in the field of magicians and sorcerers as far as many were concerned. On the other hand, there is the line that comes from splendour, clamour and so on, which refers not to special knowledge but to its effects; that is to say, to bedazzlement, wonderment and deception.

All investigators of the etymology of glamour agree that Sir Walter Scott first introduced the term into literary language in his first important original poem, published in 1805, *The Lay of the Last Minstrel*. Here it was used to signify illusion and visual deception. In Scott's *oeuvre*, themes of nostalgia mixed with imaginative recreation to forge a powerful and alluring image of more heroic times. Mark Girouard has suggested that the author's biography and personal circumstances influenced his choice of themes. He was born into a family with distant connections to aristocracy. He was conscious of his ancestry and revelled in its associations. 'In general, any relationship that could be described as feudal, or involved personal loyalty, was immediately attractive to him.' 'He got a particular romantic kick out of meeting or knowing anyone who inherited a historic name or ancient traditions – from George IV downwards' (Girouard 1981: 31). In a long series of novels, poems and ballads, which drew on wide reading and extensive research, he recounted stories of violent passions, terrible feuds, great loves, chivalrous acts and deadly battles, all of which took place in a setting of lakes, mountains, forests, castles and towers. 'Everything was depicted in high contrast,' observes Girouard. 'Even the sounds were strong and simple;

armour clanged, teeth gnashed, maids shrieked, spirits groaned, hounds howled, and every knight lived in imminent expectation of "The bursting crash of a foeman's spear as it shivered against his mail" ' (ibid.: 35).

Scott drew on this literature and the history of the period to create a version that appealed to the reading public of his own time. He gave his many thousands of readers

> a Walter Scott version of the Middle Ages that captured their imagination because it was presented so vividly, was so different from the life they themselves lived, and yet seemed to express certain virtues and characteristics which they felt their own age was in need of. (ibid.: 34)

Scott felt that the distance of time was a necessary precondition for the work of imagination in which he was engaged. 'We can only now look back on it as a beautiful and fantastic piece of frostwork, which has dissolved in the beams of the sun' (ibid.: 33).

Nineteenth-century medievalism was a curious phenomenon that may be linked to romanticism, although as prominent a romantic figure as Byron dismissed what he termed 'these monstrous mummeries of the Middle Ages' in 1813 (ibid.). Much has been written about the romantic imagination. As a cultural movement operative approximately between 1790 and 1830, it grew out of the Enlightenment but stood in opposition to rationalist narrowness. Defining romanticism has taxed many historians and critics, not least because it embraced such a wide range of intellectual and cultural fields and also influenced social attitudes and political life. For this reason it is perhaps best considered as an impulse or a structure of feeling. Gauderfroy-Demombynes described it as 'a way of feeling, a state of mind in which *sensibilité* and imagination predominate over reason; it tends towards the new, towards individualism, revolt, escape, melancholy, and fantasy' (cited in Campbell 1987: 181). The sociologist Colin Campbell adds other features to the list: 'dissatisfaction with the contemporary world, a restless anxiety in the face of life, a preference for the strange and curious, a penchant for reverie and dreaming, a leaning to mysticism, and a celebration of the irrational' (ibid.: 181). In essence, romanticism emphasised creativity and the aesthetic, not just from the point of view of the artist, but also from that of the ordinary, but unique, person. In contrast to the older Christian opposition of flesh and spirit, the romantics stressed the natural, the emotional and the sensual.

Although Scott was no revolutionary, indeed he was a deferential monarchist, much of his work catered to the romantic impulse, at least in the latter's popular dimension. The impact of his work was such that it was not confined to the imagination. It was such that aristocrats and country gentlemen built castles and filled them with weapons and armour; young girls thrilled to the thought of gallant knights, loyal chieftains and faithful lovers; young men performed romantic gestures and dashing deeds in both love and war (Girouard 1981: 30). It has been said that he so glamourised the clans and the Jacobites that he virtually created the tourist industry of the Highlands and was responsible for the obsession with baronial mansions across the whole of Scotland. Scott himself was not averse to inventing rituals and pageants. He stage-managed George IV's visit to Edinburgh in 1822 and influenced the presentation of royalty more widely. As early as 1811, a travelling Frenchman compared Windsor castle as remodelled by Wyatt for George III to 'a castle of Walter Scott's own building' (ibid.: 27–8).

Although Scott popularised glamour as a term and established its associations with illusion, beauty, magic and the supernatural, it was not until Hollywood cinema made glamour its own in the 1930s that it became widely recognised not only as a feature of fiction, but also of commercial culture. This book explores in depth what happened in the period between the early decades of the nineteenth century and the second half of the twentieth, highlighting the processes, institutions and figures that produced and sustained glamour. It will be shown that in this period crucial economic, cultural and technological develop-ments occurred that led to glamour being drawn into the interstices of capitalist society as this moved from an emphasis on production to one of consumption. It will be suggested that glamour took shape first in the imaginative realm; however, with the development of commercial culture and the modern city, it rapidly acquired a material dimension. In all instances, it preserved its initial association with illusion and make-believe. To have glamour or to be glamorous was to possess a mysterious aura of desire that attracted attention and aroused emotion.

In addition to mapping the historical origins and development of glamour as it is understood today, the book seeks to theorise and cate-gorise glamour. Although many social critics and sociologists have writ-ten about topics that impinge on a possible conceptualisation of glamour, there currently exists no theory, only fragments and sugges-tions.[1] In repairing this deficit, and hopefully opening the way to fur-ther studies of the phenomenon, we wish to draw attention to glamour as a phenomenon of material culture. Given that glamour's function has always been to dazzle, to bewitch and to seduce, and that it is primarily a visual experience, it needs to be understood as much in terms of material culture as sociological concepts. In other words, while the phenomenon requires conceptualisation, it must also be understood as a complex language of colours, materials and visual effects.

Glamour, it may be argued, is integral to capitalist modernity. It emerged at a specific point in history characterised by: the shift in terms of the general order of meanings and priorities from a society dominated by the aristocracy to one governed by the bourgeoisie; the extension of commodification into ever wider public and private spheres; the development of a new urban system of life permeated by consumerism and the importance of fashion; the closer proximity of the theatre and high society; the creation of patterns of leisure shared by virtually all urban classes; and an obsession with the feminine as the cultural codifier of modernity's tensions and promise.

Glamour became more important as modernity spread and the mass media developed. Popular magazines, cinema, radio and, later, television provided opportunities for staging, representing and inventing people, events and commodities. For this reason they were seized on by retail and cultural industries. Over time, a language of commercial seduction evolved and was codified that is still in use today. It may be suggested that, in recent times, the forms taken by this language have tended to be nostalgic or to employ pastiche. The photographic spreads that appeared in the leading magazines at the time of the fashion industry's 'glamour revivals' of 1994 and 2000, for example, had a dull and familiar feel to them. The American model Caprice (Caprice Bourret), as a contemporary embodiment of glamour, seems more like a reminder of American television shows such as *Dynasty* and *Baywatch* (which themselves were influenced by classical Hollywood cinema) than an original. The values she represents – Californian beauty, jet-set lifestyle, perfect grooming – are the common currency of commercial culture. Other, even more prominent, recent or contemporary figures of glamour, such as the model Claudia Schiffer and the actress Pamela Anderson, also seem like constructed personalities whose exterior appearance contains their very essence. There are several reasons for this. One is related to the sheer quantity of glamorous images that have been produced over the last century. Today we live in a complex, highly visual culture in which the iconic images of the past have, through repetition, acquired more resonance than everyday reality. Thus contemporary images of glamour tend to work off other images, creating a self-referential cycle that reinforces artificiality.

Glamour as it is understood today, as a structure of enchantment deployed by cultural industries, was first developed by Hollywood.

In the 1930s, the major studios, having consolidated their domination of the industry, developed a star system in which dozens of young men and women were groomed and moulded into glittering ideal-types whose fortune, beauty, spending power and exciting lives dazzled the film-going public. Writing in 1939 about American film stars, Margaret Thorp defined glamour as 'sex appeal plus luxury plus elegance plus romance'. 'The place to study glamour today is the fan magazines,' she noted.

> Fan magazines are distilled as stimulants of the most exhilarating kind. Everything is superlative, surprising, exciting ... . Nothing ever stands still, nothing ever rests, least of all the sentences ... . Clothes of course are endlessly pictured and described usually with marble fountains, private swimming pools or limousines in the background ... . Every aspect of life, trivial and important, should be bathed in the purple glow of publicity ... (Thorp 1945; quoted in Richards 1984: 157–8)

Neither the *faux* medievalism of Scott nor Hollywood seems to be persuasive as a starting point for the analysis of glamour, although both, with their common emphasis on image and spectacle, are important components of any examination of the phenomenon. Hollywood in particular, as the most systematic producer of glamorous images in the twentieth century, requires analysis if the functioning of glamour in contemporary commercial culture is to be understood. Before embarking on this, however, a definition of the phenomenon should be set out. Glamour, it may be argued, is an enticing image, a staged and constructed version of reality that invites consumption. That is to say, it is primarily visual, it consists of a retouched or perfected version of a real person or situation and it is predicated upon the gaze of a desiring audience. The subjects of glamour, which may be things or people (usually transformed through a process of manufacture), seduce by association with one or more of the following qualities (the more the better): beauty, sexuality, theatricality, wealth, dynamism, notoriety, leisure.[2] To this list might be added the feminine, because display and consumption have been heavily connoted as feminine since at least the nineteenth century. Femininity, moreover, is often considered to be a masquerade, the construction of an image that matches cultural expectations. As Jeanine Basinger (1993: 129) observes, 'a woman *is* her fashion and glamour, rather than her work'.

Any theory of glamour would have to take account of its imaginative appeal, seductiveness and artificiality. It would also need to refer to persistent class divisions, the alienation of modern capitalism and the frustrations of consumer culture. Although a great deal of work has been undertaken in recent years on consumerism, fashion, photography and the media, it may be suggested that early sociologists like Werner Sombart, Georg Simmel, Thorstein Veblen and Siegfried Kracauer still have much to offer. Their contribution is important because they were writing about luxury, fashion, conspicuous consumption and cinema in a phase that witnessed the birth of glamour as a social and commercial phenomenon. Perhaps the most important starting point, however, is Walter Benjamin's concept of the decline of the aura of art in the age of mechanical reproduction. Through reproduction, art may gain commercial potential, he argued, but it loses authenticity (Benjamin 1969). Something similar can be sustained in relation to high society or fashion. Once the privileged attributes of a given class, they became commercialised and available for public consumption through the mass media and mass production. Rita Felski (1995: 20) argues that even woman loses her aura in an era of technical reproduction since femininity as nature is demystified. These ideas stem at root from Marx's theory of labour and value in industrial society. The problem is that, without aura, imagination is impoverished and commercial potential undermined. Glamour, therefore, is the manufactured aura of capitalist society, the dazzling illusion that compensates for inauthenticity and reinforces consumerism as a way of life.

In the late nineteenth century, a shift occurred in northern Europe and America as the previous concern with production gave way to a new preoccupation with consumption. The boundless capacity of manufacturers to produce goods ever more rapidly and in ever greater quantities meant that it was no longer sufficient to rely on the secular 'democratisation of desire' that accompanied the rise of the bourgeoisie.[3] Strategies of enticement were required to manipulate wants and needs, to attract interest, to promote aspirations and create rituals that made consumption satisfying. It was in this phase that modern consumption, which Guy Debord described as 'a matter not of basic items bought for definite needs, but of visual fascination and remarkable sights of things' (1995: 32), first took systematic shape. To a large extent, strategies of enticement rested on techniques of display and manipulation of the effects created through display. Merchants and pioneers of retailing drew heavily on showmanship, magic and religion. But approaches became increasingly standardised and systematic. Great attention was dedicated to where and how goods were shown and sold, advertising developed as an industry, and technology was harnessed to maximum effect. Major cities throughout the industrial world witnessed the development of zones dedicated to consumption and entertainment. Such areas were invariably close to centres of wealth and power and they quickly acquired an allure as tourist sights, places of style and opulence, and home to all that was modern and fashionable.

The ultimate purpose of such grandiose efforts was to endow commodities with an aura, a mystery or an appeal that went beyond their use-value. Although many goods, including clothes, household items and foodstuffs, continued to be sold on the basis of their practical utility (no store missed an opportunity to claim that it offered good value), others relied heavily on the ideas that were associated with them, in particular the promise of magical transformation or instant escape from the constraints of everyday life. All goods, moreover, were inserted into sales contexts that disguised their primary purpose and engendered temporary feelings of pleasure and luxury. The self-illusory, imaginative hedonism that found a practical outlet in the distractions and shopping of the late nineteenth century and after has been identified by Campbell as a defining feature of the bourgeois mentality. The daydreaming to which novelists had become so expert in catering was sustained and further stimulated in the new temples of consumption.

Commodities needed an aura because large-scale manufacturing had stripped goods of the intrinsic value that derived from their having been made by human skill and effort. The commodity was precisely an object that was conceived and fabricated in relation to a set of market relationships. Its value derived from the mediations of the market that stood between increasingly impersonal producers and dream-laden consumers. In other words, it existed in the depersonalised world of Tönnies' *Gesellschaft* and not the traditional, organic world of the *Gemeinschaft* that was favoured by Benjamin and other leftist as well as conservative critics of consumerism. In Marxian terms, it was defined in relation to its exchange value. This abstraction formed the necessary premise for the fetishisation of the commodity, which occurred by obscuring its origins and turning it into a focus of fantasy and dreams. All the institutions of mature capitalism were geared to transforming commodities into signifiers, building them up as transmitters of ideas and meanings, and enhancing their exchange value. Benjamin (1999: 182) saw the great exhibitions as cathedrals in which commodities took on metaphysical subtleties and theological niceties.

It may be argued that glamour was born at precisely the intersection of the victory of abstraction, rationality and money with the persistence at the heart of modernity of strongly irrational impulses, romantic currents, mystery and illusion. Glamour was magic, trickery and illusion which was harnessed to, while also disguising, the commercial imperative. It was not so much a quality as an effect that played on the imagination. If something attracted attention and was found to be desirable, beautiful, enviable and intriguing, then it was glamorous.

The sexualisation of the commodity was one of the central features of consumer culture as it took shape in the nineteenth century. Consumer desire was in part a deflected form of sexual desire, with eroticised objects and images capturing the attention of the status-hungry and the fashion-conscious in the commercial centres. Although the shopper was most likely to be a woman, the particular functions of allegory, metaphor and desirability conventionally ascribed to the female sex ensured that femininity rather than masculinity supplied the visual imagery of the commodity culture. 'In becoming not only the commodity's emblem but its lure', notes Abigail Solomon-Godeau, 'the feminine image operates as a conduit and mirror of desire, reciprocally intensifying and reflecting the commodity's allure' (1996: 113). Solomon-Godeau's work on the 'spectacularisation' of femininity in the early nineteenth century highlights how the preconditions were established for 'the connotative linkage of the erotics of femininity with the commodity and its assimilation to the structure of commodity fetishism' (ibid.: 114). She suggests that within lithography, narrative and mythological motifs disappeared, along with the idea of the male body as the embodiment of ideals, leaving the female figure as a subject in itself. Print culture offered men new opportunities to acquire titillating images of compliant femininity and indulge in fantasies of possession.

The formation of the 'male gaze' has been theorised by Luce Irigaray and Laura Mulvey as critical to the process whereby modern femininity incorporated an element of spectacularity or 'to-be-looked-at-ness' (Irigaray 1985; Mulvey 1989: 19).[4] The solicitation of the gaze or, in other words, the constitution of the feminine self as desirable and desiring, became a key feature of the new, publicly focused female culture of the middle–late nineteenth century, albeit mediated and conditioned by prevailing notions of class, respectability and family. It would be mistaken to suggest that all the developments of the period that came to define modernity dovetailed neatly or complemented each other, for conflicts and contradictions were equally frequent, but certainly the spectacularisation of the feminine provided a resource for store display, the periodical market and the theatre, as well as painters, photographers and the nascent advertising industry. All of these participated in the process whereby commodification and reified eroticism were conjoined.

Peter Bailey suggests that parasexuality is 'a sexuality that is deployed but contained, carefully channelled rather than fully discharged; in vulgar terms it might be represented as "everything but" ' (1990: 148). He argues that it is 'an exercise in framed liminality or contained license that constituted a reworking rather than a dismantling of hegemony' (ibid.: 149). He develops his argument in relation to a real figure – the barmaid – who, he asserts, was given a semi-theatrical staging in the Victorian era by being confined behind the bar. She shared this stage with the commodities on sale, thus implying that in some way she might also be an article for purchase and consumption. This staging constituted the barmaid as a visually available 'sex object', a fact which made her a bearer of glamour ('a distinctively modern visual property'). Her allure was compounded by the distance from customers that was maintained by the bar itself. Thus, in principle, desire for her was artificially stimulated and then managed and channelled. As Bailey puts it, 'Distance not only sustains and protects the magical property that is commonly recognised in glamour, but also heightens desire through the tension generated by the separation of the glamour object and the beholder, a separation that also functions to limit the expression or consummation of desire' (ibid.: 152). She was a decoy, used by the publican to attract customers. Her mystery stemmed from her unknown background and provenance and from the erotic association of bars with alcohol and the night.

Bailey asserts that the actress could be claimed to constitute an earlier and clearer example of 'the woman as parasexual and modern glamour object'. 'The actress was a key figure in the promotion of glamour', he argues,

> but the particular novelty of the Victorian barmaid remains in her relative ubiquity and approachability. She was an everyday phenomenon, marginally distant yet more proximate than the actress; it was … in this sense of normality that the barmaid proved so sensational. Yet, while the particular circumstances of her employment kept her a controversial figure into the 1914–18 war, she was by then much less singularly conspicuous, for her visual impact had been diminished by the more general glamorisation of women, of which she had been such a notable prototype. (ibid.: 165)

Bailey also refers to the role of actresses, chorus girls and other women workers, shop girls and so on, who entered the public sphere bringing 'further dramatic changes to the sexual landscape'.

There are a number of problems with this interpretation. First of all, it fails to locate the visual consumption of women in relation to the broader relations of spectacularisation and consumption. Second, it takes no account of the class aspects of glamour and in particular the traits and characteristics formerly reserved to the upper class that were released on to the market in the late Victorian era. Third, the focus on the barmaid, like that of Erika Diane Rappaport (2000: 198–203) on the shop girl, seems curiously marginal. These were indeed ubiquitous figures but, even though they were abstracted in musical revues, fiction and so on, their 'glamour' was in reality very modest. They were sexualised in the context of a sexualised, commodity-laden marketplace, but they were at the bottom rather than the top of the glamour hierarchy. In this sense their image was more specific than general. They were individualised and real, rendered 'glamorous' by their simple staging. It may be suggested, in contrast, that glamour had a lot more to do with artificiality and image. Bailey is right to highlight distance, mystery and theatricality, but these properties were much more those of the courtesan, actress or performer (including the socialites who entered the realm of publicity). The image of these women had little to do with their real selves and more to do with costume, make-up, photography, lighting and publicity.

The theatre and theatricality more generally provided unique opportunities for self-invention and image-making. Writing of showgirls, Andrea Stuart argues that 'extravagant lifestyles and flair for self-promotion provided a prototype for women like Mistinguett to mythologise themselves' (1996: 32). Showgirls were rootless; they were outsiders who inhabited symbolic spaces with special connotations. 'The showgirl constitutes herself through clothing. Those feathers and sequins and furs identify her to her audience, as well as seducing and bewitching them,' asserts Stuart.

> Dazzled by their shine and their sparkle, the public does not see the truth behind their revelations, the sweat that goes into the showgirl's appearance of ease, the utter contrivance needed to create the impression of such ravishing near-nakedness. These garments pretend to show us everything, displaying the breasts, framing the face, flattering the legs, but really they reveal next to nothing. There are hidden narratives beneath these sheer chiffons and lace, concealing, on occasion, the onset of age, a lack of talent, or the frailty of the flesh. (ibid.: 170)

These points are important, for they point to the illusory, oxymoronic qualities of glamour. Sleazy elegance, accessible exclusivity, democratic elitism: these are just three of the ostensibly incompatible pairings that lie at the core of glamour. It goes without saying that its capacity to combine these reinforces its importance in the creation and maintenance of bourgeois hegemony. But it also means that glamour is extraordinarily appealing as a source of self-definition and empowerment. Far more than natural, unalloyed beauty, glamour offers anyone the chance to use artifice to transform themselves, forge a new façade and escape the limitations of the physical body. Its message to everyone is that yes, you too can be gorgeous, even if you are plain or no longer young. You can submerge your real self beneath a dazzling array of wigs, feathers, sequins and heels (ibid.: 171).

The mass media, and in particular cinema, lifted glamour out of specific contexts and made it into a generalised, everyday experience. Daniel Boorstin (1962) analysed memorably in *The Image* how a 'pseudo-reality' made up of staged events, personalities made famous by publicity and other illusions had eclipsed the realities of the world. From the 1920s, the images and figures that inhabited the media realm came to have an unprecedented purchase on the public's 'psychic energy and attention' (Schickel 1976: 12). They were at once remote yet familiar, famous yet valueless, desirable yet shallow. In this way, the media were able to generate substitute forms of heroism, ciphers of admirable qualities, to compensate for their disappearance from the real world. Boorstin was referring not only to the effect of cinema but also to the press, advertising, public relations and the tourist industry. But there can be little doubt that the film industry was a central motor of a 'surreality' peopled exclusively by the well-known in which the inconveniences of daily life were erased and everything rendered euphoric and exciting. It, more than any other culture industry, created new archetypes, 'idols of consumption' as Leo Lowenthal (1961) called them, who influenced not though their moral qualities but through their lifestyles. These processes occurred as the media realm became self-sufficient.

Writing in 1970, Jean Baudrillard refined some of Boorstin's points and laid the basis for the interpretative model that he would develop over the next three decades. The flow of pseudo-events (including 'pseudo-history' and 'pseudo-culture') did not derive from reality, he argued, but were *'produced as artifacts from the technical manipulation of the medium and its coded elements'*. The basic element was not the material of exchange but exchange itself. 'It is not "consumable" ', he continued,

> unless filtered, fragmented, and re-elaborated by a whole series of industrial procedures – by the mass media – into a finished product,

into the material of finished and combined signs, analogous to the finished objects of industrial production. ... We should be careful not to interpret this immense enterprise for producing artifacts, makeup, pseudo-objects and pseudo-events that invades our everyday existence as the denaturation or falsification of authentic 'content'. (Baudrillard 1990: 92; emphasis in the original)

'The misappropriation of meaning, depoliticisation of politics, deculturation of culture, and the desexualisation of the body in mass media consumption', he argued, 'is situated quite beyond the "tendentious" reinterpretation of *content*':

It is in *form* that everything has changed: everywhere there is, in lieu and in place of the real, its substitution by a 'neo-real' entirely produced from a combination of coded elements. An immense *process of simulation* has taken place throughout all of everyday life, in the image of those 'simulation models' on which operational and computer sciences are based. One 'fabricates' a model by combining characteristics or elements of the real; and, by making them 'act out' a future event, structure or situation, tactical conclusions can be drawn and applied to reality. It can be used as an analytical tool under controlled scientific conditions. In mass communications, this procedure assumes *the force of reality*, abolishing and volatilising the latter in favour of that *neo-reality of a model* materialised by the medium itself. (ibid.; emphasis in the original)

Baudrillard stressed that simple events or, one might add, people were not consumable unless they had been 'filtered, fragmented, and re-elaborated by a whole series of industrial procedures – by the mass media – into a finished product, into the material of finished and combined signs, analogous to the finished objects of industrial production'. This might be taken to refer most obviously to the manufacture of the film star, but the implication was more general. A similar process occurred through the application of cosmetics to the face, he asserted. This involved 'the systematic substitution of ... real but imperfect features by a network of abstract and coherent messages made up of technical elements and a code of prescribed significations (the code of "beauty")' (ibid.).

Although neither Boorstin nor Baudrillard addressed the issue of glamour directly, the linkage established here between the imaginary world of the media and the application of cosmetics suggests strongly that there is a connection between the forms of social relations that gave rise to mass communication and the construction of artificial personas, personal images and desirable exteriors. If the human face constitutes the most particular mark of the individuality of the person, a window on the soul according to theological interpretations, then the glamorous face is an abstracted assemblage of desirable and seductive attributes created through the work of photographers, make-up artists, hair stylists. A face such as that of Greta Garbo was no longer the face of a person, but an image, a free-floating signifier that signified nothing beyond its ability to attract attention and express manufactured beauty. It was, Roland Barthes observed, 'an admirable face-object' (1972: 56). From this point of view, the persistent desire to uncover the reality behind the mask, the human story that could explain the image, was doomed to failure. It was, in Baudrillardian terms, a vain search for a nonexistent source. But, on the other hand, it may be seen as an indication that, seductive and fascinating though glamour might be, it can never be completely satisfying. Just as its appeal is shallow, so too is its capacity to deliver anything more than that surface appeal. The tragedy is that contemporary culture is so permeated by seductive dreams and images that Benjamin's hope that a collective awakening might one day occur leaves one wondering not only how such an event might take place, but what exactly people might awaken to. Paradoxically, few things seem more permanent than that most unstable and ephemeral of effects and sensations that is glamour. For this reason it is necessary to understand its origins and explain it.

* * *

Part I is concerned with the origins and development of glamour as a structure of enticement. The first chapter deals with the re-fashioning of elites and behaviour in the age of consumption and democracy. The second explores the growth of consumption and its connections with the feminine and the theatrical. The third is concerned with Hollywood cinema and its impact on society in the twentieth century. Part II is devoted to an examination of the material language of glamour. It presents eight categories of glamour, each of which draws on the most varied of cultural sources. The scenarios that are described together constitute a repertoire of glamour that first emerged in a systematic form in the late nineteenth century and that still functions today.

   The interest of the authors in glamour developed independently. Stephen Gundle's concerns are directed to the historical and sociological aspects of glamour. Clino Castelli's work has mainly been concerned with glamour as a visual language and its applications in the world of industrial design. These interests are reflected in the authors' respective contributions to the present volume. Gundle wrote the entire text and is solely responsible for the Introduction, the Conclusion and the three chapters that comprise Part I. Castelli conceived the scenarios that are elaborated in Part II and prepared visual versions of them (not reproduced in the present volume) together with outline texts. Gundle developed Castelli's basic scenarios into extended texts, substantially enriching them with additional references and examples. He also added an additional scenario (Exotic Enticements).

Part I
The Origins of Glamour

1
Glamour, Consumerism and the Modern City

Glamour made its appearance in the period that witnessed the erosion of aristocratic power and the adaptation and reproduction of the aura of the aristocracy for commercial or social ends. The qualities of wealth, style, leisure and beauty that were the monopoly of the nobility in feudal society became, in bourgeois society, desirable attributes that could be earned, copied or manufactured. Glamour, therefore, was not an intrinsic allure, a part of the mode of being of a given class or person, but a commodified aura that was conferred on a variety of people, places, institutions and objects. Few of these were fixed; on the contrary, the dynamic, fast-moving pace of modern society made sure that there were constant innovations in the language of desirability and the objects of desire. But, over time, glamour became a familiar, if elusive, quality that was primarily associated with the wealthy quarters of large, cosmopolitan cities, with the temples of commerce and entertainment that were located there, and with the people who worked in these or whose lifestyles were wholly or partly based on them. It also became a significant factor in the creation and maintenance of bourgeois hegemony in so far as it bound the most attractive and stylish people to the capitalist system and indeed turned them into emblems of the system itself.

It is by investigating the particular cultural configuration of the nineteenth-century city that it is possible to identify the sources of modern glamour. The elegance, beauty and display that had once been virtually the exclusive preserve of the court became properties that distinguished the fashionable commercial centres of the modern city. Cities were redefined as places where power was visualised and displayed; within them old hierarchies were eroded and replaced with new, more flexible ones. Although the economic and political power of the landed aristocracy was only gradually displaced in most European countries, and the cultural power of this class remained significant even into the twentieth century (see Mayer 1981), those features of bourgeois society that resembled noble continuities survived – or were reinvented – because they conformed to the practices and value system of an age that was dominated by money. In this phase the allure of the aristocracy was appropriated by institutions as well as people and manufactured in a way that made it understandable and appealing to wide social groups. In this process of reinvention, elements were incorporated drawn from the street, the exotic and the theatre. The role of spectacle, theatricality, consumption and hedonism was underlined by the growing role of the Great Exhibitions, the early department stores, show business and fashion. All of these contributed to a climate in which fleeting surface impressions and sensational visual effects acquired unprecedented importance.

This chapter is concerned with three key aspects of the period. It examines the emergence of the city as a place of social display. It draws attention to the importance of theatre and theatricality in a new culture of spectacle and consumption. It also explores the forms of desire that the bourgeois mentality cultivated and the way traders developed languages and images that corresponded to this.

From aristocratic to bourgeois rule

The precursor of modern glamour was the culture of display of the aristocratic court. Indeed, so numerous are the similarities that writers discussing court society often employ the term 'glamour' to convey its splendour and luxury. For example, Jonathan Dewald (1996: 122–4) refers to the efforts of Renaissance princes to make their courts 'more inviting and glamorous' and to the way small states 'used the glamor of their courts to establish authority and legitimacy'. He also refers to the 'exclusive glamor' of the court of Louis XIV (ibid.: 133). This use of the term is inappropriate. If glamour is to mean more than simply 'luxury, excitement, display', and is to take on quite precise temporal and conceptual connotations, then clear distinctions need to be drawn between the opulence of aristocratic court society and the role of ostentation and luxury in bourgeois society. Glamour is in fact a specifically modern phenomenon that requires, as conditions of its existence, a high degree of urbanisation, the social and physical mobility of capitalist society, some sense of equality and citizenship (but not necessarily democracy), and a distinctive bourgeois mentality. Naturally, this does not mean that there are no continuities at all between splendour and glamour. Both involve the investment of resources in exterior display, extravagance and beauty with the aim of arousing interest and bolstering the standing of an elite or a system of socio-economic organisation. However, whereas splendour had the sole purpose of establishing the unalienable superiority of an entrenched, mainly hereditary, elite, glamour involves the masses, it is comprehensible and accessible to them and requires their active participation through the dreams and practices of the marketplace. It promises them a release, an escape from their real conditions of life, even if this is largely illusory. Paradoxically, it rests on a democratisation, or at least a diffusion, of exclusivity.

Courts declined in influence as cities expanded. According to the early twentieth-century sociologist Werner Sombart (1967), the court's own thirst for luxury fuelled the development of workshops and eventually industries that acquired a rationale of their own. Even in Berlin and Vienna, where court life remained robust well into the nineteenth century, 'cultural primacy passed from court to city' (Dewald 1996: 133). Courts lost 'much of their exclusive glamor, and too much was happening outside them'. In these circumstances, old and new elites had to find novel ways of asserting their social and cultural leadership.

The redesigning of major cities was in part an act of political will. No matter how ambiguously, the bourgeois era was permeated with a democratic ethos. It rejected hereditary privilege and practised a notion of wider citizenship, if only because the risk of revolt or even revolution could not be discounted in the wake of the French Revolution and the tumults of 1848. Political power needed to be organised in such a way that it spoke to the mass of the people and meant something to them. It needed, in short, a visual dimension in terms of architecture, spaces, monuments and rituals. This necessity became even more significant in the age of empire. Manufacturing, trade and finance were the core activities of the emergent bourgeoisie and, as it grew in influence, it expected that these should be valued and rewarded. The old structures of cities that in many cases dated from the Middle Ages threatened to collapse as a result of growth. They had to be modified to accommodate railway networks and wider roads. New commercial centres were required where wealth could be exhibited and the goods of the industrial age displayed for sale. The invention of gas lighting also changed the nature of city life by introducing visual effects and opening up the night.

Urban reform of sorts had begun in the late 1700s, but it developed markedly in the new century. Modifications to public spaces and facilities were informed by the bourgeoisie's basic ideas about nationalism, citizenship, public and private, self-denial and gratification, modesty and display. In an era that witnessed the expansion of the public sphere, institutions were required to signal their importance by means of their location and imposing architecture. Criteria of efficiency and rationality were brought to bear on issues of public health, transport and street lighting. Road systems were made more logical, city walls pulled down and buildings erected that were functional and standardised. Houses were not geared solely to the needs of display, as private interior spaces were broadly as important as those intended for entertaining. Houses of the middle and the upper classes differed in size and location, but were organised, in theory at least, on the basis of similar concepts of privacy, cleanliness, morality and orderliness. Yet, despite a notional sense of equality, the pattern of urban reform catered mainly to the requirements of the wealthy. Public spaces were geared to private display and private enterprise was given free rein. The city became a stage for those who were profiting from industrialism to parade their success. Because the era believed in earned material rewards, the poor were not accepted but despised.

London was one of the first major cities to undertake significant reform in the 1840s and 1850s. This was not wholesale modernisation; there was no dramatic overall shift in the profile of the city and no strategic design that encompassed all facets of urban life. Rather, the process of change and improvement was piecemeal, with some important innovations and the construction of some prestigious new locations, such as Regent Street, Piccadilly, Trafalgar Square and The Mall, while elsewhere medieval and Tudor streets and buildings remained. If London pioneered some aspects of urban reform, Paris extended these and fashioned them into a model. Napoleon III's regime, even in his day, was mocked for its carnivalesque qualities and the emperor himself compared unfavourably to his more famous uncle. But by promoting the reform of Paris, Louis Napoleon succeeded in turning the French capital into a paradigm of the modern city. He was impressed with the changes taking place in London and was aware of the civic progress of American cities such as Philadelphia and Chicago. He was determined that Paris should not be left behind and indeed that under the Second Empire it should reassert the primacy that the French royal court held during the reign of Louis XIV.

In the 1830s, Paris was still largely a medieval city. It was riddled with narrow, winding streets that let in neither sun nor air. Lacking sanitation, it stank and was disease-ridden. In 1832, 20,000 Parisians died from cholera. Although pavements had been laid, some new squares built and roads improved, reform had been limited. The old structures were collapsing to the point that not even the brilliant social life that conventionally characterised the city could conceal the squalor (see Marchand 1993: 27–8; Guerrand 1992: 205–6). Unlike some, Louis Napoleon had no sentimental attachment to the given forms of the city and he championed its radical transformation. This major task was entrusted to Georges-Eugène Haussmann, appointed Prefect of the Seine in 1853 and architect of what would become the *ville bourgeoise*. By skill, energy and determination, Haussmann substantially modified the city in the years up to 1870, depriving it of its haphazard spontaneity and imposing bourgeois criteria of rationality. Appropriately, given the emperor's desire to improve transport communications and free spaces around great monuments such as the Louvre and the Hôtel de Ville, he is best remembered for having demolished vast swathes of the centre and for creating the majestic *grands boulevards*. In this way Paris was centralised and made to fit a rational scheme. On the model of London, water supplies, sewers, parks and proper roads were introduced. Housing was also standardised in the form of many impressive but monotonous blocks that contained dwellings in a variety of sizes. Only external ornamentation provided variety and some aesthetic distinction.

Haussmann's reforms were much criticised as artificial by those who believed cities should grow and develop gradually, preserving their variety and character. Many Parisians claimed that they did not feel at home in a city whose main lines had been imposed from above. Contemporaries lamented the mixture of influences drawn from Gothic, Renaissance Byzantine and Louis XIV periods (Lameyre 1958: 282–3). The writer Emile Zola dubbed the new city an 'opulent bastard' (Marchand 1983: 97), an expression that might legitimately be applied to the whole of the Second Empire and even to the bourgeois age itself. Only later would decoration and design restore an atmosphere of charm.

The new city introduced new criteria of political and social rule. The boulevards opened out the city and imposed a long perspective that rendered its core visible and decipherable, as well as easier to occupy militarily should the need arise. The poor, who could not afford to live in the new housing that replaced the slums, were obliged to move to the east while the west was turned into a residential area for the rich and a site of public display. It was here that monuments, squares, parks, boulevards and palaces made Paris a showcase within which the regime developed its visual dimension and the wealthy and stylish flaunted their social superiority.

All redesigned and modernised cities dazzled in new and unfamiliar ways. Major cities throughout the industrial world witnessed the development of zones dedicated to consumption and entertainment. Such areas were invariably close to centres of wealth and power and they quickly acquired allure as tourist sights, places of style and opulence, and homes to all that was modern and fashionable. Zola, Valland and other writers offered accounts of the city lights of Paris as suggesting a magical fairyland. For Christopher Prendergast, the flickering lights of the shop fronts, creating the illusion of daylight, and the blaze of gas lamps on café tables 'recapitulated the myth of the illuminated city' (1992: 40). The lights of the city, he argues, were linked to the lure of the city, they were beckoning signs of what was deceptively promised by the new and fast-growing culture of leisure and pleasure.

Theatre and theatricality

The Second Empire invested massively in the outward signs of majesty. Because it was a dictatorship, uncertain of its prestige, it made ample use of colour, pomp and display. This emphasis was not in itself exceptional. What distinguished Louis Napoleon's regime was the exuberance with which it embraced spectacle. It set standards for pomp and ceremony that even outdid those of Napoleon I. But, like most things about the regime, there was something implausible, even unreal about them. Traditionalist visitors found the magnificence of the imperial household, with its vast numbers of attendants and extravagant lifestyle, to be excessive, even 'parvenu-like' (Kracauer 1937: 175). The court itself was not a centre of culture, and the emperor and empress were frequent visitors to Parisian theatres, but the costume balls, where guests were restricted to those who had been presented, were the highlights of the social calendar. Haussmann has been described as the emperor's stage designer and certainly one of his tasks was to organise the huge balls that constituted the grandest moments of the regime's ceremonial. Every year between January and Lent four were held and 4000–5000 guests were invited to each.

Dazzling displays were crucial to the Second Empire and to the new spirit of enforced gaiety that was favoured. Surfaces, theatrical effects and illusions of grandeur were important elements of its syncretic style. Siegfried Kracauer argued that Louis Napoleon was obliged to proclaim a policy of 'joy and glamour' to maintain himself in power. In order to cover over social contradictions that no amount of political dexterity could have resolved, he decided to banish all sense of realism in the hope that in this way latent antagonisms would go unperceived: 'Hence the motto of joy and glamour – the joy was to intoxicate, and the glamour to dazzle' (Kracauer 1937: 117). To this end lavish expenditure was embarked upon and sumptuous splendour became the hallmark of the round of socialising that had at its core the presidential palace and the improvised court.

More programmatically and continuously than the court, the commercial theatre was vital in creating a pattern of distraction. The new theatres of the Empire were not the same as the small commercial theatres that had been so popular in earlier decades. Most of these were destroyed as part of the urban reform and replaced by larger public theatres that were located in the centre, in contrast to the *ancien régime*, which had banished them to the periphery. One of the centrepieces of the reformed city was the giant new opera house that occupied its own specially constructed square, the Place de l'Opéra. Although it did not open until 1875, it was entirely conceived and very largely built under the Second Empire. Endowed with an elaborate, sculpted façade, a grand foyer staircase, an enormous stage and ceilings decorated with mythological scenes, it was a work in all styles and none. When she first saw the architect Garnier's plans, Empress Eugenie is reported to have asked, 'What style is that? That's no style – not Greek, not Louis XIV, not even Louis XV.' Garnier replied: 'Madame, those styles were for those times. This is the style for the time of Napoleon III' (quoted in Christiansen 1994: 394). More than anything else, Joanna Richardson observes, 'it represented the love of show, the superficial splendour of the time; it also reflected the extreme materialism of Second Empire society' (1971: 229). Like a giant wedding cake, it was 'brilliant, vulgar, gay, monstrous and imposing', the most opulent monument in the whole city (ibid.: 228).

No cultural form reflected the eclecticism and materialism of the age more than operetta. Under the Second Empire, attention was diverted from authoritarianism and dictatorship through economic prosperity and the theatre. At this time, Kracauer (1937: 129) noted, the theatre became the centre of social life. The works of Offenbach and his young imitator Hervé enjoyed great popularity. As theatre boomed, it was their operettas that appealed to wide audiences with their vivid spectacles, improbable plots and melodious, sentimental music. Offenbach is particularly remembered for the genius and wit with which he captured and satirised the contemporary obsession with money, social status and display. His work ranged from the mythological, as in *Orphée aux enfers* and *La Belle Hélène*, to the contemporary *La Vie Parisienne*, which opened in 1866 and ran for nearly 200 performances. The ostentation of abundance and the pleasure of movement and variety were vital building blocks in the construction of a pattern of escapism based on distraction. The French theatre of the 1850s and 1860s offered mild satire but, because of censorship, mainly provided noise, excitement and display – symbolised most explicitly by the crinoline and the can-can. Opulence, sensory excitement and the dream of sudden wealth constituted the stock-in-trade of operetta, an entertainment form that was driven on purely by money and spectacle. Offenbach's theatre 'was meant to be a kind of foretaste of paradise', Kracauer reflected, 'and in paradise there must be superficiality' (ibid.: 161).

Operetta was a part of a mass culture that could only have developed in the modern metropolis (Hanák 1998: 136). It was also vital in marking the origins of a modern dream world. Although politics provided the framework for this and exploited some of its possibilities, theatre and commerce played the leading role. It was through visual stimulation and entertainment that a common culture unifying urban populations took shape. Thus operetta was a quite widespread phenomenon. In England Gilbert and Sullivan emerged as its chief practitioners, while later, in Vienna, Johann Strauss and Franz Lehár, author of *The Merry Widow* and *The Count of Luxembourg*, fuelled a medium that communicated ideas about the modern city to a wide range of social strata. In all instances, operetta was an eclectic mish-mash that performed a function of social reconciliation by exchanging the sententiousness and melodrama of opera for a hybrid form which included folk motifs and catchy songs and depicted a wide range of popular figures, often drawn from the world of the theatre.

In tune with the emphasis on exterior display that musical theatre pioneered, mainstream theatre itself changed, becoming markedly more visual. In England as in France, audiences looked to the theatre for excitement and escape. 'Patrons of "high" and "low" theatre shared a predilection for variety and colour in entertainments', observes Russell Jackson, 'and the mish-mash of drama, circus and pantomime available at such establishments as Astley's [reflected] a love of novelty and brightness that appears to have transcended class barriers' (1989: 10). Costumes, 'pictorial splendours' and the pursuit of illusion were feared by some contemporary observers to be displacing the ability to treat human feeling and behaviour (ibid.: 2). Leisure took on some of the same characteristics. London's Cremorne Pleasure Gardens, one of the first dedicated sites of organised commercial leisure, opened in 1846 and remained popular until its closure in 1877. It was a sort of proto-theme park which consisted of a variety of entertainments including fireworks, a theatre, balloon trips, an American bowling saloon, bars, a supper-room and dancing. Open by day for families, it seemed more magical and alluring – even 'Parisian' – by night due to artificial illumination and a certain sexual *frisson* (see Need 2000: 118–31; Sweet 2001: 214–15).

The connection between visual splendour, eclecticism and political authority was especially marked in France but, even outside the euphoric context of Louis Napoleon's regime, the legitimation of power was becoming increasingly theatrical and theatre was acquiring new importance. The invention of colourful ceremonials around the British monarchy did not develop fully until the 1880s, not least because of Queen Victoria's personal disinterest in them, but the awareness of the utility of royal pageantry was present considerably earlier (Hayden 1987: 54). State occasions even in the first half of the nineteenth century contained novel elements of choreographed pomp. The revivalist nature of the symbolic aspects of ceremonial meant that it took on the features of a theatrical show (Burns 1972: 210). Historical re-enactments of all types were designed to impress with their false timelessness. Above all, Walter Scott's hugely popular literary works were instrumental in stimulating historical fantasies and in nourishing their development. He personally choreographed George IV's visit to Edinburgh in 1822 and contributed to the fashioning of other official rituals.

Colin Campbell (1987: 89) has stressed the importance of dreaming and yearning to a bourgeois mentality that was predicated on deferred gratification. The consequences of the development of this new mentality could be seen in both the tendency of pageantry and theatricality to be incorporated into statecraft and in the growing importance of contemporary urban life in theatre. These elements were mutually reinforcing. If theatricality in ordinary life consists of a resort to 'a special grammar of composed behaviour', as Elizabeth Burns argues, then 'the theatricalisation of public life entails a heightened awareness and manipulation of frames and settings in which action is staged' (1972: 10). The point can be seen in relation to a curious double tendency that growing theatricalisation brought. It might be said that as history plays moved from the stage to the realm of government, social life incorporated elements of façade and performance.

Far from being limited to the mannered world of the court, role-playing and fantasy became defining features of metropolitan life. In the feudal era, rank was broadly fixed and the social hierarchy only moderately flexible. Even the efforts of wealthy merchants to outdo the nobility in the matter of luxury were regulated through sumptuary laws. The bourgeois era was in theory more open. Unlike the court, which was open to the few, the city was open to all; money and economic values were dominant, not patronage. Consequently, cities became sites of social interaction where issues of impression and appearance were central. The public spaces of cities were inhabited by all manner of people who were unknown to each other and who took on roles in their social relations (Need 2000: 65). Gaslight turned the streets into a stage in which glowing illumination of the sort widely used in theatre made even the humble appear picturesque. Writing in 1839, Dickens (1957: 55) noted how 'theatrical converse' had become common currency in a London that was filled with people aspirant above their actual station. Would-be aristocrats, swaggering apprentices, shabby-genteel people, theatrical young gentlemen and bragging impostors fill the sketches he authored under the pseudonym of Boz. In the same period, Baudelaire identified the *flâneur* and the whore, two specialists of appearance and spectacle, as the emblematic figures of modernity, the embodiment of the street culture of the modern city.

The fluidity of identities in popular and high theatre resembled and reinforced the performative aspects of modern daily life. In the countries of northern Europe and the United States, where the puritan tradition was strong, a sharp battle was waged against masquerades and showy exteriors in general. In their place the ideal of sincerity was articulated and asserted. The theatre was singled out for revulsion because it was seen as 'the ultimate, deceitful mobility' (ibid.: 4). In her study of the United States, Karen Halttunen (1982) shows that the polemic against hypocrisy and fashion was motivated by fears that falsity and theatricality were becoming dominant. The concern with externals and the opportunities for impression management that the new era brought were seen as threatening. Advice manuals warned of the empty and deceptive men and women who inhabited the cities. In sensationalist novels as well as moral tracts, the metropolis was a place of uncertainty in which characters appeared and disappeared in different guises; nothing was as it seemed; confidence men abounded (Lears 1994: 55). In situations where people systematically encountered others of whom they knew nothing, 'fair exteriors' and 'winning manners' could disguise imperfections of character or background (Halttunen 1982). Just as Louis Napoleon could cast himself in the role of emperor so, at a more ordinary level, could a trickster appear to be a gentleman or a prostitute adopt the manners of a respectable lady. Halttunen argues that the phase of hostility was brief since middle-class desires to rise on the social scale informed a vogue for private theatricals in the 1850s and 1860s. She shows that social forms evolved in such a way as to accommodate the theatricality and front that were becoming key features of modern urban life.

Dreams and desires

Historically, the aristocracy had been the leading consuming class. Although merchants and other wealthy persons had in past eras competed with aristocrats in the matter of splendour, this had normally been kept under some control through hereditary privileges and other favours granted selectively by monarchs, as well as sumptuary laws. With the advance of democratic ideas and the erosion of privilege, the bourgeoisie fashioned itself as a class that asserted itself through a set of practices rooted in consumption. This did not simply involve one class taking over the customs of another. It was a complex transition that involved a clash of cultures and mentalities. As a class whose members were constantly seeking to be better or different from what they really were, the bourgeoisie selectively appropriated fragments of culture from the past and elsewhere. The desirable images of the age were shot through with appropriations of aristocratic rituals and visions of faraway places.

Campbell (1987: 8) has demonstrated persuasively that the bourgeois idea of luxury was different from the aristocratic one. 'The expression of a seignorial ethos of rank' through full-time extravagance and indulgence aroused a deep-seated moral antipathy (Elias 1983: 53), as did the aristocrat's obsession with externals, honour and the refined life. The bourgeois was internally-driven; consequently he was emotional and passionate where the aristocrat was aloof and controlled. Precisely this different emotional condition produced a desiring or yearning predisposition that fuelled aspirations and dreams (Campbell 1987: 35–8). Campbell suggests that, whereas the hedonism of the aristocracy was geared towards the satisfaction of specific pleasures, the key characteristic of bourgeois hedonism was insatiability, the apparently limitless pursuit of wants. The bourgeois idea of pleasure was more abstract and free-floating; it was emotional and psychological in nature. 'Modern autonomous imaginative hedonism', as Campbell calls it, accorded a particular role to the imaginative dimension, making desiring the satisfaction of wants a pleasurable activity in itself: 'Individuals employ their imaginative and creative powers to construct mental images which they consume for the intrinsic pleasure they provide, a practice best described as day-dreaming or fantasizing' (ibid.: 77).

This mentality is central to glamour. In the bourgeois age, the construction and consumption of attractive mental images were not purely individual matters. It was a collective process that was linked to institutions such as the theatre and to urban architecture. The earliest forms of pleasurable escape through material fantasy stressed remote historical periods; later, remote geographical places were evoked. An important part of the art of the Victorian era, like the literature of the period, was marked by fantastic evocations of the distant past. Artists specialised in producing works that refashioned Arthurian themes, classical figures or Renaissance techniques and colours. 'The new rage for many-coloured embellishments' was a trait of the period (Steegman 1987: 308). These were generally lifted out of their contexts and re-elaborated in such a way that their evocative, imaginative qualities were highlighted at the expense of any presumption of historical accuracy. The British painter Sir Edward Burne-Jones, for example, described his work in the following terms: 'I mean by a picture a beautiful romantic dream of something that never was, never will be – in a light better than any light that ever shone – in a land no-one can define or remember, only desire' (Birmingham City Art Galleries 1999). Such statements demonstrate that these images were entirely bourgeois confections; they were depictions of the aristocratic past that served contemporary purposes. Nostalgia disguised an 'anguished longing to return home; not just to go somewhere else, but to go home' (Steegman 1987: 310).

The self-illusory, imaginative hedonism identified by Campbell found a practical outlet in cultural practices that took shape around shopping. The daydreaming to which novelists had become so expert in catering was sustained and further stimulated in the new sites of consumption. Shopping as it developed in the first half of the nineteenth century was a wholly new experience that was so central that it became a vital feature of the reformed city. Urban commercial culture first captured the attention of Baudelaire in the 1840s. The prince of the decadents was the first to celebrate the new elements that comprised the spectacle of the city. His careful descriptions of the surface splendour of café life bore witness to his own 'dazed enchantment' and revealed 'the dream-machine in action', in so far as it exposed 'the terms on which the city entices into a fantasy of comfort, luxury and gratification' (Benjamin 1973: 37). What made modernity dream-like was its ability to offer a semblance of transcendence, to work on the secret hopes and fears of people and to construct imaginative realms that stimulated the senses while dulling the intellect. At first, the dream was fragmentary and restricted to certain moments and settings. But in the course of the nineteenth century it became collective and spread from the middle classes to the upper ranks of the workers.

As far as glamour is concerned, Campbell's work only allows us to understand the context of its development. He stresses a predisposition towards soft-focus projections of a modified reality and explains some fundamental reasons for the extraordinary popularity of Scott's medieval pastiches. Yet he has little to say about the actual development of the institutions and practices of modern consumerism. This needs to be accounted for because, for the first time, new methods of production brought household articles and other items within the reach of far wider groups than ever before. The boundless capacity of manufacturers to produce goods ever more rapidly and in ever greater quantities meant that it was no longer sufficient to rely on the secular 'democratisation of luxury' that accompanied the rise of the bourgeoisie. The presence of cultural obstacles to continuous acquisition meant that strategies of enticement were required to manipulate wants and needs, to attract interest, to promote aspirations and create rituals that made consumption satisfying. Consequently, techniques of persuasion were necessary as the previous emphasis on production gave way to a new preoccupation with consumption.

Writing in the 1930s, Walter Benjamin identified the elegant covered arcades that sprang up in the early nineteenth century as the prototypical setting of the consumerist dream world. In the warren of little shops with their display windows, he wrote, 'commodities are suspended and shoved together in such boundless confusion, that [they appear] like images out of the most incoherent dreams' (Benjamin 1993: 254). Shops adopted plate glass, luxurious interiors and a host of other enticements to turn shopping into a captivating event. 'Anyone who lost his way in these passages might well have been pardoned for supposing that he had entered a fairy grotto,' observed Kracauer, another critic at the margins of the Frankfurt School who focused on this period. 'The city's magic seemed concentrated here. Remote from earth and sky, it seemed a realm exempt from natural laws, preserving marvellous illusions, like the stage' (1937: 22). Lighting contributed most obviously to the function of the city as visual spectacle in the allure it conferred on the commodities, places and people. Gas lighting enhanced all private as well as public display. In Prendergast's view, 'The ostentatiously lighted interiors of Balzac's Birotteau and Crevel signify, awkwardly and crudely, the acquisition of wealth, as will later the invention of electro-plating, designed to give a fake aura of luxury to the household utensils of the bourgeoisie' (1992: 34). Some sort of aristocratic imprint in matters of style and decoration was necessary to a status-conscious bourgeoisie that lacked a confident style of its own. In the modern city wealth, prestige, class and the perceptions of these qualities were matters of social import in which everyone participated.

Commodities needed an aura because large-scale manufacturing had stripped goods of the intrinsic value that derived from their having been made by human skill and effort. The commodity was precisely an object that was conceived and fabricated in relation to a set of market relationships. Its value derived from the mediations of the market that stood between increasingly impersonal producers and dream-laden consumers. In other words, it existed in the atomised, depersonalised world of modernity and not the organic world that Benjamin and other leftist as well as conservative critics of consumerism favoured. In Marxian terms, it was defined in relation to its exchange value rather than its use value. This abstraction formed the necessary premise for the fetishisation of the commodity, which occurred by obscuring its origins and turning it into a focus of fantasy and dreams (Jhally 1987: chapter 2).

Benjamin's socio-psychological interpretation of modernity as a dream world has been widely referred to in analyses of mass consumption. As a Marxist, Benjamin used the metaphor of the dream to theorise the possibility of a collective 'awakening' in the form of the emergence of revolutionary consciousness (in Buck-Morss 1990: 253). This view is in contrast to that of Campbell, who stresses the individual satisfactions to be derived from daydreaming. Benjamin did not deny such pleasures, but he thought they would stimulate action by offering glimpses of a utopia that could never be realised in bourgeois society. He saw capitalist modernity as having brought about a re-enchantment of the world and a 'reactivisation of mythic powers' (ibid.: 254). According to his interpreter, Susan Buck-Morss, underneath the surface of increasing systemic rationalisation, on an unconscious 'dream' level, the new urban-industrial world had become fully re-enchanted:

> In the modern city, as in the ur-forests of another era, the 'threatening and alluring face' of myth was alive and everywhere. It peered out from wall-posters advertising 'toothpaste for giants' and whispered its presence in the most rationalised urban plans that, 'with their uniform streets and endless rows of buildings, have realized the dreamed-of architecture of the ancients: the labyrinth'. (ibid.: 254)

Exhibitions and department stores

Several innovations of the period were driven by the great exhibitions, mostly held in Paris, which became a hallmark of the industrial age.

They were huge encampments to which all could gain access and experience the wonders and the abundance of industry. The exhibitions were extraordinary display cases for technological innovation, manufactured products, fantasies, entertainments and goods from all over the world. They were products of the era of trade, manufacturing and empire, but the form they took reflected the nineteenth century's predilection for sensation and spectacle. Virtually every country had a section in which it presented its achievements and typical examples of its material culture. At the Paris exhibition of 1867 there were Persian gardens, an Egyptian temple, a Chinese tea-house, mini-factories, machines for making everything from shoes to soap, cookery demonstrations, hundreds of cafés and restaurants, and performances of every conceivable type. The exhibitions brought together art and commerce, technology and entertainment. The show transported visitors of all classes into a realm of possibilities that previously could not have been imagined. Consequently, they were seen as pioneers of a consumerism that was endowed with a mass dimension. They established firmly the existing links between looking, desiring and buying. For the first time, the Paris exhibition of 1855 displayed goods in a sumptuous fashion with price tags on view, giving people the opportunity to browse, explore and fantasise about potential ownership (Buck-Morss 1990: 17). They were huge in scale, highly innovative in their architecture and at the forefront of developments in applied technology.

The exhibitions were not intended merely for the elite; they reached out to the mass of the people in an effort to draw as many visitors as possible. Six million people visited the Crystal Palace exhibition of 1851 when, after the better-off had had their chance, entry price was lowered to a shilling. Five million visited the Paris exhibition of 1855 while eleven million passed through the turnstiles (then a new invention) in 1867. These figures grew to 16 million in 1878, 32 million in 1889 and an astonishing 51 million in 1900. Each time more and more foreigners made excursions to Paris for the occasion.

'The world exhibitions glorified the exchange value of commodities,' Benjamin argued.

> They created a framework in which their use-value receded into the background. They opened up a phantasmagoria into which people entered in order to be distracted. The entertainment industry made that easier for them by lifting them to the level of the commodity. They yielded to its manipulations while enjoying their alienation from themselves and from others. (Benjamin 1973: 165)

These techniques became part and parcel of retail marketing well into the first half of the twentieth century. Benjamin (1999: 182) saw the Great Exhibitions as cathedrals in which commodities took on metaphysical subtleties and niceties. The more dramatic manifestations of this process occurred in public spaces – in the construction of 'those super-windows on the commodity, the huge glass edifices of the Exposition Universelle, or in the exploitation of the large shop window in the new department store of the Second Empire' (ibid.: 34). The bourgeois era, he noted, was marked by 'a flood of deceptive surfaces' (Lears 1994: 83), by images and spectacles generated by the chaotic world of commodity culture. For Williams, 'The expositions and similar environments ... displayed a novel and crucial juxtaposition of imagination and merchandise, of dreams and commerce, of collective consciousness and economic fact' (1982: 12).

The early exhibitions contributed to the emergence and the development of the department store. Indeed, according to Bill Lancaster, 'the evolution of the department store is inexplicable without reference to expositions' (1985: 17). Although the arcades were the first buildings specifically to be erected as temples of consumption, these were fairly soon joined and eventually eclipsed by department stores. Stores stood as monuments to the grandeur and wealth of the cities which hosted them. They destroyed small shops and pioneered large-scale commerce. They contributed to the new function of the city as a 'pleasure zone', since the shopper was designated as a pleasure-seeker, defined by longings for goods, sights and public life (Rappaport 2000: 5). Like the spectator at the theatre, the shopper was a looker whose behaviour was channelled and whose fantasy was mobilised. Stores added to the brightness and magical atmosphere that marked districts characterised by wealth, power, entertainment and consumption. They extended the display culture that became a key feature of the bourgeois era as more and more objects, people and events were made visible and subjected to public inspection.

The first stores were not housed in purpose-built palaces. They grew incrementally as several small shops were knocked together and ever new departments were added. The Parisian Grands Magasins du Louvre and Bon Marché stores were at the forefront of the revolution in marketing, followed by similar institutions in England including Whiteley's and Heal's. The big stores sold huge quantities of goods to vast numbers of people at prices that were lower than ever before. The task was not to sell goods at the highest possible price, but in the largest possible quantity. Housed for the first time under one roof, the goods moreover were of every conceivable type, from household equipment and furniture to clothes, accessories, haberdashery and dress fabrics. The stores generally allowed no bargaining and denied credit. In Richard Sennett's terms, this signified a transition from the lively theatricality of the market to modern passivity. But in fact, like the theatre, the shop became the stage and provided the show (Ross 1992: viii–ix). In his novel *Au Bonheur des Dames*, published in 1883 and based on extensive research at the Bon Marché, Zola described his fictional store as a 'monster', a 'colossus' and a 'machine', terms that suggest devoration and inexorable progress. The founders of these enterprises were often outsiders, men of humble and provincial origins who contributed to the invention of the shopping metropolis. In his novel Zola (1998: 127) describes the 'Provençal verve' with which his hero, Octave Mouret, developed a spectacular style of commerce.

The stores really were miniature cities, enclosed worlds that catered to almost every need. They were part of the same phenomenon as the boulevards and the theatre. In Paris, most of them were situated on the right bank of the Seine, near Haussmann's great arteries and the Place de l'Opéra. In London, stores like Whiteley's led the way in the transformation of the districts in which they were situated. The exterior of the new Bon Marché building, opened in 1872, was stately and monumental like that of many other such institutions. The façade of grandeur gave the sense of a temple, museum or theatre. The grand style continued inside as galleries, immense staircases and halls lifted shoppers out of the everyday. One of the key innovations was display windows that led to the custom of window shopping, perhaps the archetypal expression of the bourgeois yearning identified by Campbell. The lighting systems of the boulevards and the department stores instituted a whole new set of relations between the gaze and the commodity, emphasising the process of spectacularising and fetishising of manufactured goods. The specular relation was magnified beyond measure by the Great Exhibitions, since these uniquely evoked what Georg Simmel called 'the shop-like quality of things' (Prendergast 1992: 34–5). In March 1881 *Le Figaro* wrote that 'the great bazaars are the first houses of the great city of the future. Their electric illumination is the light that protracts that of the sun into the night' (cited in Becker 1992). These stores did not draw upper-class clients, who preferred specialist boutiques and personalised service. Rather, they aimed at a predominantly middle-class clientele and as such they promoted the democratisation of luxury (a phrase that recurred in the promotional material of many stores) (Miller 1981: 165; see also Lancaster 1995; Rappaport 2000). This watchword shows how some sort of exclusivity was maintained and not abolished as the mass market developed. This paradox was vital to the development of glamour.

The Bon Marché was highly theatrical, a show, a spectacle and a permanent fair. Its founder, Aristide Boucicaut, aimed to sell the idea of consumption as well as his merchandise. He understood completely the need to create dreams, to stimulate desires and to turn shopping into a pleasurable and desirable experience. Assisted by his wife, Marguerite, he turned selling into a seduction, catering especially to the women who were his principal customers. They were drawn less by specific needs than by the excitement of the whole experience. While the theatre was, despite certain changes, an environment that was frequented more by men, the store was geared towards women. This shift of emphasis was significant; it opened the way to specifically feminine appeals that would come to be associated with glamour. The drive towards social emulation was one that accorded women a key role. A visit to the store was an event and an escape that added a new dimension to life. Boucicaut, like his fictional counterpart Mouret, was forever arranging goods in new ways, creating huge displays and linking them through themed promotions. He quickly grasped the commercial advantages of saturating merchandise with all manner of lighting. 'Part opera, part theatre, Boucicaut's eclectic extravaganza did not disappoint those who came for a show' (Miller 1981: 168). Particularly on great sale days, 'goods and décor blended one into another to dazzle the senses and to make of the store a great fair and fantasy land of colors, sensations and dreams' (ibid.: 169). Selling became a show that offered the visuals of theatre without the narrative.

Boucicaut saw that in an age that witnessed a proliferation of dreams and fantasies, it was possible to impress the store on the life of the city and more widely on the imagination. The store did not only obscure the processes whereby its goods were made and the exploitation of its own workers; it radiated a vision of newness and perfection that made the city seem wondrous, rich and stylish. Even the simple fact of the delivery of goods contained an element of splendour and romance as the store's wagons crossed Paris drawn by well-groomed horses and driven by coachmen in top hats and attended by young men in full livery. Stores could be brash and lurid, but they also embraced pomp and cere-mony, mixing stately rituals with baser passions and longings. The fla-grant falseness of the courtly appropriations was part of the store's appeal. Monumental and fantastic as it was, the store became a leading attraction, 'one of the sights of Paris,' Boucicaut claimed (ibid.: 169).

It was a tribute to his success that the first purpose-built department store in London, which opened in Brixton in 1876, was also called the Bon Marché.

The visual materials of desire, identified by William Leach with colour, glass and light, had been used for centuries by royal courts and by the military to attract devotion and loyalty and instil fear, and by religions to depict other-worldly paradises. They were now employed to suggest a this-worldly paradise that was stress-free and happy (Leach 1993: 9). The appropriation of coloured glass was seen to take selling into the realm of religion. The Bon Marché was seen as 'a cathedral of another sort, charismatically beckoning of its own world of entrancement' (Miller 1981: 177). Moreover, the cult of consumption was seen to be replacing religious devotion. Zola noted that 'the department store tends to replace the church. It marches to the religion of the cash desk, of beauty, of coquetry, and fashion' (quoted in ibid.: 177). Whereas women, the main shoppers, had previously regarded the Church as the centre of their existence outside the family, now they had a tantalising alternative.

Technology became increasingly important as capitalism moved into its corporate phase and strategies of enticement became more sophisticated and scientific. It was due, among other things, to their primacy in this field that the American stores eventually surpassed their European equivalents in both size and retail innovations (ibid.: 58). Mirrored glass proliferated in stores: it was inserted into showcases and shelving, and was suspended on walls and columns. The impact of mirrors was largely illusory; they seemed to increase the floor space; they concealed the less attractive parts of the stores; and they amplified 'the allure of goods' by 'showing them from every angle' in glass showcases. They also refracted light, enhancing the glitter that literally dazzled shoppers. Achieving the twinkle of Nirvana was no longer a chance effect but a deliberate technique. Mirrors also had the power to draw customers into a narcissistic maze of self-reflection, creating an environment in which they might interact with the goods in the most intimate and personal way. At Wanamaker's in Philadelphia in 1897, every pillar on the ground floor was encased in mirrors 'from floor to ceiling' (Leach 1993: 75).

From the 1890s, traders and commercial designers drew on myths and traditions to invest artificial things and urban spaces with plasticity and life. They aimed for theatrical effects and for a new enchantment, routinely dramatising commodities and commodity environments in ways that camouflaged and altered them (Leach 1989: 100). Department stores extended the realm of their activities to become embedded in the structured imagination of everyone, not just their customers. Several writers, including Zola and Pierre Giffard, explored the way in which the Bon Marché had harnessed a tradition of fantasy by creating a whole enchanted world of its own. 'For the bourgeois child growing up in late-nineteenth-century France, the magical, the exotic, the fantastic, and the extraordinary were still the stuff of legendary figures, fairytales, and heroes of the French nation; but they had also become the stuff of department stores as well' (ibid.: 176).

It may be argued that glamour provided the modern dream world with a material content. It was born out of the insertion of strongly irrational impulses, romantic currents and illusions at the heart of a modern culture based on abstraction, rationality and money. It was an organised form of magic and illusion that was annexed to the commercial imperative and camouflaged it. Glamour was not so much an intrinsic attribute as a manufactured quality or effect that attracted attention and rendered desirable, beautiful, enviable and intriguing those things that possessed it. It catered to the modern individual's sense of an ideal self and to aspirations for social mobility and escape from the humdrum. The nature of this aura was varied, but it increasingly involved a combination of advanced technology and rich colours which provoked proven psychological effects. A complex language of desire evolved which drew on available imagery to reach new forms of intensity.

The consolidation of consumption

In the period between 1890 and 1918 the developments that began in mid-century were rendered systematic and permanent. An interlocking commercial system was forged from which politics was largely excluded. This was the heyday of the department store, but also the period in which consumption reached out to a mass national audience due to innovations in transport, communications and advertising. It was also the phase in which the United States, having gained the economic ascendancy, began to export back to Europe techniques that had been honed in the largest mass market. Modern advertising was born in the 1890s and was greatly facilitated by another novelty of the period, the cheap illustrated press. Photographic images, rare in the middle of the century, became more commonplace and easy to reproduce. By the late 1890s motorised transport and moving pictures were quickening the pace of life, while electricity rendered light brighter and more diffuse. Higonnet (2002: 4–6) argues that this was the formal start of the age of the phantasmagoria, that is to say of the reified, self-deluding myth.

In spite of some differences, the great stores of the United States, France and Britain developed in basically similar ways. The more the market became mass-oriented, the more instinctive and spectacular the appeals. They all occupied a middle ground between exclusivity and vulgarity. Several store magnates traded heavily on sexual allusions and even reputations. Both Whiteley and Selfridge championed women's rights, but they were also notorious for their sexual exploits. Whiteley was murdered in his own store in 1907 by a young man claiming to be his illegitimate son, while Selfridge conducted a public liaison with the French musical hall star Gaby Deslys. In *Au Bonheur de Dames*, Mouret is depicted as having enjoyed a string of liaisons with female staff. Rappaport suggests that such events 'only added to the exciting image of the Edwardian department store' (2000: 5) and Lancaster confirms that Whiteley's was constantly surrounded by sexual innuendo and controversy, yet customers still appeared in droves, 'from the royal family and aristocracy to the Paddington proletarians who flocked to the January sale' (1995: 22). By injecting an element of sexuality into their marketing, store owners and advertisers blurred the boundaries between class and sleaze, thus creating the premises for one of the most enduring features of modern glamour. Although magnates wanted to define modern women as consumers, the struggle to assert this involved overlaps and ambiguities with show business, prostitution and the street. This led to Whiteley being accused of 'turning ordinary suburban women into Jezebels'. Just as stores blended elite and mass culture, 'mirroring the world of Ascot and the amusement park', so they blended classes, sexes and lifestyles (Rappaport 2000: 108, 166).

France conserved a leading role in the fabrication of glamour due to its special monopoly on a certain type of fantasy. With censorship being very relaxed compared to London or Vienna, Parisian theatre acquired an image of daring and pleasure that appealed and tantalised. Paris was more cosmopolitan than any other European city, it was a centre of the world economy and a powerful centre of entertainment. In art, fashion and spectacle, if not in the sheer scale and dynamism of its commercialism, Paris set the tone for Europe and the world. The culture of pleasure and entertainment that first developed in the 1850s and 1860s reached a new apex in the years between 1900 and 1914 – the years of the *belle époque*. With the crisis of the 1880s over and the Victorian era at an end, an atmosphere of hedonism and excess reigned. The entertainments were many and varied and helped fuel that identification of festivity and gaiety with French character that became current even before the nineteenth century (Rearick 1985: 39). 'Montmartre', Charles Rearick has written, 'was an antidote to the pomposity and stiff class rules that reigned elsewhere. In its dance halls and cabarets Parisians could temporarily free themselves from inhibitions of everyday respectability and find normal forms of bourgeois behaviour mocked or disregarded' (ibid.: 62). As entertainers, as well as poster artists including Toulouse-Lautrec, moved from Montmartre to the more prestigious locations of central Paris in the 1890s, so the reputation for frivolity and licentious-ness, which had been confined to the margins, came to be identified with the city as a whole. The connections between the theatre and the spectacle of the street along the grand boulevards became more marked than ever before (ibid.: 100, 152).

The theatre had much to do with Paris's continuing appeal as a centre of cosmopolitan attraction. After the fall of the Second Empire and the foundation of the Third Republic, it assumed such pre-eminence because it was the 'symbol of frivolity and luxury for an audience that is always right' (Spadini 1966: 97). New department stores were founded, including the Galéries Lafayette, whose interior design was explicitly modelled on the theatre. Even as the pecuniary power of the American rich made itself felt, the charm of Paris proved irresistible. An English-language tour guide to the pleasure capital published in 1914 described the sensation of being in the Place d'Opéra at night, at the intersection of many illuminated roads, as akin to standing at the heart of a star 'flung from the great heaven above, a star despised of God or, fixed ever, a mark by which the angels steer their courses, who knows?' 'And Paris is beautiful beyond words, shine your poet phrases how they will,' the author continued. 'And of her sins, well – we have not come out to go seeking for them. It is the glamour only of the place that has lured us on and the wayward magic of it' (Kelleher 1914: 60). Born in Paris of the eclectic mix of styles, classes and motifs that characterised the bourgeois era, glamour was a seduction that lured real visitors, as well as visitors of the imagination, and to which many surrendered voluntarily.

2
The Gender of Glamour

The modern mass society that emerged in the nineteenth century was often described as feminine. Although no major European country granted women the vote before the 1920s, there was a perception that 'the masses' were feminine in their characteristics. In their passivity, capriciousness and irrationality, they were devoid of the self-control and calculation that were seen as masculine traits (Marchand 1985: 69). From some points of view, modernity itself appeared to be feminine. These developments and these views perhaps testified more than anything else to the asymmetry of the categories of male and female. This fact, Simone de Beauvoir noted in *The Second Sex*, was 'made manifest in the unilateral nature of sexual myths' (1964: 175). No matter how present or visible women became, 'Representation of the world, like the world itself, is the work of men'. Woman was always 'defined as the Other'.

In industrial society, the 'Otherness' of woman was a collective drama that was played out in many different ways and in different forums by a variety of women and men. In particular, it was female figures of glamour who acted as the lightning rods of ideas, values and debates about modernity, sexuality and representation. The glamour of woman had a variety of sources. It derived from superstitions about her mysterious affinity to nature and her capacities for seduction which, in the Judeo-Christian tradition, were identified with evil. It derived from the role women took on in the course of the nineteenth century as the ornamental sex, following the masculine renunciation of fashion as display. It also stemmed from fears of the feminine that were current in the second half of the nineteenth century. Bram Dijkstra (1986) and Nina Auerbach (1982) have explored the way the anxieties about powerful, destructive feminine impulses were played out in European painting, while other authors have highlighted the rampant misogyny of much social commentary and popular literature.

Female glamour did not only derive from mythology and mystery or from a masculine crisis. It was the product of very specific processes that defined the industrial age and the modern city. Because the development of consumerism at once played on, and catered to, female desire and placed systematic emphasis on spectacle and display, it involved a commercialisation of femininity. It became a process of self-fashioning, and in some cases, of self-invention, using clothes, cosmetics and so on. Women became manufactured objects who stood as emblems of the material age. In addition, what Bailey (1990: 148–72) has termed 'parasexuality' was a feature of the period; that is to say, a generic, free-floating female sexuality became a part of commercial culture. Both of these developments provided women with opportunities to take on prominent roles, but at the same time they objectified them in general typologies and forms of spectacularisation that fitted in with the requirements of a male-dominated society.

In this chapter four categories of women will be examined, all of which were either made more visible or were created by the culture of display. All have been, in different ways, seen as bearers of glamour. These are the high society woman, the courtesan, the actress and the showgirl.

Women and high society

Nineteenth-century high society accorded a privileged if constricting position to women. They were not powerful, for the influence they exercised was almost always related to the position of their husbands or fathers. None the less, they acquired a role by means of the way women's appearance and activities became important in establishing and maintaining high social status. 'Society women signified with their bodily presence and appearance high social class and respectability, which in turn reflected on their male provider's monetary wealth' (Montgomery 1998: 6, 117). In Europe, where status was still in part inherited, this was less necessary, but in such instances prominent hostesses were 'the glamorous embodiment of traditional aristocratic social power' (Cannadine 1990: 344). Thus class and sex were profoundly bound up in the culture of display and visual signification that marked the modern period. Women writers have differed over the extent to which visibility meant only increased surveillance and social control of women or rather whether they accorded wealthy and aristocratic women powers of self-fashioning that were equivalent to those of decision-making (Montgomery 1998: 134). What seems certain is that the role of women in testifying to the status of their husbands and more widely to the stylish superiority of their class brought them new obligations to project an alluring image. The shift from the court as the main stage to the city meant that 'a fine dress was no longer something to be worn at court or at selected private assemblies; it was something to be worn in the most public manner possible', as the fashion historian James Laver noted (1937: 19). Elite women were arbiters of taste and fashion, a position that gave them a social function of considerable importance in a world where style was increasingly a key marker of status. Some became celebrities whose lives were reported in great detail in newspapers and magazines. They became public figures and offered a model of femininity that was presented as an ideal to the wider public. This rested on taste, refinement, cultivation, style and beauty.

In this phase 'the image was born of the fashionable female – the sophisticated, urbane woman who knew how to converse amusingly, how to handle servants, and how to keep up with the Mode' (Seebohm 1982: 36).

> The Mode – the word alone was enough to send frissons down the spine of an ambitious young lady at the turn of the century. If one was not au courant with the Mode, one might as well stay in Hammond, Indiana, for the rest of one's life, doomed to provincialism like Madame Bovary. (ibid.)

Because of the wealth of their husbands, upper-class women had special access to the image-makers who largely determined what was fashionable and interesting. On their own they could achieve little, but in alliance with the fabricators of splendour and allure they could establish the stylistic pre-eminence of their class. For elites everywhere, this entailed a connection with Paris, the capital of modern fashion. As the capital of the country that had witnessed the first violent revolution against the old order as well as the systematic development of consumerism, Paris was the site of the most significant shift of fashion from the court to the city. The fashion system that took shape in the middle of the nineteenth century was one in which rules and cycles were determined by a new category of cultural mediators known as couturiers. While the Empress Eugénie impressed by her extravagance and the court by its frivolity, it was the first couturier, Charles Frederick Worth, who determined the vogue for particular colours, materials and styles. Although Valerie

Steele argues that he was 'less a fashion dictator than a designer with an astute sense of what small changes his clients would be willing to accept' (1985: 80; see also de Marly 1980), he turned women's fashions into big business by making clothes for a range of moneyed clients as well as foreign buyers and manufacturers who distributed them throughout the world. Unlike his contemporaries, Worth designed a collection of models each season and then presented them to a select clientele. To turn his creations into fashion, he needed prestigious clients to wear them and draw attention to them, but at least in part this was a process he managed himself.

The invention of modern fashion gave Paris an allure that was conveyed widely across the capitalist world. It was associated with sophistication, chic and taste. Americans, Marchand notes, became 'fixated with Paris as the symbol of fashion' (1985: 128). Although a product of an expanding capitalist economy, the exclusiveness of haute couture (a uniquely Parisian phenomenon) gave it a power and suggestion that resonated widely. The moneyed classes of the world looked to Paris for fashion advice and were assisted in their desire to be informed by a fashion press that mediated between producers and consumers. The fashion press itself was not new, but the twentieth century saw the birth of a type of class publication that was aimed only at an elite. Condé Nast's *Vogue* began in 1909 as a magazine that recounted 'society, fashion and the ceremonial side of life' to the social elite of America's East Coast (ibid.: 42). The fact that it was also read by those eager to enter this elite turned it into an instrument 'of the struggle between an exclusive, hidebound, aristocratic society and the new wealth, glamour, and social ambition that were impelling America into the twentieth century' (ibid.: 39). Paris was the main inspiration for the fashion pages of *Vogue*. Indeed, in large measure the fortune of the magazine itself pre-1914 'depended on the free supply of news from the Paris houses' (Seebohm 1982: 102).

While the emergence of a new elite fuelled the growth of a commercial public sphere, the new rich remained focused on the construction of an impressive façade for themselves and their families (ibid.: 184). Just as the aristocracy's identification with titles and magnificent dwellings influenced them, so too did its historic monopoly of the arts. While their wives learned the manners, rituals and tastes of the established wealthy, tycoons built houses and collected art.

The favoured artist of the super-rich was John Singer Sargent. Sargent was in every sense an establishment painter. An expatriate American born in Florence who worked in Paris and London before returning to the US, he conferred an air of distinction and style on the newly moneyed men and women who were his main subjects. His portraits were vigorous and flattering. The overwhelming impression that transpires from his work is of a confident, relaxed ruling class, content with its mastery of money, beauty, taste and power. Subjects are surrounded with an aura of wealth and ease that suggests nobility and refinement. That Sargent also counted aristocrats among his clients constituted a guarantee that he could confer an authentic stamp of distinction on 'those who would otherwise have lingered in the between-world where class, nationality, money, and money's provenance, were matters not to be raised without a qualm'. 'One of Sargent's greatest charms, for Edwardian society, was his ability to give new money a good opinion of itself,' noted John Russell. 'For the reassurance-collector there was no other painter in the country' (Anon. 1996: 208; see also Prettejohn 1998: 25–9).

Sargent's speciality was the Society lady. His best-known work is of the wives and daughters of the new rich. There are innumerable portraits of beautiful, light-skinned women, elegant and composed in surroundings of taste and refinement. Their langorous demeanour testifies to a relaxed confidence and to immunity to problems of any type. The women are invariably elongated, with delicate hands and feet and slender waists. Although there is a certain standardisation in the images and also some idealisation, this relates less to the individuals than to their social and economic situation. According to Thorstein Veblen (1973: 107), such women displayed conspicuous leisure and appeared to be useless and expensive. As such, they had to be supported in their idleness by their 'owners' and consequently were 'valuable as examples of pecuniary strength'.

How did Sargent arrive at this model of representation? His work evolved in this direction after he excluded sexuality. Sargent's stylish conservatism was the result of a major career shift following his departure from Paris in 1884. The cause was a highly controversial portrait of an eccentric American, Mme Gautreau (Madame X), which, when it was unveiled at the Paris Salon, led to a drying-up of commissions and to a decline instead of a consolidation of the reputation of the young painter. The woman in question was a vain society figure noted for her strong Grecian profile and bluish skin tone, which may have been caused by the custom of taking small quantities of arsenic to achieve a dull pallor (Olson 1986: 102). Instead of immortalising her physical splendour and adding to her celebrity, the portrait resulted in her ridicule. Wearing a simple back gown with an exceptionally ample *décolletage* and a shoulder strap hanging down over one arm, Mme Gautreau was depicted standing with her head turned in profile. This bald statement, uncorrected by any costume accessories or background detail, was taken to suggest overt sexuality and even evil. Although the skin colour was regarded by those able to judge as being less striking than in nature, a contemporary observer recorded that 'she looks decomposed' (ibid.: 104). After this episode, Sargent shied away from the conspicuous society beauties who clamoured for attention and specialised instead in the attribution of a noble patina.

This episode testifies to the importance of respectability to the upper classes. Unmarried upper-class women were expected to be pure, and married women to maintain a good reputation. Although infidelity among the married was widely tolerated in private, it was never acknowledged publicly. Nothing could be allowed to tarnish the image of moral superiority. Because the very entry of women into the public sphere opened up unwanted possibilities of confusion with those who were indeed purchasable, there was a strong emphasis on modesty and respectability. Discreet street dress was deemed particularly important to avoid misrecognition. Although daring gowns and self-display were all tolerated and even encouraged in private, especially on the part of a few eccentric or very grand ladies, the case of Sargent's Madame X portrait showed that there was a difference between going close to the boundary and crossing it. In cities, there were respectable and unrespectable areas and there were places, such as certain parks and boxes at the opera, which were the preserve of the former. Anyone who flouted social convention was subject to swift censorship or, in extreme cases, ostracism. In Edith Wharton's *The House of Mirth*, Lillie Bart falls from grace because she is perceived to have transgressed rigid lines of respectability.[1]

Giovanni Boldini (who took over Sargent's Paris rooms after the latter's departure) can be argued to have made the portrayal of the beautiful and the fashionable into a speciality. The equilibrium between sex, fashion and distinction that Sargent so signally failed to achieve became a hallmark of Boldini. His portraits are edgy and contemporary, and explicitly sensual. They convey not Edwardian contentment but the stylish hedonism of *fin-de-siècle* and *belle époque* Paris. In this sense Boldini, even more than Sargent, was a fabricator of glamour.[2] Boldini specialised in portraits of the wives of financiers and industrialists, as well as the more daring aristocrats and other celebrities and society figures who wished to attract attention and show off their status. It has been said that he created a harem of superbly tall, elongated women whose small heads, delicate features, long necks and trailing arms turned them into fantastic, exotic creatures. Undoubtedly, he manipulated and altered the female form at will, twisting and turning it into the sort of serpentine poses that had come to be identified with the *femme fatale*.

Dario Cecchi describes Boldini's studio as 'a highly potent pictorial *maison de beauté*' (1962: 274). Particular attention was paid to fashion. Boldini was well aware of the latest innovations of Worth, Doucet, Poiret and others, and he frequently borrowed dresses and advised on choices of garment, as well as jewellery, hats and so on. His subjects were wrapped fashionably in luxury goods, while glimpses of the body and loose hair would suggest erotic thoughts. It is worth stressing that fashion by this time had ceased to be purely an elite interest or prerogative. Prints and magazines had, in the course of the nineteenth century, 'loosened their ties to a fixed aristocratic hierarchy' and instead become part of a commercial culture that 'purported to create a cultural (as opposed to ostensibly economic) elite through the promulgation of fashions diversely sartorial, theatrical, and literary' (Higonnet 1995: 151).

Yet, although Boldini's Parisian location enabled him to insert more fashion and sexual allusion than would have been the case had he been working in another capital, he still encountered some problems along the lines of those experienced by the young Sargent. In particular, his portrait of Donna Franca Florio, the statuesque wife of the Sicilian industrialist Ignazio Florio, was rejected by the latter, who refused to pay for it. The grounds were that, far from confirming his wife's position as 'Queen of Palermo', it portrayed 'a beautiful woman in the act of wiggling her hips, either before a mirror or worse: before the audience of a *caf'conc''* (Cecchi 1962: 174). Modifications were subsequently undertaken to tone down the general attitude and turn the glamorous portrait into a traditional depiction of a distinguished lady (for more detail, see Gundle 1999: 289–90). In contrast to the current of the time, the upper classes believed that there was 'a glamour and a mystery about the respectable woman' (Cartland 1971: 28), with the result that enormous weight was placed on the maintenance of a respectable public image. What this meant was that, although high society women were necessary to the market, they were not sufficient for it, even as images. The sexualisation of women in public spaces therefore passed through more conventional channels of commodification.

Figuring the *demi-monde*

The sexualisation of the commodity was one of the central features of consumer culture as it took shape in the nineteenth century. Consumer desire was in part a deflected form of sexual desire, with eroticised objects and images capturing the attention of the status-hungry and the fashion-conscious in the commercial centres. Although the shopper was most likely to be a woman, the particular functions of allegory, metaphor and desirability conventionally ascribed to the female sex ensured that femininity rather than masculinity supplied the visual imagery of the commodity culture. The feminine image both intensified and reflected the commodity's allure (Solomon-Godeau 1996: 113). Solomon-Godeau suggests that, within lithography, narrative and mythological motifs disappeared, along with the idea of the male body as the embodiment of ideals, leaving the female figure as a subject in itself. Print culture offered men new opportunities to acquire titillating images of compliant femininity and indulge in fantasies of possession (ibid.). The spectacularisation of the feminine provided a resource for store display, the periodical market and the theatre, as well as painters, photographers and the nascent advertising industry.

The solicitation of the male gaze or, in other words, the constitution of the feminine self as desirable (and sometimes as desiring) became a key feature of the new publicly focused female culture of the mid–late nineteenth century, albeit mediated and conditioned by prevailing notions of class, respectability and family. Given the male double standard around which modern sexuality was organised, an entire sub-world, sometimes dubbed the sensual subculture or, more commonly, the *demi-monde*, existed. This was a sort of parallel high society that was shadowy and illicit on the one hand, but highly visible and admired on the other. It was a profoundly unstable community centred on male pleasure. Wives and daughters of the wealthy were rigorously excluded and instead the female element was provided by high-class prostitutes or courtesans, usually of lower-class origin, actresses and performers and some women who had been banished from high society. Female members of the *demi-monde* frequented some elite public places, were widely known to the general public and were constituted as objects of desire and luxury. They displayed themselves in a way elite women could not. They were figures of fashion and celebrity who played a striking role in the development of the consumption economy.[3]

During the Second Empire, courtesans reached their apex. The two dozen most famous were ostentatious to an extraordinary degree, dressing and furnishing their residences with every manner of luxury and costly ornamentation (see Richardson (1967) for an account of twelve of the most famous). In an age that celebrated wealth and money more than anything else, a courtesan like La Païva, whose avariciousness was such that, according to the journalist Emile Bergerat, her love of money surpassed all else (Richardson 1967: 71), in some way symbolised the period. For ten years, a prominent architect laboured to construct a mock-palace for her on the Champs-Elysées, the extreme luxury of which stood as testimony to 'the presence of a single idea: the defiant, obsessive idea of personal glorification' (ibid.: 71). La Païva aimed through display of wealth to achieve a status that compensated for the rejection she had suffered at the hands of respectable society. 'Stories of the wealth of the famous courtesans were an essential part of their myth and contributed to the displacement of interest away from their disturbing sexuality', notes Charles Bernheimer (1989: 99). Yet La Païva's immorality could never be concealed. To her guests, she offered vulgar and scatological conversation of the most salacious kind. Derided and notorious, it was said that 'she would have given herself to a miner for a nugget'.[4]

The courtesans were public figures whose worldly activities were as publicised as their commercial activities were the subject of ribald comment. 'Vice did indeed wear diamonds during the Second Empire,' writes Richardson:

> In 1860, *Le Figaro* announced a fancy-dress ball at which the goddesses of Olympus were to be represented by the Parisian courtesans. La Païva had, it was said, arranged to come as Juno. 'The treasures of diamonds, pearls and precious stones she would scatter over her dazzling tunic are valued at less than 1,250,000 francs. Mme Barucci would come as Pallas ... with 250,000 francs' worth of various diamonds and jewels. Mme Anna Deslions would come as Venus, with 300,000 francs' worth of precious stones'. (ibid.: 72)

A couturier like Worth made no distinction between courtesans and noble ladies, offering his services to all fashionable women who could afford them. Indeed, he often turned to his courtesan clients first when he wanted to introduce a new style (Binder 1986: 40–1). It was for them after all that the word *chic* was first invented (Richardson 1967: 145; see also Aretz 1932: 284).

The courtesans enjoyed their heyday in the period between the Second Empire and the First World War. They were invariably beautiful and ambitious young women of lower-class origins who masqueraded as society women, taking part in all the public, money-related rituals of the high society: theatre, restaurants, shopping, races, sitting for portraits, visiting couturiers. Not only were the more prominent among them known to the public by name, but they also enjoyed a powerful fictional representation in novels, plays, opera and art. T. J. Clark (1990: 202, 109), like Christopher Prendergast (1992) and others, has suggested that it was really the prostitute who was the symbol of the new order and who, in some accounts, became a metaphor for Paris. If the courtesan was represented more than the street prostitute, it was because she was an acceptable, glamourised representation of a troubling and problematic phenomenon. In his use of the term glamour, Clark betrays a belief that authentic glamour was respectable and high-class rather than a falsification. In other words, he argues that the prostitute became glamorous by adopting the guise of the respectable, fashionable woman. In fact, to his argument must be added another: that the courtesan was also a glamourised version of the high society woman. She added luxury and style to the prostitute, while also adding commodification, heightened visibility and sex appeal to the Society figure. This unstable blend stood at the heart of the contradictions that were inherent in glamour.

The connections between the various forms of commodification were intense. The big stores, Bernheimer noted, 'revolutionized commercial practices in some of the ways prostitutional practices were changing in the second decade of the Empire' (1989: 93). The passage from the small boutique to the spectacular big store which imported its wares from Europe was matched by the cosmopolitanism of the courtesans, brilliant and expensive professionals of desire who were mostly of foreign origin. By dressing their windows garishly and in a gaudy manner with the intention of forcing the sensations of passers-by, stores were on the same wavelength as the courtesans (ibid.: 171).

The female beauty they offered was an artificial, constructed one that had as little as possible of the natural. In a phrase that recalls Benjamin's later references to inorganic sex appeal, the Goncourt brothers suggested that La Païva had a face that 'at moments ... takes on some terrible likeness to a rouged corpse' (quoted in Richardson 1967: 62). Cora Pearl, like several others, behaved like a beauty and won plaudits from admirers, but in fact had quite a plain face (Binder 1986: 40, 66). By enveloping her body in clouds of fabric and decorating herself with jewels and metal adornments, the courtesan produced herself as 'a ritualized image, a commodified cultural idol' (Rappaport 2000: 97–8). 'The exteriority of the commodity was presented as potentially delivering man from his shameful organic functions, while retaining certain imprints of his personal desire' (ibid.: 99). Alain Corbin (1990: 133–4) points out that high-class prostitutes were often 'launched' by local dressmakers and even laundresses, who would lend magnificent garments belonging to well-to-do customers. Various trades people, including upholsterers and furniture makers, set up courtesans in luxurious apartments at exorbitant rents and arranged repayment on instalment plans.

The degree of interaction between *monde* and *demi-monde* was not fixed but fluctuating, depending on moment and place. In particular the two intersected at spas, fashionable resorts and in such places as the racetrack and the theatre. If men belonged to both worlds easily, women found themselves drawn unwittingly into reciprocal competition. 'The known woman of pleasure would sit side by side at the gaming-table with the grande-dame, and although the latter might look down her nose at her she could not do so with conviction, even to herself, if the demi-mondaine wore a richer or more striking toilette than she did,' observed James Laver (1937: 54). 'The conflict of elegance therefore became instantly more desperate, the competition of luxury more necessary, if one's place was to be maintained. In Paris it might be possible if difficult, to keep a Cora Pearl in her place; in the watering hole it was impossible.'

Artists patronised by high society often drew inspiration from the sensual subculture. For example, Boldini did not start at or close to the top of society. Rather, he began by painting small-time actresses and prostitutes. Throughout his career moreover he frequented the *demi-monde* and counted the great actress-courtesans among his friends. As Cecchi (1962: 131) has pointed out, Boldini happened to work at just the time when the fashionable society beauty was being challenged and to some extent replaced by the professional beauty who had risen through the café concert or the theatre. This process was caught and possibly accelerated by Boldini, who derived a technique of representation from the entertainment world which he then transferred to new rich and aristocratic subjects in a diluted form. In other words, he did not derive his model – save in small part – from the tradition of aristocratic portraiture, but rather forged a new one that merged and catered to the tastes of the new rich and the show business elite. His trademark style blended sensuality – in the form of twisting figures, swagged gowns and uncovered flesh – with a theatricality that was evident in bright colours and a subdued exoticism. This new ideal, Cecchi notes, was

> a type of beauty that was tending to become stereotyped, and whose attitudes often reflected the provocative mawkishness of women of the stage. Boldini in fact was a master in always conferring on his models maximum elegance, but at the same time a certain daringness of behaviour that was more appropriate to the beautiful temptresses of the café-chantants or the leading representatives of the demi-monde. (ibid.: 131)

The competition between respectable women and courtesans stemmed from a situation in which it was men who controlled the purse-strings and the organisation of society. Women were sometimes exasperated by the appeal of the courtesans. 'In good faith, what do you love in those whom you prefer to your wives? Is it beauty? Spirit? Talent?' asked the female author of a late nineteenth-century French book on the rules of fashion, before replying to her own question: 'No! It is those flashy dresses ... which seduce you (dresses, moreover, which you forbid your wives, for reasons of economy). Their jewels, their make-up, their strange but real brilliance ... fascinate your eyes and your imagination' (quoted in Steele 1988: 161). In short, what appealed was their glamour.

Alluring actresses

The courtesan persisted until 1914, but her golden age ended in 1870 with the fall of the Second Empire. In the democratic Third Republic, the frivolity and excess that had flourished as a distraction from politics occupied a less general and more specific place (Richardson 1967: 142–3). The *demi-monde* did not disappear, but it found a more continuous and official anchorage in the theatre. As Gertrude Aretz noted,

> at the end of the nineteenth century the variety stage, the *cabaret*, and the *café chantant* became the accepted bridge to a life of gallantry. The women for whom men ruined themselves, just as successfully as they had ruined themselves for the *grandes cocottes*, now appeared nightly on the stage of a music hall, and wished to be known as actresses. (1932: 268–9)

In a country like Britain, where Queen Victoria's austere presence served to contain certain exhibitions, confusions of *monde* and *demi-monde* in any case occurred later and in a more partial way. Lillie Langtry, for example, began more as an artist's muse than a courtesan. Although she was a prominent lover of the Prince of Wales, he bestowed no riches on her and her married status was vital in protecting her from disrepute. Langtry only blossomed as an *objet-de-luxe* when she took to the stage and became more explicitly a self-invented professional beauty (Beatty 1999).

Like the courtesans, actresses were public figures who approximated to the elite; to some extent these women 'had to walk, talk, move and behave and dress *like* ladies' (Findlater 1976: 16). They also led free, and sometimes scandalous, lives and were associated with sex, but they were not commodities available to the highest bidder. The glamour of the actress derived from her fame (and notoriety) but also from her capacity to merge her personality with the roles she played. By playing Salomé, Cleopatra or Lady Macbeth, Bernhardt or Duse exercised a special fascination for the Victorian imagination, which indulged a morbid fascination with devilish women. No less than courtesans, actresses traded in transparent make-believe; their trade involved an arrangement of signs in which distance from reality was an accepted norm (Stokes 1988: 5). More than the former, they were drawn towards a 'modern ideal in which the glamour of unusual women would be held to depend upon their radiant transformation of the average female' (ibid.: 9).

The leading actress of the age, Sarah Bernhardt, thrilled audiences with a passionate emotional style in which actress and character were seen as indistinguishable. She built her reputation by playing a series of decadent *femmes fatales*, including Cleopatra, Tosca, Phaedra and Fedora, the latter role written especially for her by Victorien Sardou. It is striking how many of her roles involved her playing a courtesan. The most famous is that of Marguerite Gautier, based on the real-life consumptive courtesan Marie Duplessis, in Alexandre Dumas' *La Dame aux Camélias*. She played a courtesan-gypsy turned Byzantine empress in Sardou's *Théodora* and a courtesan-type in Hernani's *Dõna Sol*; even Cleopatra became a creature reminiscent of the Parisian *demi-monde* in Bernhardt's hands. In some ways, she played directly on the cultural obsessions of her time. She confirmed some misogynistic impulses by playing evil or corrupting women and specialised in drawn-out death scenes that catered to Victorian sentimentalism. Yet she actively subverted the Victorian ideology of passive femininity. She was an all-round artist without a Pygmalion. Moreover, she considered herself to be one of the great lovers of her age and her ever-evolving sex life was frequently reported in the press. In England some were scandalised by the fact she was able to enter respectable houses while exciting base instincts on the stage and ignoring totally the rules of conventional morality.

Bernhardt was widely seen as a publicity genius. She took Parisian exoticism on to the international stage, undertaking regular London engagements between 1979 and 1913 and nine American tours between 1880 and 1918, which led to her being dubbed Sarah 'Barnum'. Self-promotion had been part of the stock-in-trade of the courtesans, but Bernhardt tapped into a new and highly developed culture of spectacle that linked theatres, metropolitan newspapers, print and billboard advertising, international exhibitions, travelling entertainments, as well as stores, dance halls and other sites of amusement and pleasure (Glenn 2000: 12). Indeed, she helped shape a modern public realm and developed glamour as a personal aura linked to the means of communication. She was a modern celebrity who practised conspicuous self-display and sought sensation. Her performance style and off-stage publicity stunts blended seamlessly in a continuous effort at startling and dazzling her audiences. Exoticism and eccentricity were her hallmarks, and were reinforced by stage cross-dressing and tales of her unusual diet, menagerie of pets, including monkeys, a cheetah and jewel-encrusted snakes, and custom of sleeping in a coffin lined with pink silk (ibid.: 30). Fashion underscored the Bernhardt persona. Details of her lavish and costly dresses were extensively reported in the press. In the United States, her Parisian provenance meant that women scrutinised her wardrobe for fashion tips. In London, she confirmed her image as a creature of passion and power in contrast to the girlish Ellen Terry.

Bernhardt was the first actress to gain entry to high society. As an eccentric, colourful and foreign personality, she was seen as diverting. It no doubt helped that she had a liaison with the Prince of Wales, whose patronage of the theatre was keener and more catholic than his mother's. The actress was a pioneer figure who broke down not only the barriers between different social spheres but also the general restrictions limiting the possibilities open to women. Susan Glenn (2000: chapters 3–5) has demonstrated persuasively how the suffrage movement and modern feminism in general were aided by, and passed through, the theatre. It enabled female roles and gender identity to be put in question and permitted the projection of powerful images of ambitious, independent and sexually expressive 'New Women'.

The rise of the showgirl

Although strong female personalities were often experts at self-fashioning, their individual images always required some assistance from professionals. The couturier Worth and his successors, Paquin, Doucet and Poiret, painters including Boldini and Sargent, and subsequently photographers all created image techniques that did not rely on specific subjects. Writers were also important. Baudelaire turned the courtesan into a cult object while Oscar Wilde produced, in *Salomé*, a vehicle used by several actresses. He also collaborated with painters in the construction of the image of Langtry. Artists drew women into the realm of objects and stressed the importance of clothes and cosmetics. 'In the process of displacing nature's transience onto commodities, the life force of sexuality is displaced there as well. For what is it that is desired? No longer the human being: Sex appeal emanates from the clothes that one wears' (ibid.: 100). This macabre inversion leading to artificial humanity, in which the living body mimics the inorganic world, appealed to aesthetes who saw it as a means to gain control of femininity.

In particular, the aesthetes found a new ideal of femininity in the showgirl. 'In order to compensate for the threat represented by her sexuality and her fertility, woman must become an object,' Andrea Stuart (1996: 118–19) notes. With her exaggerated costumes, and her body disguised by make-up, lighting, wigs and other aids, the showgirl contradicted any natural ideal of femininity and offered instead a spectacle of herself as an artificial construction. As a phenomenon she can be considered entirely a product of the birth of the capitalist metropolis. Although, as Stuart notes, the 'tradition of "entertaining exhibitionism" ... dates right back to antiquity' (ibid.: 12), the particular cluster of meanings and symbolisms associated with the *fin-de-siècle* showgirl were those of the emerging phenomena of parasexuality, consumerism, theatre as a locus of meaning, artificiality and fetishism. Born in the Paris of the Moulin Rouge and the Folies Bergère, she became first an emblem of Paris itself, then a more general urban icon. For Stuart, 'Glamour and pleasure, sexuality and fantasy, beauty and desirability, consumerism and power, anonymity and stardom, these are the conceptual threads that pull the showgirl's story together' (ibid.: 2).

Theatres like the Folies Bergère first developed an understanding of the 'box office allure of a certain kind of female performer'. It was the preferred showcase for the great dancer-courtesans of the *belle époque*: Cléo de Mérode, Liane de Pougy, La Belle Otero and Emilienne d'Alençon. The Moulin Rouge specialised in the 'mass marketing of female sexuality for mass entertainment'. There performed the leading can-can dancers, many of whom began as amateurs before being picked out for the stage on account of their popularity with audiences. Stuart suggests that the word 'showgirl' was 'probably the result of a fusion of two popular terms like "shopgirl" and "showman" ' (ibid.: 5); it was 'optimistically vague from the moment it was invented'. 'It applied', she argues, 'to a specific theatrical role – those be-feathered women posing in the spectacular revues of the period whose job was to provide a feast for the eye – and was a genericism applied to all women who appeared in popular theatre, from chorus-girl to major star'.

Showgirls were icons of leisure and pleasure, symbols of sexual freedom, financial autonomy and adventure. They shimmered, glittered and provoked, achieving fame for their decorativeness and sexuality.

In this sense they were products of that culture of visual spectacle which was such an important hallmark of bourgeois consumer culture. Just as the street life of the new Paris following Haussmann's restructuring was alluring, eye-catching and spectacular, so the gaudiness and ostentation spilled over into the theatre. The showgirl was like the city: vulgar, showy, opulent, ostentatious. The emergence of overt female sexuality in entertainment was a great novelty. The way this occurred reflected the times. The emphasis on prostitution of the period was matched by a concern with the physical, and especially the lower-class physical, which Zola caught in his depiction of Nana. Her sexual appeal was directed and unmediated; it was inscribed in the crude and unmoralistic liberty of her body. The danger, the *frisson*, stemmed from the idea of a voracious, hedonistic and lower-class female sexuality. The lower-class element was as important as the female one. Up to now, we have considered glamour to be a property of the false 'lady', but it can never solely be this; the presence of the low Other is essential as it is vital to the maintenance of the dialectic between class and sleaze.

One of the key features of the showgirl was the capacity for transformation. Showgirls were essentially ordinary young women who could, like Mistinguett, 'act' beauty, disguise any physical disadvantages and turn themselves into creatures of 'overwhelming glamour' (ibid.: 25). They inhabited theatres that became more important than the arcades or the stores in setting the tone for the imaginative landscape. They were glittering, brash, ostentatious. Their false façades found display not in the private *hôtels particuliers* of the Second Empire courtesans, but palaces of entertainment. Stuart says that the showgirls were 'the direct descendants of the great courtesans of the Balzac era ... . From the courtesan the showgirl inherited her unique social place, reputation, and lifestyle'. The difference was that this role was now institutionalised. The *demi-monde* became the café society and sucked the *beau monde* into it. Although the showgirls were often also *cocottes*, they were no longer false ladies or imitation duchesses. They took elements of class but also aspects of *nouveaux-riches* and the *petit-bourgeois* – in particular, the explicit and repetitive reference to money and the love of money. Their sexuality was codified as displaced fetishism. The mythologising and self-mythologising was a combination of self and press. Stuart argues that the

> extravagant lifestyles and flair for self-promotion provided a prototype for women like Mistinguett to mythologise themselves, and they also provided her with many of her themes. Just as the courtesans

exploited and helped create popular perceptions of the showgirl as *femme fatale* and gold-digger, so would Mistinguett, in her many performances and songs which irrevocably linked 'love and money', borrow from them. (ibid.: 32)

Showgirls were rootless. They were outsiders who inhabited symbolic spaces with special connotations. Their costumes dazzled by their contrivance and created a frame for the body which concealed and revealed in deliberate measures. This coding and camouflaging, and the repertoire of costumes, references and gestures that comprised the process, were constitutive of glamour as a visual euphemism.

The chorus girl was an invention of the 1890s and initially she connoted a range of other figures. As a working young woman on visible display, she occupied the position of the prostitute, but her independence also aligned her with the new women who were defining new roles in the public arena (Mizejewski 1999: 66). This ambiguity was crucial to her appeal. In the public imagination, chorus girls happily embraced the opportunities and contradictions of their position. They were breezy, cheerful and carefree; women on the make who were also busily making themselves. Vital to projecting the look of youth and happiness was the smile, which was as taught as were their steps (Glenn 2000: 170). But although they were new, they also confirmed the idea that women's main function was sex and to 'make themselves presentable for show' (Mizejewski 1999: 87).

The sexual exhibitionism of the Moulin Rouge was moulded in the early years of the twentieth century into something less explicit and more acceptable.[5] In the United States, there were several brand-name chorus girls. Of these the most famous was the 'Ziegfeld Girl'. Invented by the showman Florenz Ziegfeld as a key figure in the Ziegfeld Follies, which in various versions ran from 1908 until 1931, the girl was a glorified American girl. Initially, Ziegfeld had traded on European exoticism, importing and presenting Anna Held, a strongly individualised figure somewhat in the Bernhardt mould, who offered high-profile discourses about Paris fashion and style. But subsequently he developed a standardised patriotic version for whose authenticity and quality he personally vouched.

The Ziegfeld Girl was a visible ideal, a body on show. Her creator 'produced glossy sexual images as upscale commodities for a middle-class market' (Jarrett 1997: 8). Although stage clothing was usually revealing, titillation was firmly controlled. The upscaling disguised the promiscuous connotations of theatre women. But the young female body was none the less a core part of the attraction. Such bodies did not merely present commodities or accompany them, they actually became the commodities. This embodiment occurred through exaggerated dress designed to attract attention and provoke desire, through the display of the person and through multiplication and standardisation: chorus girls were levelled and homogenised, manufactured in a word, and there was always a ready supply. They were available for visual consumption by those who purchased tickets to the shows. In one show, *Glorifying the American Girl*, the chorus girls, who often mimicked the processes and products of machinery, directly became living mannequins in a department store. 'The Ziegfeld stage-as-department store, with chorus girls graduated into mannequins, is perhaps the apotheosis of modern entertainment as consumerism,' comments Mizejewski (1999: 91).

The chorus girl added a number of features to glamour. First, her advent confirmed glamour as a packaging of female sexuality. Transformed women were presented as pricey, barely obtainable items in which sexuality was disguised beneath the flashy sensationalism of the publicity-hungry *nouveau riche* and the controlled aloofness of the lady. To achieve this effect, there was an erasure of origins as a premise to the assumption of a new identity. Although the semblance of the poise of the lady made for the controlled distance necessary to arouse interest, this was quite clearly a pose in contrast to the real haughtiness of the Society woman. The glamorous ideal was to be at once unattainable and irresistible (ibid.: 191). Remoteness and availability combined to create an 'upscale version of female sexual display for male pleasure' (ibid.: 176). In this sense glamour involved a tantalising cross of social opposites: the debutante and the *demi-monde*, the lady and the streetwalker. Commodification was also integral and indeed was the means whereby the crossover occurred. For the first time personalities were packaged as products and actresses were identified with fashion and consumption. Glamour was unequivocally a product of a society in which looks, display and goods were pervasive and unavoidable.

In addition, popular theatrical revues such as the Ziegfeld Follies posited the body as necessary to glamour. Without the young, attractive bodies of the girls, the ideas and practices of fantasy and consumption remained loose and free-floating, ungrounded and of imprecise utility. The Ziegfeld Girl, however, was a regimented and controlled figure, a comforting alternative to the *femme fatale* or New Woman. It is striking, as Mizejewski persuasively argues (ibid.: 32–3), that she was rigorously and deliberately white. Not only sex and class, but also race was a vital component of the image of the glorified American girl. Whiteness of skin was traditionally a feature of the Western upper-class woman, which various courtesans such as Cora Pearl had mimicked. But the emphasis on whiteness in this context was not simply a matter of class; it needs to be related to the specific conjuncture of American society in the early twentieth century. Ethnic whiteness took on a central position in American glamour and would, through the means of communication that the US came to dominate, become one of its recognisable and non-negotiable hallmarks.

3
Hollywood Lifestyles

After having undergone a lengthy formative phase mostly in Europe, glamour was transformed in the interwar years into a mainly American and cinematic phenomenon. The American film industry in the 1930s and 1940s was widely known as 'the dream factory' or 'the glamour factory'. Like the automobile industry, it furnished products in large numbers for mass consumption. The only difference among the motor cars, household products and clothing produced by American manufacturers and the movies furnished by the motion picture industry was the fact that the latter catered not to practical needs and situations but precisely to the imagination. Of course, more practical goods were often sold in alluring settings (stores, catalogues, etc.) and modern advertising, which developed from the 1920s, weaved spells of aspiration and desire around even those that were not. But the movies were both product and spell, and this latter aspect was underscored by the environments in which they were shown. It has been argued, most notably by Charles Eckert (1991) and Douglas Gomery (1992), that picture palaces developed out of the department store. They imitated the plush environments, the mock-palace atmosphere, the opulent ornamentation and the exotic architecture as well as the commitment to lifting audiences out of their everyday lives and stunning them with sensation. First-run movie theatres were often situated in the immediate proximity of stores and a mutual dependency soon developed. While stores advertised films and featured still pictures of stars in their window displays, films and related publicity directed the material desires of the public towards given products, and cinemas offered opportunities for commercial enterprises to exhibit their goods. Thus, established strategies of commercial seduction very specifically informed the manner in which American cinema spoke to the dreams and desires of its audiences.

Hollywood films, produced by companies that had a firm stake in the exhibition and distribution sectors, conformed largely to the escapist imperative. They offered a range of options for audiences to choose from, including European-style decadence, American aristocracy, theatrical opulence, showgirl glitz and youthful beauty as well as city savvy, down-home Americanism and pioneer virtues. But above all Hollywood created a unique blend of the aristocratic, fashionable, sexual, theatrical and consumerist appeals which had emerged and uneasily coalesced in Europe and America in the preceding period. This blend, which emerged as the American motion picture industry's signature style from the 1920s, exercised an unprecedented influence over global aspirations, desires and lifestyles. The success derived in part from the synthetic nature of the industry's products. The creators of Hollywood glamour were very largely Europeans, émigrés and exiles from Germany, Hungary, Russia, France and Britain.[1] But the strong traces of European decadence and exoticism that were apparent in the films of one of the five major studios, Paramount, were balanced by a predominant emphasis on optimism, democracy, the mass market, social mobility, individual aspiration and the possibilities for self-transformation. Because it was located in California, far from the main centres of privilege and style, the film industry reinvented glamour as an enticing image that was removed from specific social referents and that relied solely on technique, artifice and imagination. What Hollywood offered was a unique blend that mixed a plausible pastiche of upper-class ways and styles with established spectacular cultures and low cultural appeals. Thanks in part to the extraordinarily dazzling qualities of Hollywood glamour, American cinema expanded forcefully in Europe after the First World War, establishing a hegemony that it would retain for the rest of the twentieth century.

This chapter provides a broad picture of the nature of Hollywood glamour, its formation and applications. It focuses not on film texts, but rather on the way in which movie stars, having been constructed as desirable images, penetrated and transformed the public sphere.

Publicity and the media

The rise of photography, cinema and the press contributed to the redefinition of reality as a mediated phenomenon not solely reducible to direct experience. The chaotic mix of seductive atmospheres, deracinated motifs and gaudy colours which had previously characterised store decoration and theatrical publicity found an extension – and, to some extent, a complement – in a new, media-based phantasmagoria. Like the Frankfurt School Marxists and other critics, Kracauer argued that this 'lacked any authentic and materially motivated coherence except possibly the glue of sentimentality' (1995: 327). The assault on the senses and the emotions conveyed, 'the *disorder* of society'. Moreover, the flood of images impeded understanding and swept away 'the dams of memory'; 'the "image-idea" ', he maintained, 'drives away the idea' (ibid.: 58).

More than any other, the film industry contributed to the development of a second-order realm of experience that significantly modified the way people lived their lives.[2] Movie companies not only created performers, like Douglas Fairbanks and Mary Pickford, who quickly became world famous and were often confused with the type of personalities they played; they were also masters of ballyhoo. Films were marketed as events and interest stimulated by press coverage, premières, street parades and commercial tie-ins. Hollywood soon became a new outpost of fable and legend. For people all over the world, it was a place of fantasy, not so much a real community as a distillation of pure essence that was a type of 'unreal estate', a new form of commodified space created by movie agents and local promoters.[3]

American cinema was all the more powerful because the men who created the film industry were refugees who gave rise to an imagined America as a land of freedom, tolerance, wealth and personal realisation. Neal Gabler's (1985) work on the Jewish influence on Hollywood glamour suggests that there was a connection between cinematic fascinations and the earlier ones identified by Lears (1994). Nineteenth-century peddlers were often German or East European Jews too, and this was a factor in their liminality and their association with the mysterious East, as well as sorcery and magic: 'In a world of shifting identities, fraudulent representations, and frequent changes of status, the encounter between the peddler and his prospective customer was both exciting and disturbing' (Lears 1994: 69). Like the peddlers, the movie moguls offered dazzling images which promised instant personal transformation and provided rich material for daydreams. The difference was that these images were no longer conjured up by the oral and presentational skills of individual salesmen operating face-to-face. They were embedded in the 'surreality' that overlay daily life and was experienced purely through the media (Schickel 1976: 12–13).

The figures who came, in the twentieth century, to embody the most complete form of existence as commodified spectacle were Hollywood movie stars. In his writings on stars, Richard Dyer (1979; 1987) develops the idea of the 'star text'; he sees the star image as an intertextual construct produced across a range of media and cultural practices, capable of intervening in the working of particular films but not being limited to these. According to this view, the off-screen lifestyles and personalities of prominent film actors are not simply part of the extra-filmic para- phernalia of movie marketing, but an integral part of what makes an actor a star. The 'charisma' of a star is not precisely the 'certain quality of an individual personality' which Weber (1968: 329) saw as the exceptionally rare feature that set certain figures of history apart from ordinary people (see also Dyer 1979: 34–6); rather it is a *perceived* exceptionality arising from a deliberate publicity strategy and as a con- sequence of the place of movies in society. As personalities constructed in function of the public's tastes and aspirations, stars are primarily images (their glamour derives in part precisely from this, the fact that they are first and foremost enticing images). They therefore do not on the whole *do* anything, they simply *are*. 'Celebrity is an industry like many others,' Joshua Gamson writes: 'Celebrities are manufactured as attention-getting bodies, a process complicated but not negated by the fact that celebrities are human beings. Knownness itself is commodified within them' (1994: 104–5).

The first generation of movie stars enjoyed unprecedented fame and financial rewards. Charlie Chaplin, Mary Pickford and Douglas Fairbanks achieved a worldwide prominence and power in the industry that virtually no subsequent star would obtain. The consolidation of the industrial structure of Hollywood in the second half of the 1920s ensured that production strategies were stronger than any individual performer and that corporate power was the determinant factor in the industry. The arrival of sound and the impact of the Depression in the early 1930s reinforced the near-monopoly of the five major film studios. In a situation in which the methods of Fordism were finding application in the film industry no less than the rest of the American economy, the production of star figures also became an assembly-line matter, subject to precise codes, procedures and practices. The movie star was a standardised product which came in a limited number of varieties and was subject to continuous revision and modification. Thus the empha- sis in any analysis of American movie stars must fall on the *system* of star production and distribution, because it was precisely the high degree of organisation that distinguished Hollywood stardom from that of other cinemas.

More than any other studio, Metro Goldwyn Mayer (MGM) turned glamour into a corporate product. It was the largest and most successful studio of the sound era; in 1932 an anonymous contributor to *Fortune* described its list of stars as 'vastly the most imposing' in the industry (quoted in Balio 1976). Paramount was its only serious rival in the matter of star production. The other studios, 20th Century Fox, Warner Brothers and RKO, plus the minors – Columbia, Universal and United Artists – placed less emphasis on stars. Fox, for example, had under contract only four top-ranking stars between the mid-1930s and the late 1940s: Shirley Temple, Betty Grable, Tyrone Power and Gregory Peck; Warners relied on James Cagney, Bette Davis and Humphrey Bogart (Gomery 1986: chapters 2–5). The point, ultimately, was one of cost. 'There are only two kinds of merchandise that can be made profitably in this business – either the very cheap pictures or the expensive pictures,' wrote David O. Selznick to his treasurer when he left MGM to found his own company (quoted in Sklar 1975: 191); this was as true in the 1930s and 1940s as it had been in the 1920s. Although some performers went over with audiences without any particular preparation, the heavy investment that was normally required to mould and successfully launch a star persona could only be made by the big studios.

Gorham Kindem (1982: 86) calculates that, in the 1950s (the first period for which such an estimate exists), the marquee value of movie stars accounted for around 16 per cent variation in box office, but this interacted with other factors, including the title and subject matter of a film. Companies like Warners, which did not share MGM's commitment to a Veblenesque 'general finish and glossiness' (Anon. 1932; in Balio 1976: 269), or smaller companies which could not afford the luxury of high-cost production values, did not develop promising actors or invest in lavish sets, but instead concentrated on familiar genres, characters or settings. 'The glamour of MGM personalities is part of a general finish and glossiness which characterizes MGM pictures and in which they excel,' wrote a *Fortune* correpondent:

> Irving Thalberg subscribes heartily to what the perfume trade might call the law of packaging – that a mediocre scent in a sleek flacon is a better commodity than the perfumes of India in a tin can. MGM pictures are always superlatively well-packaged – both the scenes and personalities which enclose the drama have a high sheen. So high a sheen that it sometimes constitutes their major box-office appeal. (ibid.: 269–70)

The special allure of Hollywood cinema derived from a combination of factors including the genre system, screenplays and the great investment in the overall look of films. But Hollywood's most precious products were the stars that it so carefully groomed and manufactured. These human commodities were the main object of Hollywood fantasy, and in the 1920s and 1930s vast amounts of effort and money were invested in their creation. The construction of a star was no less a process of transformation than the turning of a bare set into fantasy environment. In contrast to Ziegfeld, who concentrated on transforming raw young women into stage icons, the studios took Broadway actors, foreign star-lets, athletes, beauty pageant winners and others and moulded them into fully-fledged screen personalities. Often the starting point was daunting. When she arrived in Los Angeles in 1925 Greta Gustaffson, the future Greta Garbo, was just short of twenty and 'an unretouched Swedish dumpling'; her front teeth were crooked, her hair was frizzy and there was a hint of a double chin (Tapert 1998: 206). She was taller than average and had a rangy, boyish frame. Marlene Dietrich was plump by American standards and wide-nosed; her manners are said to have been coarse and Teutonic. Joan Crawford was brassy and unsophisticated; she was shorter than most, had wide eyes, flared nostrils and freckles. Even as a chorus girl, she had not demonstrated any great talent. Carole Lombard's curvaceous figure and athletic ability seemingly suited her to be one of Mack Sennett's Bathing Beauties but nothing more.

In each of these women studio bosses detected a certain quality. In addition to some acting ability, youth was important and so was beauty, but more significant were two more elusive attributes: a photo-genic quality and personality. The first of these was not always as simple as it might appear. In the case of Garbo, Louis B. Mayer spotted some hidden potential. Legend has it that when he saw one of Mauritz Stiller's Swedish films, with a view to offering the director a contract, he imme-diately spotted Garbo and exclaimed, 'Look at that girl! There's no physical resemblance, but she reminds me of Norma Talmadge – her eyes. The thing that makes Talmadge a star is the look in her eyes' (ibid.: 74). However, bringing out the star quality was no easy task. Garbo did not photograph well under strong lights and initially had developed a nervous tic in her cheek when filmed in close-up. Her first MGM screen test did not impress due to poor lighting and only when the master of soft-focus effects, the cinematographer Henrik Sartov, was brought in was her potential revealed. According to her biographer, Sartov's lens and its magical ability to 'clean out' the face through spot lighting finally brought out her beauty (Paris 1995: 88). The sort of beauty that showed up well on screen featured good bone structure, an oval or square-shaped face with a high forehead, expressive eyes, generous lips, possibly of an interesting shape, and a winning smile.

Personality had to shine through on screen; stars had to have magnetism and a talent for holding attention. 'I always looked for the actor with personality first,' one MGM talent scout, Al Trescony, said. 'I've found that a person with a fantastic personality will attract the attention of everyone in a room, not unlike a beautiful young woman. But people will look at the beauty and after a moment return to their conversation. The one with personality will hold their attention' (quoted in Davis 1993: 83). A performer had to be able to make people believe him or her and this too was perceivable mainly through the eyes. 'The eyes show everything a person is thinking. It comes through the celluloid right out to the audience,' Trescony continued. To enhance this effect, stars were wrapped in a romantic aura; biographies were falsified or invented and names were often changed (Greta Gustaffson became Greta Garbo, Lucille LeSueur Joan Crawford, Archie Leach Cary Grant, Marion Morrison John Wayne and so on). Often the humble origins of American stars were played up, while aristocratic or well-to-do backgrounds were developed for Europeans. Stars were portrayed as confident, seductive, exotic, debonair, paternal or funny in accordance with the type of roles they played.[4] The intention was to mingle reality with illusion and fantasy to make quite ordinary people into fascinating ciphers of individual dreams and aspirations.

To achieve this, film companies also drew on the culture of sexual representation which had developed in the theatres of Europe and the United States. Gertrude Aretz argued that 'the chosen beauties of the film world' had become the bearers of the erotic femininity that was previously the preserve of the *Parisienne*. There was a continuity, she argued, between their tastes and 'the luxurious *demi-monde* of the Old World' (1932: 294). Garbo repeatedly played fallen women or courtesans, including the title role in *Mata Hari* and Marguerite Gautier in *Camille*, the film version of the old Bernhardt vehicle *La Dame aux Camélias*. The 'sex appeal' that was a vital quality for every star (and, according to Hortense Powdermaker (1950: 230), for *all* movie actors, 'whether hero or villain'), was not however the same as the commodified sexual appeal of the courtesan and showgirl. Indeed, it was regarded by some European observers in the 1930s as a mysterious quality.[5] Blaise Cendrars (1936: 83–4) found that in Hollywood great emphasis was placed on symmetry and harmony of the face and body in achieving the 'flash', the 'magnetic attraction' that was central to sex appeal; the contribution of the artifice of hairstyling was also deemed of central importance. Perplexity arose because there was no immediately recognisable connection between the calculated strategies of the professional seductresses of a previous generation and the less explicit, subdued fascination of the stars. The latter combined class and sleaze no less than the Parisian courtesans but, instead of holding the two qualities in precarious equilibrium, they blended them in a fascinating original synthesis. Sexuality was highly mediated and recast as a manufactured appeal that did not cause offence to mass audiences. This adaptation was necessary as the growth of film audiences led to objections to the movies' alleged immorality. What infuriated critics and censors was the identification of luxury and wealth with commercialised sexuality, a phenomenon that recurred in the many 'fallen woman' films made between 1928 and 1942 (Jacobs 1991).

Packaging the stars

The inventor of 'sex appeal' in cinema was in fact the middle-aged English novelist Elinor Glyn, author of a scandalous novel, *Three Weeks*, which portrayed the passionate seduction of a young British aristocrat by a Balkan princess.[6] She taught Gloria Swanson and other protégés how to project 'star quality', that is 'a kind of ever-warm but slightly aloof benevolence when seen socially or at public functions' (Lavine 1981: 38). Crucially, Glyn also taught filmmakers how to encode sexuality, first coining the term *It* (the title of one of her stories, which gave rise to a 1927 film of the same title featuring Clara Bow – the 'It' girl) which evolved into sex appeal (Walker 1968: 36–43). The point was to make sex secondary to magnetism; women, Glyn advised, 'ought to remain mysterious and elusive in order to keep their men interested, even after marriage' and the same applied to movie stars and their audiences (Rosen 1973: 118). This view reflected the background of Glyn, who was basically a romantic conservative, but her usefulness lay 'in providing a safe span between turn-of-the-century innocence and a modern world in which men and women dealt with each other not only as creatures of fancy, but as friends, business acquaintances, and potential sexual partners' (ibid.). She brought to Hollywood a certain European and extra-European (Glyn was very keen on the exotic) eroticism, which allowed popular notions of the 'daring' and the 'fast' to be incorporated into the movies without giving excessive offence.

As Glyn and others conceived it, sex appeal was primarily a female matter. In this sense its cinematic application opened a new chapter in the culture of woman as spectacle. The development of cinema allowed male producers and artists new possibilities for moulding women and creating figures of fantasy, even to the point of reconstructing ideals of femininity. The practical aspects of stardom, with its attention to beauty, artifice, display, fashion and luxury, were considered by many to be exquisitely feminine, and indeed film American audiences and fans were largely female. While there was no shortage of young men keen to get into the movies, aspiring youngsters were most commonly summed up in the phenomenon of the 'movie-struck girl' (Sklar 1975: 74–7).

The physical appearance of the film star was not a casual matter. Once it had been decided to turn an actor into a star, a radical reshaping process began: stars were not born but made according to what, by 1930, was a routine. 'Hollywood moguls had definite ideas about how a star should look and re-fashioned their new talent accordingly,' writes Ronald Davis (1993: 83). Women were usually put on a rigid diet and subjected to intensive massage treatment to lose excess pounds that would look unflattering on the screen. In this way cheek bones showed through and the face acquired an angular quality that the light could capture, while the body took on a sleeker look. Teeth were fixed, corrective plastic surgery was applied if necessary, hair was smoothed out. Even the men were compelled to undergo the same physical modifications; they were sent to the gym, and – like Clark Gable – had their ears pinned back and other imperfections attended to.

After this, the make-up department went to work, thinning out and redesigning eyebrows, lengthening eyelashes, enlarging eyes, reducing noses, removing beauty spots (although some stars, including Gloria Swanson and Arlene Dahl, kept theirs as a trademark) and covering freckles. The perfect 'Max Factorised' faces of the stars bore witness to their role in representing an ideal rather than the real. They became in some respects standardised and generalised. Make-up depersonalised the face, removing its eloquence, but 'in order to super-personalise it'. This did not, contrary to popular opinion, turn stars into modern-day gods; for Morin, 'make-up in cinema does not counterpose a sacred face to a profane, everyday face; it raises everyday beauty to the level of superior, radiant, incontrovertible beauty. The natural beauty of the actress and the artificial beauty of the make-up join in a unique synthesis' (1972: 43). Perhaps the most obvious point of synthesis was in hairstyling. Mary Pickford's curls, Jean Harlow's platinum blonde tresses, Claudette Colbert's bangs and Veronica Lake's 'peek-a-boo' style were all influential.

Several female stars built on Bernhardt's penchant for masquerade and the unusual. No small part of the allure of Garbo and Dietrich, not to mention Crawford, Katherine Hepburn and Bette Davis, derived from the androgynous nature of their appeal. 'From birth, Garbo's physique united the two sides of her nature, the feminine and the masculine,' writes Alexander Walker (1968: 102). In her acting, she brought this androgynous element to bear most forcefully in love scenes, 'where the almost male intensity of her attack was played off strongly against the feminine spirituality of her looks'. For Kenneth Tynan, Dietrich – cinema's most celebrated cross-dresser – 'has sex, but no particular gender. Her ways are mannish: the characters she played loved power and were undomesticated. Dietrich appeals to women and her sexuality to men' (1954: 88). At a time when independent women still aroused curiosity, these stars embodied widespread fears and aspirations.

In the black-and-white stills that constitute the most enduring and readily available examples of Hollywood glamour, all of which had to receive the stamp of approval of the PCA, the balance of light and shade is crucial in dramatising and conferring an atmosphere of sexual allure on the subjects. The actors may be very well known, but the visual descriptions that emerge in the photographs are of icons not individuals; the subjects are ideals of youth and beauty, figures of fantasy (Kobal 1976: x). Photographers emphasised sensuous surfaces of skin and hair, dwelt on furs, silks and satins, and alluded to sex by having actresses lie on rugs or wear loose gowns or a negligée. In contrast to photographs of royalty or other important personages, the shots of stars lingered on their physical perfection and communicated seductive appeal. Highly retouched, the stills revel in artificiality; indeed, precisely their abstract, constructed character made them 'consumable' by the viewer. In the Depression, they offered poor and hungry people a dream of perfection, an image of a sexual and material heaven. For Hurrell, the 'glamour look' was quite simply a 'bedroom look' (Kobal 1993: 15). 'You know, glamour to me was nothing more than just an excuse for saying sexy pictures,' he told John Kobal. 'In other words, my interpretation was entirely one of saying "Come on, we're going to take some sexy pictures" ' (ibid.: 9). 'You can create glamour totally, I think. But a woman in our business generally has some quality of it,' he added. It was his task to get the sexual electricity into a still in a suitably mediated way or else use artifice to create a simulacrum of it.

On occasion, still photographers like George Hurrell and Clarence Sinclair Bull were brought in for close-ups, but on others cinematographers and even directors took charge. Sternberg took the decision to position a key light directly over the head of his protégée Dietrich, which brought her makeover into stark focus. It illuminated her bone structure, emphasised her deep-set eyes and achieved a halo effect that made her hair glisten. Bathing her in light created a moody, seductive effect (Engstead 1978: 72; Tapert 1998: 230–1). In general, women were washed with light, with backlighting eliminating any residual shadows. This endowed them with a glowing image that was sometimes enhanced by glistening materials and hair gel, as well as white sets, costumes and accessories. The objectification of female sexuality and the sexualisation of the object world went hand in hand in Hollywood cinema, where both male protagonists and, by extension, spectators were turned into voyeurs who derived pleasure from the fetishisation of the female star. In her essay theorising this phenomenon, Mulvey singles out Sternberg's use of Dietrich as the 'ultimate fetish': 'The beauty of the woman as object and the screen space coalesce; she is no longer the bearer of guilt but a perfect product, whose body, stylised and fragmented by close-ups, is the content of the film and the direct recipient of the spectator's look' (1989: 22).

High fashion and star style

Whereas 'good' women in films were placed in traditionally decorated contexts, sexually promiscuous, independent, modern women were often associated with architectural modernism as well as the exterior trappings of wealth: furs, jewels, fashionable attire, cars (Jacobs 1991: 56). Cecil B. De Mille was the first director to use upper-class settings, and MGM in particular persisted with the upscale image; Mayer thought that wealth would automatically be assumed to be moral. The connection between the gold-digger's ability to manipulate male desire and the rewards of her activity was often so strong that the latter could be mistaken for the former; i.e. the furs and modern apartments appeared as the tools of seduction of the predatory woman. One of the pioneers of star style was Gloria Swanson. The elegant clothes and costly jewels she wore on screen produced expectations that she should be the same in life. As one of the first to bear such expectations, she defined what the movie star should look like, attending premières in magnificent gowns and furs, looking for all the world like a queen.

Mansions, swimming pools, limousines, fine clothes and an exciting social life were the recurrent features of the star lifestyle. Robert Sklar argues that Thomas Ince was 'the first movie figure to join the oil magnates when he built a mansion in the Spanish style and inaugurated the Aquarian life style of outdoor sports, big cars and weekend parties' (1975: 77). Others followed with dream castles and costly houses overlooking Hollywood and in Bel Air and Brentwood. The purpose was not just to impress each other, but also the public. The larger-than-life image of the star involved, stereotypically, exaggeration and attention-grabbing at the expense of taste.

With the rise of consumerism and the cult of materialism, stars tended to take the place of the new rich and fashion-enticing lifestyles. Because of the extraordinary global fame of film actors, the visit of a movie star was certain to gather publicity everywhere. The movies were above all about motion and both on and off screen stars travelled a great deal. Photographs of stars in stylish coats and furs, standing by trains, planes and luxury automobiles with quantities of leather luggage, convey some-thing of the identification with class and modernity that they embodied. Like the upper classes, they seemed to live a magical, leisure-oriented *vie sans frontières*. This image of wealthy leisure was a key component of the dreamscape of the period. 'Travel is one of the best means for a society to maintain a permanent state of absentmindedness,' observed Kracauer. 'It assists fantasy along mistaken paths', creating desires among 'little shop girls ... to get engaged on the Riviera' (1995: 299).

From the late 1920s, Hollywood acquired a distinctive style leader-ship. Thus it tended to displace existing influential fashion centres. The films themselves were the most important factor in giving Hollywood a design edge. Although art directors have received far less attention than producers and directors, the house style of the major studios, as well as the particular appearance of given films, was largely their work. While the Oriental imagery of the early 1920s testified to cinema's reliance on the stage, the clean Deco lines of the 1930s were products of a process that saw moves towards an independent concept of set design. The most prominent art director was MGM's Cedric Gibbons, an influential figure who took overall responsibility for the look of every single film produced by the studio between 1924 and 1956. He personally designed the sets for several of MGM's most luxurious film vehicles. Gibbons was respon-sible more than anyone else for linking the manufacture of glamour to contemporary aesthetic trends. Anne Massey (2000: 31) argues that he maintained a simple approach to designing for film, abandoning cluttered grandeur for Art Deco and turning this modern style into 'a powerful symbol of transatlantic glamour'.

Starting from 1925, the year Gibbons undertook a visit to the Paris Exposition of Decorative Arts, which pioneered what, at the time, was known as the *moderne* style, Art Deco furnishings and geometric interior designs were used to frame and locate screen characters who were associated with jazz music, 'fast' behaviour and a generally decadent lifestyle.[7] The simplicity of the Deco look should not be overstated. Although, with hindsight, it looks spare and elegant in its emphasis on streamline and two-tone effects, it was in fact 'a promiscuously eclectic style, drawing on the art of many cultures and countries – and indeed periods' (Hillier 1983: 81). In this sense it tied in well with the eclectic jumble of sensations and effects that marked mass culture. The Paris exhibition drew the strands together and helped bring about some kind of fusion, but ultimately it was the United States that gave the style a distinctive stamp and made it into an emblem of glamorous modernity.

Hollywood style appealed greatly to the new rich, to whom it offered a vision of life imbued with the values of wealthy modernity. At all levels, MGM specialised in pristine perfection. Mary Astor wrote in her memoirs that, at Metro, 'all automobiles were shiny. A picture never hung crooked, a door never squeaked, stocking seams were always straight, and no actress ever had a shiny nose'. If an actor or actress was spattered with mud in one scene, somehow the mud had disappeared by the next (quoted in Davis 1993: 225). More than at other studios, actresses looked at all times as if they had just come from the beauty parlour. 'You practically had to go to the front office if you wanted something as real as having your hair mussed,' Astor recalled. This superlative quality was a crucial aspect of Hollywood glamour.

In the 1930s Hollywood also developed an original fashion identity. Fashion was vital to Hollywood glamour and was one of the key ways that America took over the leadership in the field of glamour from France. Although Paris never ceased to be a reference point, the film companies found ways of their own to produce garments and accessories that were effective on screen. The wardrobe departments of major studios were small factories employing hundreds of workers and it was the job of chief designers (Adrian at MGM, Travis Banton and Edith Head at Paramount, Orry-Kelly at Warners) to provide costumes for the stars and to develop detailed wardrobe plots showing the sequence of ensembles a star was to wear in the scenes shot (Lavine 1981: 28–30). The designer had to conceal defects – often using special undergarments – and stress good points in order to 'create an illusion of physical perfection'. Stars like Garbo, Dietrich and Crawford could have as many as twenty costumes for a film, each requiring up to six fittings (ibid.: 33). The costliest materials were used and clothes were designed cinematically, i.e. in an exaggerated manner and using textures, colours and effects that would achieve the greatest impact on screen. Not even the men were overlooked. The elegance of Fred Astaire and the impeccable casual clothes of Cary Grant were mainly the work of Giles Steele at MGM.

Feminist film historians have recently analysed the role of costume and have stressed the importance attached to it by the moguls, several of whom had begun their working lives in the garment trade (see Gaines and Herzog 1990; Bruzzi 1998). For millions of women film-goers, star personas were associated with fashion and there was intense interest in what new costumes actresses would wear in a film. Film publicity agents promoted the idea that every woman should draw inspiration from a star personality whose face, figure or temperament broadly resembled her own. To assist the process, fashion and beauty advice ostensibly dispensed by stars appeared regularly in magazines and stores, and pattern companies made garments seen on film commercially available (Wilson and Taylor 1989: 98–100). These, of course, were cheap adapted versions, for actual star looks were extremely costly and incorporated the fantastic as well as the realistic. In a market in which there was as yet little interest in labels and brands, the stars were vital to the launch of new fashions (Rémaury 1991: 217).

Many films either incorporated fashion shows or were little more than a sequence of episodes linking display set pieces. *Roberta*, *The Bride Walks Out*, *Artists and Models*, *Vogues of 1938* and *Mannequin* all relied on fashion as spectacle and took advantage of the opportunities for *mise-en-scène* and luxury that the fashion show offered.[8] Several of these films were musicals and the fashion parade blended with revue sets and musical performance (Berry 2000: 56–7). Berry argues that these elements of film glamour were not escapist; rather they drew on the carnivalesque traditions of popular theatre. They were playful and deliberately exaggerated, stimulating the imagination by stressing the entertainment value of luxury and style (ibid.: chapter 2). It is this reliance on vaudeville that reveals the populism of Hollywood fashion. It was not on the whole deferential towards established style hierarchies or the class images associated with them. Haute couture was often parodied and demystified, its elitism and eccentricity becoming an object of mirth. In this way elite forms were appropriated and rendered accessible. 'In films about fashion and couture, populism emerges through an emphasis on making high-fashion's glamour accessible rather than on exclusive design or elite fashion culture itself,' Berry argues. 'This accessibility is provided, in spite of opulent and "impractical" displays of clothing, through the evocation of traditions of popular spectacle, melodrama, and masquerade' (ibid.: 48). Hollywood effected a major shift in the way fashion worked by creating a glamorous blend of high fashion, popular spectacle and street style that was both theatrical and reproducible.

As fashion icons, stars exercised a new and highly important role. Their emergence marked a redefinition of taste elites as they were the first to take fashion to the masses, to display expensive materials, creative designs, original gowns and furs, all of which had 'connotations of high society, European "taste" and exclusiveness' (Dyer 1979: 42). In essence, stars dressed to excite attention; their look was sumptuous and theatrical. 'Dietrich's things were more than fashion – they were super-fashion,' the designer Head once said (quoted in Tapert 1998: 238). This conformed to Dietrich's own definition of glamour as 'something indefinite, something inaccessible to normal women – an unreal paradise, desirable but basically out of reach' (quoted in Fox 1995: 56–7). Stars inevitably influenced style and invaded the fashion magazines that had once been the preserve of the social elite. For example, Horst P. Horst photographed Dietrich and many others for *Vogue*. It was a measure of Hollywood's growing confidence and autonomy in this sphere that in the late 1930s designers like Orry-Kelly and Head were releasing their own retail collections. Although the European connotations of fashion were never eliminated, the presentation was distinctively American.

The role of the studio publicity departments in building careers and images was crucial. They manipulated news, inventing stories, suppressing others, rationing still more. As MGM publicity chief, Howard Strickling was responsible for constructing and maintaining star images. In his accounts actresses did not drink or smoke, they did not even have babies; each of their usually many romances was made in heaven. They were presented and photographed only in the most ideal circumstances. Metro staff were instructed never to mention what stars earned, as quoting money placed commerce ahead of glamour. Moreover everything was puffed up. 'If you had a farm, it was an estate. If you had a field it was full of horses,' said Warner Brothers' Celeste Holm (Fox 1995: 139–44). By these means stars were turned into larger-than-life figures who everyone, including ultimately the publicists themselves, believed were special.

The public and the mass market

Unlike other elites, the stars spoke directly to the dreams and aspirations of the masses. Watching films in the dark on a big screen, people projected on to the protagonists their own interior lives and aspirations. According to Jib Fowles (1992: 156–7), exposure to stars affected the emotional state of the audience. Specifically, they either *identified* with performers (i.e. became them in their fantasies) or *interacted* with them (making them an ideal object of sexual desire). Morin (1972: 24) linked the phenomenon of stardom to the rise of the working classes, a fact which, he argued, should be considered 'a total human phenomenon'.

'On the plane of daily emotions', he argued, the class struggle 'translated itself into new aspirations, new forms of individual participation'. Improvements in material conditions combined with new leisure practices to produce a situation in which workers and salaried employees 'join the spiritual civilisation of the bourgeoisie'. Alongside material demands, they made a new 'basic demand: the desire to live one's life, that is to say to live one's dreams and to dream one's life' (ibid.: 24). The studios were as aware of this as they were of most if not all aspects of audience behaviour on account of the close attention they paid to fan magazines and subsequently to the data furnished by market research organisations. The strong emotional content of most films was designed precisely to respond to the modern individual's desire for romance and sexual excitement by proxy (ibid.: 162).

Issues of 'front' and appearance became particularly important in a fluid social context. Choice of goods was linked to expressions of identity. This applied equally near the top and at the lower reaches of the social scale. Fitzgerald explored the problem of defining exactly what made a 'gentleman' in *The Beautiful and Damned* and returned to the theme in *The Great Gatsby*.[9] In both works, façades were important. As a poor boy who had reinvented himself, Jay Gatsby concealed his humble origins and ill-gotten wealth behind a glitzy lifestyle and an illusion of heritage. Yet, as Graham McCann (1996: 12) has argued, the need to erase earlier poor identities diminished in the course of the twentieth century. Thanks largely to the synthetic capability of the movies, the figure emerged of the polished everyman, symbolised by Cary Grant, who contained a core element of the working-class mongrel. The movies had an unrivalled capacity to induce longings and aspirations that was emphasised by the press. In this way, the popular media rather than Society became the arbiters of all other types of consumption.[10]

During the Depression years, the Hollywood studios toned down the off-screen image of the stars. The image of celebrity in popular magazines was domesticated and reduced to a blown-up version of the typical. Stars shared the basic values and pleasures of regular Americans, people seemed to be being told – they just had more opportunities to enjoy their substantial and varied leisure. Pictures proliferated of stars at work, on vacation, attending to their children, engaging in outdoor pursuits. There was a strong ludic element in the star lifestyle; parties, receptions, promotions and even filmmaking appeared as 'fun' and a 'game' to ordinary Americans, who came to see Hollywood as a leisure utopia; but in essence they did not seem too different from anyone else.

'Such ordinariness', Gamson writes,

> promoted a greater sense of connection and intimacy between
> the famous and their admirers. Crucial to this process was the
> ubiquitous narrative principle of the 'inside' journey into the 'real
> lives' of celebrities, lives much like the readers. Other common
> themes in entertainment celebrity texts of the time – love lives, the
> 'price they pay for fame', the desire to be just like the reader, the hard
> work of gaining and retaining success – further tightened the narrative
> links between the audience and the celebrated. (1994: 29–31; see also
> Baritz 1989: 94–8)

By drawing attention to appearance, clothing and self-presentation in
general, the visual media stressed the fact that, in a commercial and
mobile society, maintaining a good appearance was an important part
of the performance of daily life. This applied especially to women,
who were encouraged to see parallels between the studios' struggle to
maximise their stars' glamour value and popular appeal and their own
efforts to make the best of themselves (Berry 2000: 93). Cosmetics
companies led by Max Factor highlighted the artifice of Hollywood
make-up, celebrating 'the artificiality of the made-up face ... as evidence
of the democratization of beauty' (ibid.: 106).

The diffusion of cosmetics as well as other beauty products gave rise to
an idea of beauty as a construction requiring purchases. Commodity
culture posited the high-maintenance woman as its beauty ideal. Beauty
products stood in the mainstream of glamour because they were about
surfaces and façades, but also because they were predicated on the promise
of instant, magical transformation. Department stores made lipstick,
face powders and creams, rouge, vanishing cream and eyebrow pencils
available to provincial and lower-class markets. The type of beauty
preferred was standardised and increasingly industrialised. The world of
self-presentation was a 'giddy, glossy' one in which gloss was precisely
the dominant aesthetic (Frisby 1988: 166). In the popular imagination,
cosmetics were a way of creating a glamorous persona, a key prop in
the performance of seductive femininity, along with clothing and style
(Rappaport 2000: 198). As one make-up artist asserted, 'We can literally
manufacture' facial glamour 'right out of the paint-pot' (quoted in Peiss
1998: 151–2).

This democratisation was not widely appreciated by elites, intellectuals
and the Left. In all West European countries the arrival of American ideas,
products and seductions gave rise to objections and protests. But they

dovetailed with popular aspirations and found success, leading to local responses, imitations and re-elaborations. Marina Coslovi has shown that the advertisements for American beauty products that appeared in the Italian press drew attention to the role of knowledge and science:

> Therefore glamour implies a democratic divulgation of the discoveries that can improve life – and presupposes a democratisation that is presented as typical of American society. It is in that society that scientists feel a duty to put all their discoveries immediately at the disposal of everyone, and it is there that cosmetics companies like Max Factor take on the task of spreading the word about beauty. (n.d.: 3)

Cosmetics were still widely regarded as not respectable especially for young women, even as late as the 1930s. However, the years between 1909 and 1929 witnessed a doubling in the United States of perfume and cosmetics manufacturers and a tenfold increase in the volume of sales (Peiss 1998: 97). The movies, with their historical fantasies of Egypt, Turkey and Persia (Cleopatra constituting a recurrent motif), contributed decisively to this. As a result, a transition occurred from a local, small-scale beauty culture dominated by women selling to women to a corporate system run by professionals and managers which rolled out national systems of mass production, distribution, marketing and selling. Women were still prominent, but old practices were displaced by a business culture that fuelled the development of consumption. Advertising, radio sponsorship and magazines helped generate 'mass produced images [that] distinctly and powerfully began to influence female self-conceptions and beauty rituals' (ibid.: 134).

The movies were also vital to the development of mass fashion. Although Warner Brothers actually licensed costumes in 1934, many of the most notable commercial initiatives in this sphere were independent or indirect in nature. For example, Waldman's Cinema Fashions, a chain of stores with a flagship outpost at Macy's in New York which mass-produced the work of some studio designers, was an officially approved operation; neither were the endorsements which stars offered free of charge to Max Factor. Advertising was something that producers and some stars were uneasy about because it undermined the element of mystery that was essential to glamour. Mary Pickford turned down a potentially lucrative advertising contract on the grounds that it would be undignified and risky to have her name 'bandied about in all sorts of good, bad, and indifferent commercial projects'. Other top stars followed suit (Schickel 1976: 53). Nevertheless, commercial tie-ins were a central part of movie promotion; some involved national deals between studios and manufacturers over specific films, while others were left to the local initiative of exhibitors. 'Product placement' – the strategic placement of products in films – began in 1933 when MGM signed a $500,000 deal with Coca-Cola. And, as Charles Eckert (1991: 30–44) shows, star images were frequently seen in stores and were regarded by sales departments as merchandising assets. Like mannequins, stars could show clothes, cosmetics and other products to best effect. Moreover, after their box office standing had declined, many stars traded on their celebrity by offering fashion advice and sponsoring products.[11] In the era before labels and brands, stars offered an appeal that could spill over on to products. In America especially, there were direct connections between department stores and movie theatres; both in their own way were palaces of consumption (Albrecht 1991). The movies helped people to dream and the apparatus of consumerism assisted them in partly turning those dreams into lived experience. The ostentation of luxury was part of this. 'When Metro did a shot with Joan Crawford dragging a fifteen- or twenty-thousand dollar mink coat along the ground', MGM screenwriter William Ludwig said, 'every woman in the audience thought, "Boy, would I like to do that! That's the way to live!" ' (quoted in Davis 1993: 368). 'By the mid-1930s', Berry notes, 'Hollywood-endorsed fashions were available everywhere, from Saks to Sears Roebuck'. The tradition of home-sewing meant that many middle- and working-class women also produced their own versions of screen style. The advent of movie-influenced fashion had two main effects: it undermined the influence of traditional social leaders and it concealed the facts of mass production beneath an alluring veneer.

The feminine ideal that Hollywood projected signified excitement, luxury and sexuality at a time when the lives of most women in America and elsewhere were dominated by scarcity and dowdiness.[12] Although surface image was vital, 'star glamour was understood not only in terms of appearance, but also as signifying confidence, sophistication and self-assurance, which was perceived by female spectators as desirable and inspirational' (Baritz 1989: 154). Precisely this perceived gap, which in later years would result in sharp critiques of the tyranny of glamour (e.g. Wolf 1990), allowed women in the middle decades of the century to dream and use that dream to form pictures of their ideal selves (Stacey 1994: 110). The fashioning process of stardom in this sense paralleled the work of femininity, which required the consumption and absorption of images even in the relative absence of products. Young working women in their late teens or early twenties were particularly reliant on their contemporaries and the mass media for their source of orientation and as such were just the sort of 'other-directed' personalities that the sociologist David Reisman (1950) saw as the new American character-type emerging with consumer society. They were less 'inner-directed' (i.e. reliant on values assimilated at an early age) than the older generation and placed more importance on exterior self-fashioning and personal relationships. Even in the workplace, they were less likely to think of themselves as loyal and efficient assistants than as 'glamor-exuding personalities' (ibid.: 265).

The picture of the pre-war working-class girl as being lipsticked, silk-stockinged and dressed 'like an actress' is one that derives from the writer J. B. Priestley (quoted in Alexander 1989: 245). But, as Sally Alexander points out, young women in London really did want to live their lives differently from their mothers and, if education had failed them, this feeling derived 'enormous impetus from the cinema' (ibid.: 263). 'Via the high street or the sewing machine', she argues 'the mantle of glamour passed from the aristocrat and courtesan to the shop, the office, or factory girl via the film star' (ibid.: 264). The advantage of the film stars was that they were unlike women of the older generation or actual aristocrats. In their polished allure they were also different from local, homely entertainers and more like the confident well-dressed women of the East End. Unlike the prostitutes and courtesans of the nineteenth century, the glamorous screen heroine offered the fantasy that she was little more than the girl next door who was her fan (ibid.: 265–6).

Glamour was a vogue word of the 1930s and many commercial enterprises bought into it. Even *Vogue* was not exempt. Condé Nast decided to exploit the opportunities of the mass market by founding first Patterns of Hollywood in 1932 – these were distributed through chain stores rather than exclusive *Vogue* pattern outlets – and then, in 1939, a new magazine, *Glamour of Hollywood*. The aim was to make available to ordinary women the knowledge of maximising appeal and attractiveness that movie designers, costume departments and make-up artists had developed for the stars (Seebohm 1982: 323–5). The magazine exploited the sex-and-style publicity power of the film industry and signalled this by publishing the picture of a film star on most covers. It may be questioned how far such operations achieved respectability. Peiss suggests that the figure of the painted woman continued to haunt cosmetics companies and the ideals they elaborated. Make-up was no longer the mark of the prostitute, but too much 'still implied female coarseness, promiscuity and low social standing'

(1998: 152). It is possible that this mattered less to consumers than to manufacturers, since she also reports that when one company put out two products, one branded *Lady* and the other *Hussy*, the latter outsold the former by five to one (ibid.: 3–4). Given the traditional associations of cosmetics with seduction, it is scarcely surprising that some sexual connotation aided sales even in a context where the made-up face was becoming normative. No company did away completely with the suggestion that its products could aid users to attract men.

The Lady, however, did not disappear. In the course of the 1930s, Hollywood became more respectable, and tailored its appeal to the conventional domestic aspirations of its female audiences. This trend did not substantially relent for over twenty years. A primary thrust of Hollywood glamour in the 1950s was a refinement and extension of the earlier bid to embrace respectability. At precisely the moment when conventional high society ceased to be influential, the lady-like ideal prospered as a deracinated mood or look. As Erica Carter's examination of postwar German womanhood has shown, the popularity of this ideal could also be seen in women's magazines and advertisements. It may seem strange that in just the period in which mass culture was becoming predominant, consumerism was beginning to take shape and the old rigidity of the social hierarchy was undergoing sharp erosion, there should have been a flowering in Europe of images so evidently shot through with aloofness and elitist chic. The tall, slim, angular woman, perfectly groomed and cool, proliferated in magazines and advertisements. In fact, although these images were unapproachable for some women, they were not as removed from the average as might be thought. First, as Carter (1997: 209–25) has pointed out in her examination of German women's magazines, there was an emancipatory element in that these images often showed women acting in a confident and sophisticated way in public places, unencumbered by family and domestic duties. Second, they portrayed womanhood as fashion, taste and consumerism, in other words as a process involving pleasures. Third, the upper-class woman was historically the most at home with things that were now coming within the reach of the many: surplus spending, home comforts, domestic help (appliances now, not servants), beautification, fashion. Fourth, images of a model like Lisa Fonssagrives, and by extension those of other models of her type and some 'class' film stars, actually 'seemed accessible to every woman', David Seidner has written. They offered grace, balance and reserve, combined with a certain energy 'that resonated in the subconscious of generations of women to whom [Fonssagrives'] appeal was irresistible' (Seidner 1997: 20). Such women appeared to be in control and true to themselves. Fonssagrives' 'dance experience gave her a sense of theatre so that the elaborate costume never looked mannered or affected – a comfortable masquerade'.

In the 1950s Hollywood glamour presented itself with at least one face other than the Lady, namely the pin-up. Although the golden age of the studios was over and film-going was in decline, Marilyn Monroe provided 1950s audiences with an unrivalled body spectacle. In contrast to stars like Joan Crawford, Jean Harlow and even Rita Hayworth, whose elaborate wardrobes and grooming signalled their particular relationship with female audiences, Monroe relied to an unprecedented degree on her body for her appeal to men. Although the sexualisation of star figures dovetailed with the central importance that sexuality was assuming in the dynamics of individual identity in consumer society, Monroe's compliant availability was far more restrictive a view of femininity than had been offered by any previous major star (Dyer 1988). Her nude calendar shot for the first issue of *Playboy* opened the way to a narrow but persistent definition of glamour as soft pornography that is still prevalent among photographers.

Monroe was the last seductive image produced by the studio system before its final demise due to the challenge of television, anti-monopoly rulings and the rise of domesticity. Her suicide, Morin wrote, signalled the end of an era. It revealed that tragedy lay behind the polished image of the wonderful, rich, happy life of the stars. After this, Morin writes, 'There is no longer any ideal star, no longer any happy Olympus' (1972: 160). This disenchantment was accompanied by a fragmentation and diffusion of glamour. None of this meant that glamour disappeared. In a culture in which consumerism remained a central experience and in which media images were ubiquitous, this could not be so. But the very plurality of enticing images, produced by magazines, the fashion industry, film and television producers, advertisers and public relations companies created a situation of saturation that undercut the distance necessary to cultivate mystery and arouse envy. The mundane qualities of television in particular militated against glamour because these rendered everything immediately visible, accessible and without mystery. In these circumstances four responses flourished: irony and pastiche; re-proposition of the gestures and visual clichés of the Hollywood glamour of the past; cultivation of elitist forms of glamour relatively unexploited by the mass market; invention and deployment of new vehicles of visual seduction by adapting old codes to contemporary conditions.

Part II
The Visual Language of Glamour

The material culture of glamour is paradoxically both rich and poor, lavish and worthless. It is an extraordinary repertoire of colours, images, emotions, sensations, visual spectacles and façades built up over time and which consists of visual tricks and effects that have, at different times, proved romantic, stimulating or magical. There is little or nothing of enduring aesthetic value in glamour. Although various of its manifestations may approximate to art, they have no truly artistic goals. The aim is fantasy not art, and the intention is not to reveal any truth to the spectator but rather to conceal it. Indeed deception is the primary purpose of the material culture of glamour. To this end it is highly seductive; it speaks primarily to the eyes, aiming through spectacle to dazzle and enchant with the goal of concealing the mundane and the commercial. Glamour, therefore, is not normally tasteful. Precisely because it is an aesthetic of persuasion, albeit a mediated and sometimes a disguised one, the desire to attract attention overrides all other considerations. In this sense it is always marked by display; to attract and distract is its simultaneous programme.

The Great Exhibitions of the nineteenth century constituted the first arena in which the culture of commercial seduction found its first systematic deployment. Observers lamented the aesthetic hotchpotch that met visitors, who found themselves transported to magical, faraway places in which approximations of real historical and geographical contexts acted as stimuli to the creativity of the imagination. All devotion to accuracy and philology disappeared in evocations that owed more to the theatrical stage set than to the museum. Like later film sets or television shows, the pavilions of the exhibitions employed cheap, brash materials to create an illusion of luxury, pleasure and abundance. This very persistent commitment to impressions of things other and better than what they are is a feature of all the materials and images associated with glamour.

One of the first sources of the appeal of this deracinated culture of pure image was the exotic. By eclectically assembling beautiful faraway motifs, the unfamiliar and the past into a chaotic but desirable mélange, designers and image-makers created one of the most potent vehicles of escape from humdrum realities. This overarching significance of the exotic, although never the exclusive inspiration for the material culture of glamour, may lead to the conclusion that glamour is a sole language, a portmanteau aesthetic into which anything may be put and from which anything may be extracted. In fact, it is possible to determine quite distinct currents within the language of glamour. Although these elide and overlap, and may also combine and reinforce each other, it is not artificial to distinguish them. On the contrary, as the materiality of glamour developed out of the exhibitions and invaded stores, quarters and whole cities before finding a special home in photography, the press and the mass media, it developed distinctive practices and themes. The aim here is to map out in eight scenarios the main strands within the material culture of glamour. That is to say, the intention is to illustrate and categorise the variety of visual effects and sensations that have been associated with glamour over the last 150 years. Together, these constitute a system of visual enchantment: the glamour system.

The chapters that follow are primarily evocative. Although there is some analysis of the purposes and uses of each permutation of glamour, the aim is to show the extraordinarily eclectic sources that constitute each visual effect. Some are related to colours, others to metals and yet more to pure effects. Precisely because glamour is all about imagination, deracination and sensation, the visual language it employed was fashioned from materials that include classical and Celtic mythology, ancient civilisations, religion, Renaissance painting, and signs of monarchical and aristocratic distinction. Each scenario seeks to examine these sources while also paying particular attention to the development of this source material into a visual language of persuasion in nineteenth-century commerce, Hollywood cinema and contemporary advertising and culture.

4
Exotic Enticements

In his classic study of the West's distorted view of the Islamic and Arab world, *Orientalism*, Edward Said ([1978] 1995) explored the ways in which political and economic domination produced representations and misrepresentations, forms of knowledge and recurrent attitudes of fear and attraction. Formed in the nineteenth century in Britain and France, the two countries which exercised the greatest influence in the Middle and Far East, Orientalism, understood as a Western conception of the Orient, shaped institutions, practices and modes of perception which still to some extent govern the way the West views the Arab world. Said was concerned mainly with the origins and organisation of the discipline of Oriental Studies, but in the course of his argument he also examined broader cultural representations and imaginings. The Orient, he argued, was 'not an unlimited extension beyond the familiar European world, but rather a closed field, a theatrical stage affixed to Europe'. 'In the depths of this Oriental stage', he continued,

> stands a prodigious cultural repertoire whose individual items evoke a fabulously rich world: the Sphinx, Cleopatra, Eden, Troy, Sodom and Gomorrah, Astarte, Isis and Osiris, Sheba, Babylon, the Genii, the Magi, Nineveh, Prester John, Mahomet, and dozens more; settings, in some cases names only, half-imagined, half-known; monsters, devils, heroes; terrors, pleasures, desires. (ibid.: 63)

This repertoire provided nourishment to the European imagination from the Middle Ages to the eighteenth century and produced myths which became accepted at all levels of culture and politics. Said did not consider developments in Western consumer culture, fashion and film, since he confined his study to intellectual and high culture, but he did allude to them, when he indicated that 'the Orient is an integral part of European *material* civilization and culture' (ibid.: 2).

In fashion and advertising the *frisson* of danger associated with the Orient derives from its status as the *locus classicus* of sensuousness, perversion and debauchery. It also offers a ready language of desire in strong colours, powerful scents and associations with luxury and splendour. As with all the influences on which contemporary fashion draws, the Orient may be topical one season and old news the next. In reality though, it is only particular permutations of the myth that fall out of fashion, for the Orient is so varied and rich in its possibilities as a reservoir of ideas and inspirations that it may be identified as a structural aspect of Western fashion. The Orient, divorced from any time or place, simply serves as background, a way of adding elements of dream and escapism into fashion items and commodities which possess only a distant link to Eastern culture.

The Oriental reference point became a rich source of inspiration for the beauty and cosmetics industry. During the First World War, Elizabeth Arden first drew on 'the glamor of the mysterious East' to win new customers for her toning cream *Ganesh*. 'She completely repudiated the assumption that *Ganesh* had anything to do with the lower jaw,' wrote her biographers (Lewis and Woodworth 1972: 82). 'According to the copy, Ganesa was the Hindu god of wisdom, "Near whose temple in India, Mrs. Adair [i.e. Arden] first learned the secret of the now world-famous muscle cream" '. Fragrances, beauty treatments and cosmetics soon all harnessed the allure of the East. The appeal of the East in this context was essentially twofold. On the one hand, it was a source of timeless wisdom and ancient knowledge. On the other, it offered the allure of the dark, the sensual and the forbidden. In make-up, the Orient often offers an excuse for a total exaggerated look that serves to awaken desire for a single product. Consumers are offered something exotic, sensual and transgressive, to appeal to their 'dark sides'. The sexual allusions typical of advertising for fragrances such as *Mitsouko, Vol de Nuit* and *L'heure bleue* by Guerlain, *Tabac blond, Bellodiga* and *Narcisse Noir* by Caron, and *Cuir de Russie* by Chanel are often understated on the surface, masked by an imagery of deserts, dreaminess and timeless settings. But, precisely because of the traditional associations of these with the erotic and the transgressive, they are actually more deeply arousing.

Certain Oriental films have left deep traces of the collective imagination; these include *Casablanca, Lawrence of Arabia* and *The Shanghai Gesture*. But also many recent films are set there: *The Last Emperor, Shanghai*

Surprise, The Lover and Chinese films such as *The Red Lantern*. The addition of films from China and other countries is a novelty; but the exotic background to adventure or colonial films is still typical. One such film is *Indochine*, in which Catherine Deneuve changes costume 22 times against a turbulent South-East Asian background.

The origins of the West's long love affair with the fabrics, scents and spices of the East is as old as trade with the Orient. Chinese textiles were imported regularly from the seventeenth century, and silks, satins, painted materials and embroidery exercised a fascination which remained. More specifically, Napoleon's expedition to Egypt led to the replacement of neoclassical influences on fashion with a new cult of the Orient. 'It brought the discovery of a new exoticism, a country of the imagination as yet unexplored, and hieroglyphics and Sphinx's heads soon mingled with the old classical *motifs* in interior decoration and in jewelry,' James Laver wrote (1937: 21–3). 'Antique cameos were succeeded by scarabs and reproductions of the Egyptian funerary figures; but the scholarship necessary for the understanding of ancient Egyptian art was lacking, and so the Egyptian mania tended to merge into a revived Orientalism, an enthusiasm for the things of the Near East. Turbans began to make their appearance as female headdresses, and lasted, as was natural enough, well into the Romantic period.' Thanks to this vogue for the Oriental, Indian shawls made of the most varied fabrics became an indispensable article of women's toilet. Military uniforms, furniture and architecture were also influenced.

The Orient has always been loosely defined. Since it was always an imaginative construct more than a geographical reality, there was never any need to fix its contours precisely. Consequently, the lure of the exotic could be found at different times in China and the Far East, the Arab world of the Near and Middle East, or even in Southern Europe. For northern Europeans in the late eighteenth and nineteenth centuries, Italy, Spain and Greece were countries which had made fundamental contributions to Western culture in the past, but had since relapsed into primitivism. Like the Orient proper, examined by Said, these countries were infused in the northern imagination with sex, violence, mystery and inferiority. No less than Asia or Arabia, they were reconstituted as stages on which a spectacle was constructed for northern consumption.

Venice, the historic crossroad between West and East, offers the most striking example of the Orientalism of the West, although travellers to southern Italy and Spain did not have to look far to find there Arabic influences in architecture. John Pemble cites early nineteenth-century authors who found in Venice the legacy of Byzantium, of which it had been for 400 years a frontier city. 'The variety of exotic merchandise', wrote William Beckford in 1782, 'the perfume of coffee, the shade of awnings, and the sight of Greeks and Asiatics sitting cross-legged under them, made me think myself in the bazaars of Constantinople' (quoted in Pemble 1995: 118). Théophile Gautier described Venice as 'an oriental dream', while others found in St Mark's something resembling a mosque. For Pemble, ambiguous attitudes to Venice reflected ambivalent attitudes towards the Orient. This was no longer viewed with the hostility of earlier centuries as the empire of the infidel; on the contrary the Islamic world was viewed with some admiration by Goethe and Carlyle, and more broadly it was seen as a place of seductive and chaotic dreams. But underlying these were residual fears and hatreds of barbarism and malignancy.

The connections between Romantic sensibilities and consumerism have been brought persuasively to light by Colin Campbell. 'The cultural logic of modernity is not merely that of rationality as expressed in the activities of calculation and experiment', he has argued; 'it is also that of passion, and the creative dreaming born of longing' (1987: 227). The dynamism of the West relies on a restless energy that is the fruit of the tension between dream and reality, pleasure and utility. In the particular conjuncture in which it became an integral part of the developing retail industry, the culture of imagination and hedonism, found great source material in the culture of Orientalism. Indeed, it might even be argued that the Oriental myth became so important culturally because it satisfied so many of the impulses – for escape, dreaming and the desire for novelty – that had fuelled Romanticism and Sentimentalism.

The myth of the Orient and more generally of the culturally different was present in a wide variety of texts and fields from the early nineteenth century. 'The logics of imperialist expansion generated an inexhaustible supply of references to and representations of cultural otherness,' Rita Felski (1945: 140) states. Orientalism was a resource which was used to the full by advertisers and by the great commercial exhibitions of the second half of the century. Exoticism was to become central to mass culture; 'the nostalgic representation of the enigmatic and primitive ceased to be a prerogative of artists and became part of a more general modern cosmopolitan sensibility'.

As a sort of tableau for the obsessions and dreams of the West, the Orient was suggestive and powerful. While racist theorists and scientists of one sort or another all struggled to demonstrate the inferiority of the peoples and cultures of the South and the East, other writers and explorers helped to popularise interest in religions, beliefs, practices that were alternative to Western rationality and materialism. This interest would be renewed at various intervals with the discovery of new treasures of the past, such as the tomb of Tutankhamen in 1923. However, even without a material basis it was kept alive in fiction. Here, 'the East was perceived as a realm where mystical unknown forces still held sway', Felski has written. 'Numerous novels and stories by H. Rider Haggard, Rudyard Kipling and other writers of the period situated lurid descriptions of supernatural or paranormal events in the exotic outposts of Empire, as a liminal zone not yet fully bound by the laws of Enlightenment modernity' (ibid.: 136). In these novels, romantic exoticism triumphed. The Orient offered 'a magic carpet of the imagination' which could go anywhere, above all into realms of mystery, plenty and erotic transfiguration. Outside of history and modernity, the Oriental stage furnished sublime figures to tempt the bored Westerner.

In his study of the Paris Arcades, Benjamin noted that the resemblance to Christian churches of the first commercial centres to use iron and glass was replaced in early department stores by a new reference point. With their great glassed-in roofs, they 'seemed to have been modeled after Oriental bazaars', he noted (quoted in Buck-Morss 1990: 111). The agents and architects of the new consumer culture used materials to create myths and turn places of commerce into stages. It was in the United States, above all, that aesthetic desires led to the creation of mass commercial forms. William Leach has explored the way in which the display and decoration of goods, with the intention of manipulating and extending consumer desire, became a matter of great seriousness from the 1890s. Traders and commercial designers drew on all myths and traditions to invest artificial things and urban spaces with plasticity and life: 'they strove for theatrical effects and for a new enchantment, systematically interpreting and dramatizing commodities and commodity environments in ways that disguised and transformed them into what they were not' (Leach 1989: 100).

The modern approach to display involved the use of an abundance of glass, light and artificial colours. To stimulate desire, department stores, theatres, restaurants, hotels and movie houses were all decorated with lavish murals, mirrors, luxurious fittings and glassed ceilings. The visual effects were intended to draw consumers into an unfamiliar and exciting system of aesthetics and endow commodities with imaginative and dream-like properties. American cities vied with each other in the early years of the twentieth century to produce stunning colourful visual displays. 'Urban jeweled forms appeared as vertical monuments flooded with light, symbols of the fairy-tale orientalism that overtook public dream culture,' Leach observes (ibid.: 105). The prototype was the Tower of Jewels at the 1915 San Francisco World Fair, a festival totem pole of 50,000 jewels in five colours. These jewelled forms dazzled the viewer and beckoned Americans to the pleasures of a new era of consumerism.

Although the invasion of public spaces was probably uniquely American, similar trends occurred elsewhere in department stores and other commercial outlets. 'Sydney's shops', Gail Reekie has observed, 'with their brocade chairs, gilded Napoleonic furniture, Venetian framed mirrors, lead-lighted doors ... were described in 1919 as "Eastern bazaars – rich in colouring and designs, and wonderful in display" ' (1993: 89). New York stores were probably at the forefront of the drive towards atmospheres of sensual pleasure, which drew freely on Oriental culture and design, but Marshall Field's in Chicago left little to be desired. In order to stir up longing for luxury, the store's display director from the mid-1890s, Arthur Frazer, conceived and executed theatrical settings for commodities which included golden temples and pillars, carved animals, green and blue drapes, plush cushions and huge goddess figures (Leach 1989: 118). The aim was to amaze and arouse desire and stimulate impulse-buying. The trance effect of the exotic and of rich colour extended to the stage decor of the Ziegfeld Follies and even the Metropolitan Opera House (ibid.: 124).

Orientalism was never respectable. As literature, popular entertainment or merchandising theme, it always offered a dream of escape from the constrictions of the official and the moral. But it offered such a variety of languages, symbols and possibilities of expression to the protagonists of the burgeoning culture of consumerism that it became an irresistible and integral part of their strategy of desire. The 'Oriental stage' referred to by Said was affixed to the West as a consequence of empire but it also possessed resources that went beyond those of the West itself. In particular the very features which in Western perceptions marked it as inferior – its taste for luxury, impulse, desire, primitivism and excess – became institutionalised in popular culture and entertainment.

Film, Broadway, opera and the theatre all featured works with Orientalist themes, ranging from Puccini's *Madam Butterfly* to movies of Cleopatra's life. The most ambitious of these was D. W. Griffith's Orientalist phantasmagoria *Intolerance*. In the film's hyberbolic Babylonian scenes, there was little pretence of historical authenticity. Instead, a fetishistic gaze was cast over a range of commodities: decor, statues, exotic animals, costumes and headwear, large numbers of bodies and war machinery. The monumental ambition of the work and the deliberate desire to stun with excess and the unfamiliar should be connected, Miriam Hansen has argued, to the World Expositions of the 1851–1915 period. In fact, there is evidence to suggest that it was the Tower of Jewels which particularly led Griffith to aim for grandiosity and to make use of the vogue for Orientalism (Hansen 1991: 237). Although Hansen highlights some discontinuities, a line may clearly be drawn from *Intolerance* to Douglas Fairbanks' huge 1924 hit *The Thief of Baghdad* and Rudolph Valentino's *Sheik* films. All provided otherness, abundance and polymorphous eroticism (ibid.: 238–9).

Given the development and the importance of the Oriental vogue by the early twentieth century, it should not be at all surprising that Diaghilev's *Ballets russes* enjoyed such universal success and such wide and lasting influence. Performing in Paris in 1909, the company's approach to choreography, music and dance was hailed for its dynamism and absolute originality. But the visual impact of the sets and costumes of *Schéhérezade* was no less, so dramatic, Oriental and in shocking taste were they. Bakst's designs stimulated a new vogue for the Oriental in the 'harem look', but also provided new ideas about dress, form and colour that exercised a vital influence at just the moment when modern fashion was struggling into existence. The *Ballets russes* opened a kaleidoscope of colours and possibilities previously undreamed of. However, it was only an eccentric *grande dame* like the Marchesa Casati, the Venice-based aristocrat whose personal menagerie included a macaw, a leopard, an albino gorilla and a large snake, who could actually wear a Bakst-designed dress. Most rich fashionable women found their Oriental tastes catered for more satisfactorily by Paul Poiret.

According to Laver (1937: 89–90), Poiret and the Russian Ballet developed at the same time and independently of each other. Certainly Poiret always denied that he copied the Russians and refused to execute dresses from Bakst's designs. Poiret first worked for the houses of Doucet and Worth and then set up on his own. From the beginning he made himself the apostle of the Oriental influence in fashion, designing the Confucius cloak, proposing turbans and introducing harem pants. By doing battle against the formalism of haute couture and the restrictions of the corset, Poiret produced a fashion that tied in with the demands of modern women. Poiret's influence on Parisian society was rapid and remarkable, not least because of his flair for publicity. Learning the lesson of display from the expositions and the stores, he turned fashion parades into spectacular events, using music, luxurious settings and art to arouse desire. He also worked as a scenic artist and staged extravagant thematic *fêtes* to which fashionable Paris was invited. At an Arabian Nights ball in

1911 he doused the guests with *Miniaret* and *Aladdin*, perfumes invented by him for the occasion (*Vogue Italia* 1995: 108). As they entered, guests found coloured tents, fountains, black servants, parrots and monkeys and a dark bar with luminous liquors (Laver 1937: 92). When pictures of this and similar entertainments appeared in the foreign press, the Oriental vogue travelled more widely than ever before.

The figure who more than anyone else brought southern Europe and the East into the centre of the Romantic imagination in the English-speaking world was Lord Byron. The Romantic hero *par excellence*, Byron associated himself with the Orient, with Italy and, finally, with Greece. After his death in 1824, Laver notes, Orientalism triumphed once more, with turbans, flatter than those of the Napoleonic era, being worn again (ibid.: 30). However, Byron's appropriation of Arabic chic revealed a deeper aspect of Orientalism than a merely exterior fashion. In his poem *Don Juan*, he created a fantasy in which the Orient figured as a place of sexual and sartorial instability, where the rigid gender identities of the West ceased to hold sway. As Marjorie Garber has observed (cited in Cook 1996: 62), Byron mobilised all the conventional traits of a mysterious East for the purposes of both fantasy and social critique.

The exotic was always intimately linked to the erotic. In Corelli's novels, Felski finds that, 'against sultry stage sets of palm trees, lagoons, and pyramids, men and women revert to a primitive condition, magnetically drawn together by extremities of passion and desire in an eternal pattern of domination and submission' (1995: 138). In women's popular fiction, the figure of the masterful male whose sexual power is linked to his non-Western origins was as common as the powerfully seductive *femme fatale* in men's adventure fiction. The former offered the *frisson* of transgressing imaginatively the barrier of ethnic and racial difference, while the latter played on masculine fears of being destroyed by irrational femininity. The 'blurring of sexual boundaries', which was one of the options the Orient offered, was not simply a fantasy, but was referred to quite explicitly by the most famous explorer of the Victorian era, Sir Richard Burton (see Showalter 1990: 81–2). Whether real or not, the setting of novels in this area, using figures from its stage, left novelists free to escape from convention and play with the fantasies of readers. In the Western imagination, the Other was always feminised. One of the reasons the Orient appealed, while also being feared, was precisely its subversive ambiguity in areas where no such ambiguity was officially admitted. The Orient in short seduced men into effeminacy or at least took them out of their black and grey uniforms.

The exotic-sadistic *femme fatale* was not always a figure of the Orient or the South. Even if she was located there, she might be white, like

Ayesha, the heroine of Rider Haggard's *She*. But many of the character traits or costume features of the *femme fatale* were drawn from an Oriental repertoire. Her morbid associations with death, the natural and the supernatural fitted the image of the East as a place of cruelty, superstition and danger. In fact, as Mario Praz has shown in his magisterial study *The Romantic Agony* ([1948] 1986: 172), the *femme fatale* was born in Spain, albeit the imaginary Spain of Merimée's *Carmen*. She then moved to Russia, before Gautier and Flaubert located her definitively in 'a climate of barbaric and oriental antiquity, where all the most uncontrolled desires can be expressed and the cruelest imaginations can take on a concrete form'. It was Gautier, 'the true founder of exotic aestheticism' (ibid.: 179), who turned Cleopatra into 'a sort of oriental Lady Macbeth' and made her a prototype of the *femme fatale* (ibid.: 183).

The *femme fatale*, Bram Dijkstra (1986) has shown, was the product of a profoundly misongynist culture. She encapsulated and played out all the fears of the feminine, the irrational, the degenerate and the racially impure which permeated Victorian culture. As such, this figure mesmerised and fascinated. Although some examples, notably Salomé, were colourless, the opposition the *femme fatale* offered to the standard image of virtuous womanhood lay rather in the way she combined 'authority and vigor with intense sexual power' and 'imperiously [expressed] her disdain for the world and values of men' (Felski 1995: 139). For this reason, she may well have appealed to some women; certainly the great actresses of the period, from Sarah Bernhardt to Eleonora Duse and Ellen Terry, revelled in such roles. The masquerade they performed was not wholly removed from the experience of ordinary women. Kathy Peiss points out that make-up was associated with the primitive and barbarous; it was seen as a leftover from the past which hindered the progress of civilisation. 'The dominant discourse on cosmetics ... placed paint outside the truthful representation of personal and social identity, identifying cosmetics with disrepute and deceit, a debased female and non-European "other" ' (1996: 316).

The *femme fatale* drew her power from mastery of nature and sorcery. In her costume, she bore exterior witness to the eternal animal in woman. Feathers, elaborate head-gear, animal skins, capes, an abundance of jewellery and make-up testified to the role of woman as nature and as the chief artificer of civilisation (Paglia 1998). These features of costume became more apparent and more a part of the collective culture following the development of cinema into a mass entertainment. The extreme heroines of the silent era, including Theda Bara, Lyda Borelli and Asta Nielsen, brought a repertoire of gestures bordering on madness to the screen that would be short-lived but not without influence. In a more realistic vein, Greta Garbo and Marlene Dietrich carried on the tradition.

Because of her association with Joseph von Sternberg, a tireless Orientalist, Dietrich is perhaps the most interesting case. Each of her early Hollywood films, from *Blonde Venus* to *Shanghai Express, The Scarlet Empress* and finally *The Devil is a Woman*, contains elements of exoticism as eroticism and this is reflected in Travis Banton's costumes. Indeed, Hollywood glamour can be seen in part as a creation of the Dietrich–Banton partnership. 'Their collaboration created the "exotic, super high-fashion look" (characterized by feathers, veils and other glamorous accessories) that required Banton to create it and Dietrich to pull it off,' Sybil DelGaudio (1993: 27) has argued. As the studio which most leaned towards Europe for its look and appeal, Paramount was more intent than others on surrounding its stars with mysterious allure and a deep erotic fascination; MGM, for example, preferred a standardised surface glamour which was more identifiably American in its final effect. In all her films, Dietrich is a dislocated (fallen) woman and/or a woman who exercises her power over men without mercy. Sternberg's characteristic attention to surface and background detail produces a great number of set-piece scenes in which the deceptive nature of cinema and of woman is highlighted and explored. Frequently, as in *Shanghai Express*, where Dietrich's character is called Shanghai Lil, the seductiveness of a foreign city or place is linked to Dietrich's allure. Even when the setting is Western, Sternberg's love of the rich, cluttered, constricted space produced films that were beautiful and pleasurable to look at. They possess an Oriental richness. 'Exoticism is a term frequently used in describing Sternberg's style', Frank Krutnik has written, 'e.g., what is seen as his animation of the "dead space" of the image, a hyper-charging of the visual field by set and dress design; stylized object and character emplacement; the use of veiling, masking and lighting effects; and the measured dissolves and the slow exploratory camera tracks and cranes' (cited in DelGaudio 1993: 53).

The costuming reflects the mixing of the bizarre, the barbaric, the dangerous, the pagan and the animal. Pioneered in *Blonde Venus*, Dietrich's cross-dressing became, following that of Sarah Bernhardt, a hallmark. On other occasions, the particular sumptuousness of the costumes matched the setting: furs in *The Scarlet Empress*, set in the Russia of Catherine the Great; lace and veils in the Spanish context of *The Devil is a Woman*; and feathers in the Far Eastern location of *Shanghai Express*. All served simultaneously to heighten the exoticism of place and develop Dietrich's allure as star. Such indulgence was of course possible only with a female star on whom could be piled the meanings of the barbaric, the animal and so on. Claudette Colbert was given the treatment in De Mille's 1934 Egyptian fantasy *Cleopatra*. Banton draped her figure in shimmering lamé and gave her a heavy jewelled collar for her role as the Queen of the Nile. Her operetta-like costumes, however, paled by comparison with the extraordinary peacock feather costume worn by Theda Bara in 1917 for the first film version of Cleopatra (see LaVine 1981: 38–9, 140–1). Although Banton worked with many stars, he loved best to indulge Dietrich's sense of showmanship and taste for scene-stealing. He created the most extraordinary designs for her, once dressing her as Leda, complete with a swan's head and a costume covered with thousands of tiny feathers, each carefully painted by hand to create a subtle shaded effect. On another occasion, she was adorned as a white rose, here body encased in a full-length leotard covered with green bugle beads (ibid.: 171).

What do furs and feathers mean? It has been argued that bird symbolism was a recurrent feature of Sternberg's work, and that birds are employed in the films to add religious, sexual and poetic significance (ibid.: 27). The symbolism of birds and their relation to the feminine has been highlighted by Camille Paglia (1998). Plumage may be seen as one of the most easily appropriable of the animal kingdom's tools of seduction. The mythical resonance of plumage was understood and employed by Druids and Siberian shamans, as well as Merlin. The special costume in which the shaman shamanises, and in which Merlin is reputed to have disappeared beyond the human realm, was typically made of bird feathers, feathers representing 'the bird-soul which detaches itself from [the] body during the ecstatic trance, and flies aloft to the heavens' (Tolstoy 1985: 145–6). Animal skins enabled medicine men to 'acquire a means of becoming more than human'. Because 'the mythical animal-ancestor is conceived as the indestructible original of the life of the species … by becoming this mythical animal, man becomes something much greater and more powerful than himself' (ibid.: 149). They also have associations with power and sex. As Colin McDowell has argued, 'the woman in a fur coat has for many men this same primitive association. Magnificent in her borrowed skin, she betokens sex and power, to be overcome but also to overwhelm in her turn' (1992: 30).

On and off screen, furs became an integral part of the image of the Hollywood star between the 1930s and the 1950s. The image of material extravagance, which carried connotations of sexual excess (Emberley 1997: 9), combined with residual mythical meanings to create a powerful signifier of feminine stardom. Fur also carried with it a history of associations with absolute power and mastery which added further to the star's symbolic resonance. This association was famously inverted in Leopold von Masoch's late nineteenth-century novel of voluntary sub-jugation *Venus in Furs*, in which through 'the fantasy of the feminine despot, European bourgeois femininity is mapped onto the occidental fantasy of Oriental despotism' (ibid.: 87). By wearing furs, stars offered a model which middle-class women who lacked economic agency could copy in order to acquire symbolic agency 'from the erotic power and material wealth represented by a fur coat' (ibid.: 138). In fashion today, feathers and furs come and go, although the latter has got stuck in a well-defined role and symbolism. Both do better when fashion takes an opulent or theatrical turn, for they add drama and danger. 'With fashion increasingly taking its cue from the glamour of old Hollywood and the allure of silver-screen sirens, the feather is regaining prominence', wrote Hamish Bowles in American *Vogue* in 1994 (1994: 261–7). Perfect for women who wanted to make an entrance, to look different or spectacular, they were associated with women of a certain age or period, like Mae West or Barbara Cartland, who in her later years was rarely seen without pink ostrich feathers.

Leopard prints represent a curious example of the way in which an old look can be reappropriated and reinvented. Made a trademark by Hollywood stars of a certain type, like Jayne Mansfield, the leopard skin became a stereotype of the look of the sexually available woman. Leopard prints became the stock-in-trade of experienced working-class woman; as such they were a regular part of the wardrobe of the pub landlady Bet Gilroy in the British television soap opera *Coronation Street*. In the mid-1990s leopard was rescued from the depths of the fashion dustbin and reinvested with new postmodern desirability by Dolce & Gabbana. They took it upmarket and made it desirable for clothes and furniture. They could do this because of its continuing association with brazenness and self-confidence. It was therefore appropriate to queens of the media jungle, women for whom animal prints had nothing to do with camouflage and everything to do with attracting *paparazzi* like a magnet.

5
Sensational Gold

Gold is primarily associated with royalty. From time immemorial kings and queens have surrounded themselves with symbols of their status and power. Material splendour served to consolidate glory. As a page at the court of Louis XVI observed: 'Ceremonies are one of the most important pillars of regal authority. Strip the prince of the splendour that surrounds him and he will be no more, in the eyes of the multitude, than an ordinary man, because the people respect their king less for his virtues and his rank than for the gold with which he is covered and the pomp that surrounds him' (quoted in Bertelli 1990: 12). Even in the 1960s, long after the decline of absolute monarchy, the wedding of Britain's Princess Margaret to Anthony Armstrong-Jones offered the British royal family an opportunity to display its accumulated magnificence. As Kitty Kelley writes, 'The wedding was a dazzling spectacle of royalty, from the bride's diamond tiara to the five gold carriages transporting members of the royal family. Inside Westminster Abbey, the setting sparkled with more shades of gold than a Fabergé box. From the Queen's gilt chair to the Archbishop's polished miter to the solid gold altar plate, everything gleamed, reflecting immense wealth' (1997: 82).

Even more than the major ones, lesser monarchies have resorted in the twentieth century to opulent display. The ceremony at the Aga Khan III's Golden Jubilee in 1936 which saw the Imam receive his weight in gold had no precedent in the Ismaili faith. Although it is not entirely clear that the Aga Khan's mother was responsible for the idea, Anne Edwards argues that there is no doubt that 'this plan was developed and set in motion during the time of Lady Ali Shah's visit to an England observing with great enthusiasm the King's Silver Jubilee and that she was a moving force in arranging a Golden Jubilee for the Aga Khan' (1995: 128). Drawing on legends about early nineteenth-century maharajahs and ancient Hindu monarchs, a ceremony was fashioned which would enable each subject, from the richest to the poorest, to contribute to the gold that would be given in tribute to the Imam. By receiving alms in this way, the Aga Khan not only reinforced the bond between himself and his subjects but also attracted the attention of the world's press. For Edwards, 'To weigh him against gold ingots – at a time when Great Britain could no longer afford to be on the gold standard – was a stroke of sheer publicity genius' (ibid.: 129). 'The vast throng of over thirty thousand of the Aga Khan's followers were crushed together waiting to be blessed by their divine ruler and to see him receive his weight in gold in the style of moguls of an ancient time' (ibid.: 3).

The connection between gold and monarchy is an ancient one. Gold was associated by ancient peoples with the sun. Sun worship was one of the earliest, if not the earliest, manifestations of religious practice. This association meant that 'when ... man obtained pure gold from rocks and rivers, as soon as he saw it gleaming in his hand he was to identify it with the sun' (Hawkes 1962: 48). 'Gold was the first metal to be worked by man and was already in use between five and six thousand years ago,' Jacquetta Hawkes continues.

> Its colour and bright sheen, and above all the fact that it was eternally bright, incorruptible and untarnished, meant that it was instantly recognized as the metal of the sun. Through all the history of civilization gold remained as it were the solar garb, dressing heaven knows how many solar disks (of which the one raised by the Incas in their great temple at Cuzco is only the most famous), kings and queens, images and crowns, haloes and hosts of other solar forms. (ibid.: 72–3)

Sun worship reached its peak in ancient Egypt. Although the complex religion of the Egyptians was concerned with the three powers of the earth, animals and the sun, it was the sun which was supreme. Many names were given to the sun god, but in time it came to be identified with the person of Pharaoh. The ruler was not a steward of god but was himself a divinity. Everyone who saluted the sunrise in Egypt with prayer was also rendering homage to their divine king. The treasure of the pyramids bears witness to the golden allure with which, beginning with Akhenaten, the pharaohs were endowed. Similar practices were to be found in the Inca civilisation, at the apex of which was an hereditary monarch, a 'gold-encrusted solar king' (ibid.: 129). In India, religion possessed at least one solar divinity who, together with other gods associated with light, dwelt in 'a celestial palace of gold with a thousand columns and a thousand doors' (ibid.: 171–2). There was also the figure of Savtir, 'an all-gold god – with yellow hair, and eyes, hands, arms and tongue of gold' (ibid.: 173).

For the Greeks and Romans, Zeus and Jupiter were dominant and so the sun god never exercised the same supremacy. Within Olympus, Apollo appears to have originated as a god of the light and the sun. He is often described as radiant and his arrows could be exchanged for sunbeams. Moreover, when he was born on the small island of Delos, the foundations of the island turned gold while a round pool shone with a golden light (ibid.: 199). The final triumph of Christianity in the West did not mark the end of solar beliefs and practices. The conversion of the emperor Constantine, formerly a devotee of sun worship, heralded the absorption into the Christian religion of solar motifs and an emphasis, previously rejected, on temporal power and glory. Just as Judaism had been affected by the spiritualised solar vision of Persia, so Christian leaders drew on other materials and customs. The hybrid of pagan and Christian could be seen in numerous ways, not least in the ritual use of golden robes and gold crosses and altar ornamentation. In Exodus, God tells Moses how to make the Tabernacle and its furniture, indicating that the table for bread should be covered with pure gold, that the lamp-stand should be gold and so should the priests' vestments. The latter were to include a breastplate of gold, fastened with gold ropes and gold rings. Christian monarchs did not renounce the use of many-pointed golden crowns or other solar symbols; the most striking example being that of Louis XIV, the Sun King. His passion for terrestrial splendour conferred on him, even in his own view, an Apollonian radiance.

Whereas the other universal religious myth, that of the Earth Goddess, was feminine, the divinity of the sun was generally seen to be masculine. There were obvious symbolic reasons for this. For Hawkes, while the earth is ploughed and receives the seed, it is 'the sun which strikes down to germinate the seed [by means of] the sunbeams with their phallic suggestion' (ibid.: 60). More profoundly, light and dark seem, from almost the dawn of time, to have been broadly associated with the sexual principles. Femininity has been associated with darkness, mystery and instinct, whereas the light of reason and energy has been taken to be masculine.

The alchemists' attempts to turn mercury and other substances into gold reflected religious urges more than anything else. They too associated gold with the sun and, by extension, with salvation. The alchemists' stone was often identified with Christ and gold with a spiritual value.

It was not difficult to find Biblical comfort for this belief. In the Book of Revelation (21: 10–19), the city of God, the new Jerusalem, is described as shining with the glory of God and possessing the radiance of some priceless material:

> The foundations of the city were adorned with jewels of every kind, the first of the foundation stones being jasper, the second lapis lazuli, the third chalcedory, the fourth emerald, the firth sardonyx, the sixth cornelian, the seventh chrysolite, the eighth beryl, the ninth topaz, the tenth chrysoprase, the eleventh turquoise, and the twelfth amethyst. The twelve gates were twelve pearls, each gate being made from a single pearl. The streets of the city were of pure gold, like translucent glass.

The problem for both Judaism and Christianity was that the worship of gold itself was often more tempting and real than the worship of an intangible God. The Old Testament contains various examples of such a substitution. While Moses was on the mountain receiving the word of God, Aaron grew impatient and called on the women to strip off their gold jewellery, which was cast into the image of a bull calf. When Moses eventually returned, he was so angry that he burned the golden calf, 'ground it to powder, sprinkled it on water and made the Israelites drink it' (Exodus 32: 20).

The temptation to see possession of gold and, in certain instances, communion with the sun as signs of divine approval has always been strong. In any event the owner of gold possessed wealth and was regarded as fortunate. Despite the unfortunate fate of Midas, whose ability to turn everything he touched into gold led him to turn his own daughter into the precious metal, in common parlance the possessor of a 'Midas touch' is not regarded as cursed but is admired. Nevertheless, there are questions about how far the outward signs of wealth should be displayed. Whereas the ostentation of gold in religious rituals and the ceremonies of monarchy is seen as intrinsic, a confirmation of the splendour of God or of the institution, the display of gold for its own sake, divorced from any superior purpose, is often seen as vulgar, an inappropriate secularisation of a sacred metal. Despite this, wealth has always been envied and has therefore enjoyed a special allure. In general, this dichotomy has been dealt with in modern times by according value to the display of small quantities of gold (wedding and other rings, earrings, necklaces and so on), while developing cultural obstacles to excessive display.

The glamour of gold, however, relies on excess, and the attempt to tame it encounters constant failure. The primacy of money in the modern capitalist economy provides an unceasing impulse towards the accumulation and valorisation of gold for its own sake. If, for Dick Whittington, the streets of London were paved with gold, for most Europeans it was Paris more than any other city that in the nineteenth century represented the allure of gold. 'Paris was the ultimate stage on which to act out the drama of seeing and being seen,' Valerie Steele (1988: 10) has remarked. 'The arcades of the rue de Rivoli were "set up like theatre scenery in a transformation scene." The boulevards were "a dream of gold" where "everything ... overexcites you" '. For Alfredo Niceforo, writing in 1911, Paris was a rich city that expressed its wealth in luxury. Above all, it was women who were called upon to turn themselves into *objets d'art*, vehicles for luxury 'covered with jewels and gold'. 'Today', he wrote,

> high fashion demands that the showy feminine *toilette* – whether concealed (that is to say, the skirt and the petticoat) or the camisole, the corset and the modest slip – are covered with gold. It is the triumph of gold. A symbolic triumph! From plaits of golden ribbons in the hair, gold flecks in the trimmings, gold brooches – slim, shiny, harmoniously worked over – down to the scarves. The dress must have golden transparencies and be textured, in its ornamentations, with threads of gold. The impalpable and luminous *tulles* must be studded with a sand of gold. Even on hats are placed – like tired butterflies desirous of rest – open flowers of gold on stalks of gold. And on the silk cloaks that drape the feminine body to protect it from the bite of the nocturnal cold are embroidered stripes of gold and are attached flakes of gold. And strip – if you can – the *Parisienne* of her dress: gold brooches appear on the knees alongside pink or blue ribbons, and there will be flakes of gold on the corset and ribbons of a yellow-gold in the candid triumph of perfumed underclothing ... . The whole woman, from head to foot, is made of gold. (Niceforo 1911: 178–9)

In some cases, the aesthetic of costly display served to hide society's underside. The sociologist Georg Simmel, for example, believed that in prostitution both women and money were degraded and that the latter abasement was as serious as the former. 'Money loses its dignity', he wrote, and can only regain it if the price of the sexual act is increased beyond reason, until the sheer glitter of gold obscures the woman's tarnished reputation (cited in Clark 1985: 102). 'Thus', T. J. Clark concludes, 'the great courtesan redeems money and sex simultaneously, allowing them to put in an appearance arm in arm in the best society' (ibid.: 102).

Courtesans might not have been respectable, but they were style leaders and as such set the fashion trends for polite society. One aristocratic woman who revelled in excess, as well as many other guises, was the society eccentric Luisa Casati, who once attended a Roman gala dressed as a sun god. 'She was a real divinity, all resplendent in gold, a magnificent Queen of Saba with all her gifts and treasures,' wrote Witold Lovatelli (1949: 126). 'From her long hands, lengthened by long gold fingernails, si erge su un lungo stelo a gold flower, everything on her and around her was gold. Even her priests were draped from head to foot in gold.'

Such a phenomenon can be accounted for by reference to what Veblen called the cult of pecuniary beauty. Gold, Veblen recognised, possessed a high degree of sensuous beauty, but the utility of gold or other valuable objects to their possessor 'is commonly due less to their intrinsic beauty than to the honor which their possession and consumption confers, or to the obloquy which it wards off'. Contemplation might gratify a sense of beauty, but exclusive enjoyment gratified the owner's 'sense of pecuniary superiority' (Veblen 1899: 96). According to Veblen, the two could not be completely separated. 'The canon of expensiveness also affects our tastes', he wrote, 'in such a way as to inextricably blend the marks of expensiveness, in our appreciation, with the beautiful features of the object, and to subsume the resultant effect under the head of an appreciation of beauty simply. The marks of expensiveness come to be accepted as beautiful features of expensive articles' (ibid.: 97). In other words, there is an aesthetic of costliness which, while it may frequently transgress canons of what is deemed to be good taste, is widely seen as attractive and appealing.

This aesthetic enjoyed unprecedented popularity in the later nineteenth century. The market ruled and the god of religion appeared to have been replaced by the god of money. The identification of the world of money and consumption with the feminine represented a deadly challenge to conventional masculinity. Commodification was worrying for men because noble values were dissolved in the melting-pot of the market, in the hybrid world of goods, in which shabby competition and selfish endeavours prevailed. Gold represented to anti-modernists a fearful demand to coalesce into 'the mass into which men are transformed by the market' (Theweleit 1989: 285). In fact, this feeling of corrupted purity, of diminished authenticity, was by no means new. Referring to the decline of heroism in the modern world, Thomas Carlyle argued in the early years of the nineteenth century that candidates for reverence and obedience had to be carefully evaluated:

> They are all as bank-notes, these social dignitaries, all representing gold; – and several of them, alas, always are *forged* notes. We can do with some forged false notes; with a good many even; but not with all, or the most of them forged! No: there have to come revolutions then; cries of Democracy, Liberty and Equality, and I know not what: – the notes being all false, and no gold to be had for *them*, people take to crying in their despair that there is no gold, and that there never was any! – 'Gold,' Hero-worship, *is* nevertheless, as it was always and everywhere, and cannot cease till man himself ceases. (Carlyle 1901: 14)

The mystery and timeless prestige of gold may be overwhelmed by a wave of imitations and fakes but the desire for it is unchanging.

In another perspective of the later nineteenth century, women were seen as seeking to appropriate the gold which men had acquired through empire and endeavour. The *fin-de-siècle* male's fantasies about the primal woman, 'voracious in her hunger for gold', combined with a fear that women wanted not only to waste man's money but also his seed. For the writer Frank Norris, 'it was clear that women hungered for a power they did not possess, and if male potency was what women desired, then the material symbol of that male potency – gold – became equally desirable and, in a sense, obtainable to them in a way in which "maleness" itself never could be' (Drijkstra 1986: 368). This accounted for women's inordinate desire for gold. But

> the desire for gold displaced women's true function in civilization: motherhood and the passive nurturing of the generations of the future. Relieved of their nurturing role, however, women could only degenerate. Thus their very yearning for what they had lost – their virginal purity, innocence and beauty, and the sexual power bestowed on them by virtue of these qualities – was symbolized by their desire for gold, which thereupon became the source of their reversion to bestial instincts. (ibid.: 368)

Painters such as Carolus-Duran produced works which were infused with this misogynistic ideology. In 1891 he depicted Danae reclining in a luxurious manner while a shower of gold coins began to fall from the sky. Similar motifs appeared in the works of Chantron, Antoine-Auguste Thivet and Carl Strathmann (ibid.: 369). Women's alleged hunger for gold also found an indirect articulation in the Victorian literary and artistic obsession with golden hair. While gold stood, in one interpretation, for the market and the degeneration of the feminine, in another, particularly when associated with blonde hair, it indicated uncontaminated youth and innocence. It was the latter that was intended by Dante Gabriel Rossetti when he painted the Virgin Mary or A. C. Swinburne when he wrote of the Madonna's 'curled gold hair'. The painter Edward Burne-Jones made ample use of yellow and Oscar Wilde popularised it. The British actress Ellen Terry, with her blonde hair and golden costumes, managed to combine both appeals. The artist Graham Robertson much admired her Portia, especially for the chromatic allure. The memory of it 'is like a dream of beautiful pictures in a scheme of gold melting into one another; the golden gown, the golden hair, the golden words, all form a golden vision of romance and loveliness', he wrote (cited in Booth 1988: 75).

According to Michael R. Booth, Terry was as much art object as actress. By looking as she did and presenting herself in a manner that was redolent of cultural associations,

> she carried on stage all the complicated associations of innocence, temptation, and the feminine ideal, of legend and poetry, of art and decoration, of symbol and romance, of the medieval, the Venetian, and the Victorian, all before she even opened her mouth to speak her lines, it is surely true that Ellen Terry expressed a meaning and a significance to her audience, a quality of being, over and above her performance as an *actress*, however meritorious that was. (ibid.: 76)

Gold also needs to be examined in relation to associated or derivative qualities, including fair hair. Despite the contamination of gold in the marketplace, blonde hair retained and even enhanced its value as a mark of distinction. The heroes of Greek legend were blonde and the poetic tradition of Dante and Petrarch ensured that the idealised woman in the romantic canon was usually fair-haired. In Renaissance paintings the Madonna, as well as secular examples of ideal female beauty, were generally fair. Winckelmann's championing of the clarity of skin in Greek statues gave a new impulse to classical ideals. The rise in the nineteenth century of race theory in the writings of the romantic Carl Gustav Carus and, more influentially, de Gobineau contributed to the belief that blonde, blue-eyed people belonged to a lost superior Germanic race which had

6
Clamorous Chroma

Because of its recurrent and complex use in fashion and cosmetics, the colour red has prospered in these fields in a variety of shades. This does not imply that simple meanings can be drawn from different shades, as red itself, for all its immediacy and apparent lack of ambiguity, can be employed to signify everything from anger to regal authority, from defiant refusal to sexual availability. The language associated with red underlines a narrative of fire, heat, directness, passion. In the formulary of fashion, red-speak is the most constant, the least subject to variation. As Laird O'Shea Borrelli notes, 'Fashion's rhetoric is one of absolutes and extremes, allowing only for bangs, never for a whimper' (1997: 254). The bang caused by red does not get bigger through the addition of hyperbole, for hyperbole is the required tone.

Examples of red-coloured products and red names are frequent in cosmetics, fashion and other status-related commodities. In the 1940s and 1950s, all Arden beauty salons had trademark deep red doors (*Red Door* is the name still used for one Arden product line) (Lewis and Woodworth 1972: 195). There are also signatures and marques which employ red so predominantly or sensationally that the colour is indissolubly associated with them. In fashion, Christian Dior and Valentino are red designers and key purveyors of the glamour of red. In the field of cars, red has always implied exhibitionism, especially in American convertibles of the 1950s and sports cars. Ferrari's use of red has inspired a vast range of imitators and is probably responsible for its popularity as a colour even for modest saloons and hatchbacks. In Stephen King's *Christine*, a teenager is seduced, beguiled and possessed by a blood-red Plymouth Fury.

Red conveys a variety of attitudes, all of which are upbeat and forceful. The person in red is (or is projecting an attitude that is) confident, sassy, defiant and assertive. They also convey an upfront sexuality and heroic aura. 'It is generally agreed that of all the colours, red has the strongest chroma and the greatest power of attraction. It is at once positive, aggressive and exciting. It is strong, simple and primary,' Alexander Theroux (1994: 155) has written. While the twentieth century's *femmes fatales* have typically been blonde, the truly bewitching woman, the exceptional magical figure, is usually a redhead. In his novel *Venus in Furs*, von Sacher-Masoch described the Biblical Delilah as 'an opulent woman with flaming red hair [who] lay extended, half-disrobed, in a dark fur-cloak, upon a red ottoman, and bent smiling over Samson who had been overthrown and bound by the Philistines' (cited in ibid.: 220).

Red is theatrical and is associated with dramatic entrances. It demands attention, drawing eyes to it with its boldness. The theatrical connotation is often explicit in advertisements featuring red backgrounds, which may include drapes reminiscent of a theatre curtain. One of the most effective marketing campaigns built around red and its associations with sexuality and scandal was the launch of Revlon's Fire and Ice fragrance in 1952. The two-page advertising spread featured a model, Dorian Leigh, who was both elegant and glamorous (Revlon boss Charles Revson notoriously demanded that his models should be 'Park Avenue whores', 'elegant, but with the sexual thing underneath') (Tobias 1976: 120). On one page, Leigh posed in a silver sequin dress with a fiery scarlet cape; on the facing page, the slogan 'Are You Made for Fire and Ice?' appeared, followed by eight questions which were intended in the affirmative. These included: 'Have you ever danced with your shoes off?' and 'If tourist flights were running, would you take a trip to Mars?' The idea was to play on the duality of women ('There's a little bit of bad in every good woman', Revlon marketers felt), but also 'to create a sense of indignation at all the attention European women had lately been getting at the expense of the supposedly more tame American women' (ibid.: 117–20). The scheme for marketing the company's new red nail enamel in this way was suggested by the success in the United States of the Italian starlets and was intended, as Revson put it, 'to answer all the publicity going on that Italian women are the most exciting women in the world' (ibid.: 122). In reality, responses to a questionnaire showed that the women who most epitomised Fire and Ice in the public mind were Marilyn Monroe, Antonella Lualdi, Silvana Mangano and Rossana Podestà. Far from contrasting the success of the fiery Italians, the enamel was indirectly associated with them.

In the nineteenth century, the meanings of red were even more clearly drawn than they are today. Red was not a part of mainstream culture, inserted powerfully or ironically in its interstices. Rather, it was marginal or exceptional. Red signified first and foremost blood, the blood of the revolution or of the commune, the blood of dead soldiers, the blood of France or England. As such it was bound up with glory and tragedy, with life and with death. A blood red 'guillotine' choker was worn as a macabre accessory by French aristocratic women at balls after the Terror (Butazzi 1991: 62). Soldiers' uniforms often featured red; indeed in Stendhal's *Le Rouge et le Noir*, the red referred to the uniforms of Napoleon's soldiers, whereas black represented clerical habits. The glory of the former was contrasted with the dark reaction of the latter (Steele 1988: 95). In Vallès' guidebook to Paris, the symbolism of the wounded and the dead from the revolutionary conflicts metaphorically coloured public spaces and parks with red; in his account, the pretty red flowers of Impressionist painting 'are trampled by the crush of history and run the colour of blood' (Prendergast 1992: 188). Red appealed to poets because of the way it could be used to inject intense impressions. In his verist *Idolatri*, the Italian poet D'Annunzio included brief references to splashes of blood or to a copper-coloured sky; C. H. Herford wrote that these betrayed 'his passion for the crude effect of flame and scarlet, most often where they signify death or ruin ... his voluptuousness here feeds not in the lust of the flesh, but in the lust of wounds and death' (1919: 424; cited in Woodhouse 1998: 33). But D'Annunzio was also tempted by the theatricality of red. Woodhouse writes that around 1909 in western Tuscany, 'his red Fiorentia speedster with its motto *Per non dormire* (No sleeping!) was a danger to the small towns where, like Tarsis in the opening scenes of his latest novel, he raised dust-clouds with the velocity of his passage' (Woodhouse 1998: 248).

Scarlet brought to mind the passion of Spain, of the gypsies and the Orient. Through these places and cultures, real but also imagined, red's association with sex and the unrespectable was codified in art, literature and social behaviour. The interiors of theatres were usually plush red, as were bordellos. Both, of course, conventionally traded in sex. 'Mon bordello' ('my knocking shop') is how Bordenave insists his theatre be referred to in Zola's *Nana*. 'Visiting many turn of the century brothels had become like a night at the music halls,' according to Andrea Stuart. 'Many were decorated in the distinctive red and gold of the theatre, and the interiors of some of the more up-market establishments were as improbable and baroque as the shifting backdrops of any of the more extravagant revues' (1996: 22).

Prostitutes themselves became more visible during the Second Empire. Emboldened by the brash commercialism and culture of display of the shops and offices of the new boulevards of the Haussmanised centre of Paris, they emerged on the street in search of bourgeois clients. 'Illuminated by the bright lights of the city, the prostitute's visual appearance was increasingly the source of her eroticism. She had become woman as spectacle' (ibid.: 36–7). The upmarket prostitute could be distinguished by her make-up, use of bright colours and fashionable clothes. Both marginal (in relation to the social order) and central (to the new culture of the city), she added to the 'red shimmer' which Kracauer identified as a core feature of the bustling night-life of the boulevards (quoted in Frisby 1985: 138). However, if Kracauer identified this redness with 'the upper world of the boulevards', Benjamin associated it more with the modern underworld of the sewers and metro, which he connected to the most ancient underworld, Hades (quoted in Buck-Morss 1990: 102). To complete the metaphor, it might be suggested that the prostitute brought the underworld to the surface and turned its flames into the surface shimmer of the modern metropolis. Certainly, this is what Auguste Blanqui would have argued. In a powerful image of negativity, the old anarchist quite explicitly identified the phantasmagoria of commodity society with Hell (ibid: 106).

In nineteenth-century Paris, red became codified as the modern colour of sex. As such it was employed by actresses and prostitutes, and only sparingly by respectable women, unless they were explicitly flirting with the subculture of sleaze. More than any other fictional figure, Nana symbolised the virus of degeneration that was contaminating society with her taste for pleasure and the money of the upper class. Zola likened her to a fly on a dunghill, and used discreet references to indicate how the language of commercial sex and woman as spectacle was corrupting even the aristocracy. In *Nana*, 'the red silk upholstered chair in the countess's drawing room appears to the journalist Faucbery to signal "le commencement d'un désir et d'une jouissance" [the beginning of a desire for pleasure]' (Bernheimer 1989: 218). The virus had perhaps turned into the feared epidemic by the time Proust wrote of the fashion sin of the Duchesse de Guermantes in wearing black shoes with a red dress. It is not the redness of the dress that was cause for comment but the mismatching shoes, which, when pointed out by her husband, causes her more distress than the announcement by her best friend Swann that he has only six months to live. For the Duchesse, to dress appropriately for a party was the most important thing. As Proust's narrator points out, this episode indicated that aristocratic exclusivity was breaking down. 'He is surprised that she exhibited "in her dresses the same anxiety to follow the fashions" as if she were an ordinary woman', writes Valerie Steele. 'He spies on her, and sees her on the street, gazing "admiringly at a well-dressed actress", and is shocked that she might compare herself with passers-by and consider them "a tribunal competent to judge her" ' (1988: 204–5). He considered this concern with fashionableness to be unworthy of her.

Although it became more common to wear red in the early twentieth century, it retained its associations with 'fastness' and consequently with disrepute. While it was deemed tasteful for rooms in Edwardian houses to contain *une note de rouge* (Beaton 1954: 310), it was seen as a particularly unsuitable colour, for example, for young, unmarried women.[1] In her memoir of the 1920s, Barbara Cartland recalled the notorious 1924 divorce between the Hon. John Russell and his wife Christabel. It was the latter who most drew her affection. In the middle of her long drawn-out case, she walked into the Savoy and down the flight of stairs which led into the restaurant, 'wearing a vivid scarlet dress which was tightly fitted to show off her extremely good figure … . She looked lovely, striking, dramatic and what everyone thought was "very fast" '. 'It was', Cartland commented, 'an act of defiance, a typical gesture of the twenties against the disapproval of the old brigade who thought we didn't care. But brave though it might be – it wasn't wise or sensible at that particular moment. But none of us were very wise' (Cartland 1971: 71).

Baba d'Erlanger was another woman who typified the shock-and-be-damned attitude of the new generation. In 1921 she 'gave up trying to look "pretty", which she wasn't, painted her large mouth brilliant red, which was sensational, and became *chic* and *jolie-laide* overnight,' Cartland wrote. Having taken this step, 'She grew her nails long and wore dark red nail-varnish. "Her fingers look as if they were dropped in blood!" my mother's generation said in horror' (ibid.: 126; see also Beato 1971: 142). Another woman who draws comment in the memoir is the 'electric, compelling, magnetic' actress Tallulah Bankhead: 'She was redheaded, with a smouldering, pouting face. But much more than that, she had a vibrant personality and a strangely arresting voice like hot honey and milk' (ibid.: 179).

There are numerous examples of women who donned red out of defiance, refusing to be intimidated by potential criticism. Cleveland Amory (1960: 181) cites the instance of a society woman who responded to the death of her mother by putting on 'a defiant red hat with a gay veil and a ridiculous plumed bird climbing up the side of it' and going to a party. Because the news was not common knowledge, however, the defiance was private; or it was until she announced the sad event to her host. 'How charming,' he replied sweetly, passing on to the next guest.

For some women, the gesture took on the connotations of a strategic choice. Diana Vreeland, legendary editor of American *Vogue*, was one such woman. 'I adore artifice. I always have. I remember when I was thirteen or fourteen buying red lacquer in Chinatown for my finger-nails,' she wrote (1984: 27). For the night of her coming-out party in 1923, she wore, as was expected, a white dress. But she also wore velvet slippers that were lacquer red and carried red camellias. 'My mother disapproved,' she later recalled. ' "You should know", she said, "that red camellias are what the demimondaines of the nineteenth century carried when they had their periods and thus weren't available for their man. I don't think they're quite ... suitable" ' (ibid.: 28). Her penchant for red resulted in her being considered 'fast' and 'flamboyant'. In consequence, she stuck with it, even, many years later, applying for the French Légion d'Honneur because the little red ribbon had stuck in her mind from when she saw it as a child (ibid.: 195). However, she never reached the excesses of the fashion designer Charles Molyneux who, according to Elsa Maxwell, had the curious habit of bathing in red ink (see Etherington-Scott 1983: 44). Other prominent women of Vreeland's generation who demonstrated a penchant for red lipstick were Wallis Simpson (the Duchess of Windsor), Maria Callas and Eva Peron. In the case of Peron, her bright red lips were taken by political enemies as a sign of her talent for fellatio.

The meanings that red accumulated in the late nineteenth and early twentieth centuries were taken up and incorporated into the symbolic language of Hollywood cinema. It was not necessary to wait for the advent of colour film for red to resonate in the stories and titles of the movies. As Caroline Morin notes in her novel *Dead Glamorous*, 'even if a film was in black and white, you knew from an actress's behaviour that her lips were red' (1996: 45). In Warner Brothers' 1938 film *Jezebel*, a red dress was central to the story-line. Bette Davis played Julie Marsden, a Southern beauty of the mid-nineteenth century who flouted convention and wore a red gown to an all-white cotillion. As a result of her defiance of tradition, she lost her fiancé, played by Henry Fonda, who was so appalled that he left town the following morning. Excluded from polite society, Davis is forced to undergo a succession of humiliations, eventu-ally being allowed to rejoin her one-time fiancé, who had since married another, more traditional woman, on a quarantined island for sufferers of yellow fever. Designed by Orry-Kelly, who experimented for days seeking a colour that would suggest scarlet in a grey tone, the dress symbolised the failure of Davis to accept the given rules of society (Levine 1981: 87). In the most celebrated of all Southern melodramas,

Gone with the Wind, a red dress is imposed rather than chosen, but the connotations are the same. Rhett Butler forces Scarlett O'Hara to wear a crimson dress to Ashley Wilkes' birthday party, which she did not want to attend, because she had earlier been caught in an embrace with Ashley. Rhett insists she should go and 'look her part', the dress, like her name, becoming 'almost an objective correlative of what she symbolizes' (Theroux 1994: 233).

Such a usage of red was perhaps more plausible for being located in the past, but there were also contemporary examples. *The Bride Wore Red*, a 1937 film starring Joan Crawford and Robert Young, related the story of a cabaret singer, Anni, played by Crawford, who is briefly introduced into high society. Given money to spend on her wardrobe by a count who has wagered that she could be mistaken for a society girl, she immediately reveals her true nature as a fallen woman by purchasing a shimmering red evening dress. Having reached the elegant hotel in the Italian Tyrol where she is to stay for two weeks, she is about to wear the dress to dinner when the chambermaid (an acquaintance, it turns out, from her early days as a showgirl) warns her against it. 'You can't wear that here. You might as well wear a sign,' she exclaims. Guided by the staff, she manages to conceal her origins, despite a flirtation with the local postman. On her final evening, Anni is determined to win an offer of marriage from the wealthy young man who has fallen for her, even though his respectable fiancée is in attendance. For this crucial evening, she dons the fatal dress. In a significant scene she holds the dress up in front of her in a mirror and, as the image becomes clear after a brief dissolve, the dress appears on her. The message appears to be that she is revealing her true self, although she is unaware of the construction others will put on her wearing a colour for which she feels a special affinity. In the event, her true identity is revealed by the arrival of a telegram from the count and the evening is a disaster. Back in her room, Anni once again confronts herself in the mirror: 'Will you dance with me, you in your lovely red dress? Lovely red dress fit for a ... fit for me. I don't like it anymore. It's too red, too loud and too cheap. I don't like it. I hate it.' Turning to the maid, she says, 'Hang it on your wall and tell people it's a picture of me.' Only when she removes the dress and gives up her gold-digging ambitions can she return to her appropriate level and find happiness with the postman. The mirror scene is interesting because of the way it suggests that clothing can interfere in the balance between what Freud referred to as ego-libido and object-libido. In his essay 'On Narcissism' ([1914] 1991: 68), he suggested that the more one of these was employed, the more the other became depleted.

What Crawford's dialogue with herself shows is that she could only overcome her excessive attraction to herself by discarding the object through which she had defined and established her own definition of her attractiveness.

In the 1930s and 1940s, red still served to mark out an unrespectable woman; entertainers or prostitutes were permanently marked by their extramarital (and usually professional) sexual experience. In *The Angel Wore Red*, a Spanish Civil War drama starring Ava Gardner, Dirk Bogarde and Vittorio De Sica, Gardner is a cabaret singer who causes a priest to abandon his vocation for her. Although she plays a noble role in rescuing a religious relic and helps save 200 prisoners from execution, she can only free herself of the taint which gives her her allure by dying. However, films did not simply confirm the dominant morality, they also subverted it by associating transgression with powerful and attractive star figures. Ava Gardner, for example, did not just appear as a cabaret singer in several films including *The Barefoot Contessa* and *Pandora*, she also wore red outfits off-screen, which were designed for her by the Roman designers the Fontana sisters. Moreover, through both her films and her life, she linked herself to Spain, the country so often imagined as a place of blood and passion. 'Ava Gardner became Spanish quite naturally', Edgar Morin remarked, 'because it is the Spanish character which best synthesises passion, pride, nobility, greatness of spirit and sensuality' (1972: 183).

Marilyn Monroe never achieved the same passionate iconic intensity as Gardner, but her easygoing sexuality was often highlighted by red clothing and lips. In *Niagara* she played 'a shallow, sex-obsessed adulteress who wore too much make-up and vulgar, flaming red dresses' (Guiles 1989: 158). One red dress was 'cut so low you can see her knee-caps', a character in the film remarks. Precisely this quality appealed to Andy Warhol, whose 'permutated colours used in his various silkscreen pulls of Marilyn suggest a cheap, peroxide blonde with too much lipstick, smudged'. Based on *Niagara*, Warhol's 'Marilyn' forever associated her with an image that her studio favoured, but which she consistently rebelled against (ibid.: 159). Another overtly sexual star, Brigitte Bardot, is seen driving a red open-top sports car in the opening scene of *La Parisienne*, a light comedy that was her first film following the unprecedented scandal of *Et Dieu créa la femme*. Red was entering the mainstream, but it still carried connotations of 'the wrong kind of sexy', of the cheap and vulgar. In Tennessee Williams' *A Streetcar Named Desire*, Blanche Bubois dresses publicly in a white suit and white accessories. In private she wears a red kimono, which the stage directions refer to a 'scarlet satin robe', 'thus revealing', according to Alison Lurie, 'that she is really impure, in fact a nymphomaniac (1981: 196)'. The ostensibly pure Ingrid Bergman, elevated to secular sainthood following her role in *Joan of Arc*, could hardly have chosen more unintentionally confessional garments for a tense meeting with the gossip columnist Hedda Hopper in 1949 in which she was concerned to deny that she was pregnant by her adulterous lover Roberto Rossellini. 'For the occasion, Ingrid was dressed from head to foot in red, from the blouse to the skirt, including the shoes,' Laurence Lerner (1987: 326) reveals.

Without doubt, the star most associated with red is Rita Hayworth. She is the only sex symbol produced by Hollywood in the 1930s and 1940s who was consistently red-haired. Others, such as Clara Bow in *Red Hair* and Jean Harlow in *Red-Headed Woman*, went red occasionally, but no other star associated herself so completely with the allure of the red-head. The fact that Hayworth, in real-life the half-Mexican Margarita Cansino, was not a natural redhead makes the association more significant rather than less. As part of the transformation she underwent at the instigation of Harry Cohn, the tyrannical boss of Columbia Pictures, her hair was died a rich red for her launch in *Strawberry Blonde*. The most famous pin-up of the immediate postwar years, Hayworth was the first good-bad girl, a vamp with a heart of gold, who in *Gilda* taunted Glenn Ford with her infidelity. The nightclub sequence in which Gilda sings 'Put the Blame on Mame' is one of the most erotic in cinema. Backlit in the best Hollywood manner, and brought teasingly in and out of close-up, Hayworth throws back her mane of red hair as she sings, and slowly and daringly removes her long white gloves. Although the film is in black and white, the audience knew from garish posters advertising the film that her hair and magnificent, strapless evening dress was scarlet. Only the sudden entry of Ford on to the stage prevents her from completing her striptease. Other films underlined Hayworth's chromatic fixity; in *Miss Sadie Thompson*, for example, she dances provocatively in a closefitting sequinned red dress.

In films made in the late 1950s, red was generally used to signal entrances on the part of women whose sexuality will prove central to plot development. Douglas Sirk's melodrama *All That Heaven Allows* is a case in point. Jane Wyman plays Cary, a middle-class, 45-ish widow with two adult children who is drawn to Ron, the handsome, younger gardener, played by Rock Hudson. She rejects the gallant, but sexless, attractions of Harvey, an older man who is seen by both her children and friends as an appropriate suitor, in favour of the more vigorous appeal of the passionate, but socially inferior Hudson. The story and the film are constructed in such a way that the audience sympathises with Wyman and rejoices in her final union with Hudson. But she must overcome obstacles in order to be able to achieve a relationship which quite evidently emphasises sex over social decorum. Wyman's vibrancy is signalled in an early scene in which she wears a red dress to go to a club dinner. The occasion explicitly marks Wyman's emergence from mourning; implicitly, the dress marks her desire. The choice of red gives rise to numerous comments, all of which underline how daring it is perceived to be. 'Holy cat's mother!' her son exclaims, before remarking that the dress is 'cut kind of low' and saying that he hopes it will not scare off Harvey. At the club, a gossip whispers to another, 'There's nothing like red for attracting attention, is there? I suppose that's why so few widows wear it. They'd have to be so careful.' As if to confirm her comment, the woman's husband dances with Wyman and leads her outside where he tries to force himself on her.

More recent films have used a clamorous chroma either for ironical citation or in ways that conserve little of its associations with once rigid codes of morality and social behaviour. In *The Woman in Red*, Kelly Le Brock dazzles Gene Wilder with that colour. Red clothing is used to signal the entrance of a dark lady in the 1992 film *Final Analysis*. Dressed in a scarlet suit, Kim Basinger arrives at night in psychoanalyst Richard Gere's studio. They are sexually attracted, but Basinger also has a hidden agenda involving her sister, Uma Thurman, whom Gere is treating. The red suit adds drama and sends a warning signal to the audience. Although red no longer is the prerogative of the prostitute or actress, it communicates desire and desirability. When Julia Roberts wears a magnificent red gown to go to the opera in *Pretty Woman*, she is not signalling her profession or committing a social sin but rather highlighting her attractiveness. As Stella Bruzzi observes, 'The red dress in *Pretty Woman* carries the meaning: "*Vivien* is pretty." ' Although 'iconic clothes serve a proclamatory function in film', the majority of costumes 'are "real" in that they are given meaning only in terms of how they pertain to and are informed by character and narrative, are dependent on character and narrative, [and] are dependent on contextualisation for significance and do not impose meaning' (Bruzzi 1997: 17). Thus it is only in the specific context of *Rebel without a Cause* that Sal Mineo's red shirt is used as a code for homosexuality and in that of John Singleton's film *Boyz N the Hood* that red polo necks and 'Dukie Ropes' distinguish gang members from law-abiding males. However, textual readings do not always work. In *Schindler's List*, not even close study of character and context can fully explain the significance of the little girl's red coat, the sole note of colour in an otherwise black and white film.

Generally, red has come to mean excess, an excess of drama, of sexuality, of power, of visibility, of violence, of ambition. Not by chance has it always been the most frequent colour in cinema posters and advertisements. The reasons why red became such a culturally significant colour are complex. Goethe noted the long-standing association of crimson with folly and misbehaviour, citing French expressions such as 'sot en cramoisi' and 'méchant en cramoisi'. However, it is clear that there can be no automatic and unilateral translation of colour into meaning. There is, in other words, no natural reason why red should carry certain connotations. For Alida Cresti, red can only be ambivalent in meaning because it 'takes on itself every possible expression of life and death, of love as of death' (1998: 63). The ambivalence stems from a physical phenomenon. Red is held to be the first colour seen by children and by people emerging from long periods in the dark. It is the first tone to be perceived on waking up. ' "Hot colour" *par excellence*, it is the nearest to the wavelength of infra-red, which effectively produces a sensation of heat,' Cresti continues. 'Perhaps for this reason red is believed to have the physiological effect of accelerating the heartbeat, stimulating the emission of adrenalin in the blood and giving a sense of heat' (ibid.: 64).

The gender identification of red is complex. There is no automatic reason why red should be bound up with the feminine. As Luce Irigaray has argued, 'the incarnation of the divine, of man, of woman, cannot be imaged without colour' (quoted in Harvey 1995: 15n). As noted above, Mars, anger and war are masculine. For Goethe, moreover, red was essentially a masculine colour. The 'red river', the flow of blood, contains within it both masculine and feminine. Because red can stand for both Eros and Thanatos, it can be linked to both fecundity and death. Its seductive power derives perhaps in part from its structural ambiguity.

> Red is blood, linked to life and fertility, the triumphant Eros, but also, because of the bipolarism of blood itself, it is an indicator of aggression and death, a manifestation of Thanatos. ... There are two red rivers that run through the veins of life: a nocturnal, deep, feminine red, that courses through the bowels of the earth and has a centripetal power of attraction ... . But there is also another red, a masculine, daylight variety, linked to the solar values of the flame, which is itself sometimes an indicator of death, since it can burn like a destructive fire. (Cresti 1998: 139)

This suggests that woman's blood is hidden, whereas man's attains value and meaning through display. As Theroux points out, woman's blood was often strictly taboo. 'There was a centuries-old caveat that it should never be shed,' he has claimed: 'The Old Testament, which specifies stoning as the proper punishment for adulteresses, doubtless set the pattern. Smother her, poison her, drown her, burn her, or boil her in oil, but shed not a single drop of her blood! In medieval Christian Europe, when men no longer understood the atavistic reason for the ban on woman's blood, women were never beheaded or drawn and quartered as were men' (Theroux 1994: 166–7).

These observations point to an understanding of why red was an approved colour for men, why it stood for grandeur, authority, monarchy and religion, fields which were dominated by men. They also point to why it was not usually an appropriate colour for women, since it carried a reminder of what was concealed and should remain concealed. But even this is not unambiguous. Because of its associations with life and with fertility, red also carried positive connotations for women in some cultures, and was even, as in the peasant costumes of the Black Forest, deemed an appropriate symbolic colour for unmarried women. In Spain, it was married women who exercised the traditional prerogatives of red. It was this custom which inspired the designer Valentino's passion for red. 'My first vision of the power of red came when I was a student visiting Barcelona,' he remarked in an interview. 'I had been invited to the opera, where I stared in astonishment at all the boxes. They were filled with these beautiful Spanish women almost all dressed in red, while the exteriors of the boxes were covered with vivid red roses. It was sublime.' From that moment, he realised that 'red is a fascinating colour – it's life, death, passion, love as well as the best remedy for sadness. I feel strongly that a woman dressed in red is always great-looking and will always stand out from a crowd' (Middleton 1997: 134).

The association of red with vanity and excess means that it can, depending on period and context, take on positive and negative meanings at different times and also be associated with either the masculine or the feminine. It is this complex structure which underpins the use of glamour of red today.

7
Captivating Metals

According to Valerie Steele (1988: 24), Louis XIV 'desired the precise regulation of clothing according to minute distinctions of rank', a fact which placed severe restrictions on sartorial choice and linked dress unambiguously to power. In particular the right to employ 'woven material and trimmings of gold and silver' was reserved to himself, the princes of his family and those subjects on whom he conferred the privilege. At his marriage to the Infanta Maria Theresa of Spain in 1660, the Spanish grandees dressed in sombre black velvet were 'symbolically opposed [by] the French nobility in the baroque splendour of beautiful lace and gold and silver braid' (ibid.: 23). Many years later, Louis XIV let it be known that he wished the court to be especially magnificent for the marriage of his grandson. Although he had dressed simply for some time, he planned on this occasion to don 'the most superb raiment'. 'This was sufficient to launch a mad rush to attain the height of richness and invention,' Steele notes. According to Saint-Simon, 'there was barely enough gold and silver' (ibid.: 23).

In the succeeding period, these combinations lost their narrow exclusivity but retained their noble associations. In combination silver and gold suggest abundance and taste; they imply balance and luxury. Whereas pure gold signifies unalloyed magnificence, the tempering of gold by silver conveys at once a sense of a plurality of treasures and somehow a measure of restraint. In other words, together they suggest a certain limitlessness and variety of wealth and resources while at the same time indicating that the person, residence or occasion that is distinguished by this combination has no need to flaunt their status and is concerned with matters of taste. Although he never formulated the idea explicitly, in *The Glass of Fashion* (1954) Cecil Beaton broadly regarded taste as the ability to see beauty not only in the expensive but also in the simple, the cheap and the primitive. Whereas silver could not be regarded as cheap, its lesser value with respect to gold allows it to act as a balancing factor which sets off the more precious metal. In this sense, silver and gold may be seen as an aristocratic combination, and perhaps as a symbol of aristocracy itself. Above all they stand for sophistication and elegance. Pinocchio shows not merely the extent of his aspirations but also his good taste when he promises Geppetto that, when he has acquired some money, he will buy him a gold and silver coat (Collodi 1998). On its own, however, silver can be disappointing. Truman Capote once slighted the chairman of Tiffany, giving as his reason the fact that the publicity the store derived from his *Breakfast at Tiffany's* had been inadequately acknowledged. 'When I moved into my new apartment', he said, 'they finally sent me a silver breakfast service. Should have been gold!' (quoted in Fine Collins 1996: 122).

The origin of the association of the combination of silver and gold with balance and privilege is not entirely clear. However, at the root of this captivating duality lay the ancient belief that gold and silver were precious metals which represented the sun and the moon. For the alchemists, the theme of the marriage of sun and moon stood as an analogy for the work to be accomplished. In their system of thought, there were clear correspondences between material elements, the planets and self-development. The solar dimension was right-handed, day-oriented and masculine, while the lunar was left-handed and feminine, 'the realm of dreams, intuitions and non-verbal communication' (Weil 1980: 245). A similar division could be found in Tarot cards, where the male figure of the magician was associated with yellow while the high priestess was 'a blue-robed virgin'. Together they stood for balance and completeness, an objective which the alchemists sought to achieve by compounding silver and gold.

The symbolic linkages established between metals and the planets show the common root of alchemy and astrology. In their Western form, Titus Burkhardt (1967: 76) argued, they both derived from the Hermetic tradition. Whereas the latter interprets the meanings of the zodiac and the planets, the former is concerned with the meanings of elements and metals. The relationship between them is derived from the law of 'whatever is below is like that which is above'. It was held that the metals were generated in the dark womb of the earth under the influence of the seven planets that were visible to the human eye. This view shows how the alchemists believed in the complementary nature of heaven and earth which they interpreted as being active and passive poles of existence. According to Burkhardt, 'The sun, or gold, is in a certain sense the incarnation of the active, generative pole of existence, whereas the moon or silver incarnates the receptive pole, the *materia prima*. Gold is sun; sun is spirit. Silver, or moon, is soul ... . Thus it is that gold unites in itself all "metallic light" or all colour, while silver, like a mirror, is colourless' (ibid.: 77–8). According to this perception, *materia prima* is the bearer of all forms. Quicksilver is the 'womb' of all metals, 'while silver resembles the virginal condition of pure *materia prima*' (ibid.: 81). This explains why the alchemists represent the 'material' or feminine cause by both the moon – or silver – and quicksilver.

The powerful symbolic suggestion of gold and silver had a broad-ranging cultural resonance. Because it was the aesthetic effect that was desirable as much as the metals themselves, silver and gold could equally be represented by white and gold or by white garments and blonde hair. White itself, when employed in a context of wealth and luxury, similarly functioned to convey splendour and restraint. It also stood for purity, innocence and godliness. It was surely not casual that Margherita, youthful consort of Umberto, king of Italy between 1878 and 1900, should have caused such commotion in the country by her first public appearances as queen. Fair-haired and dressed in white, she dazzled intellectuals and common people. The poet Carducci even wondered aloud if she was not 'one of those divinities that surround the wagon of Febo as it triumphantly ascends into heaven (Bracalini 1983: 96). For Marina Warner, blondeness was identified with 'heavenly effulgence ... . It appears to reflect solar radiance, the totality of the spectrum, the flooding wholeness of light which Dante finds grows more and more dazzling as he rises in Paradise' (1994: 336). Radiance and innocence are also combined in the gold and silver costume worn by Ingrid Bergman at the coronation of the Dauphin in the 1948 film *Joan of Arc*.

While gold is by definition the material of the heavens and masculine regality, virginal white has many vaguer connotations of spirituality. In ancient China it was the colour of mourning and of the transcendence of the soul. In Islam it is associated with masculinity, leadership and mysticism (Lyle 1990: 102). In the West white took on a variety of meanings, which have been explored by Richard Dyer (1997). Although the altar furniture, ceremonial robes and the very vision of heaven in Christianity were all gold, the religion was also 'thought and felt in distinctly white ways for most of its history'. As causes of this, Dyer (ibid.: 17) cites the role of the Crusades in racialising the idea of Christendom, the gentilising and whitening of the image of Christ and the Virgin in painting, and the appeal to the God of Christianity in the prosecution of doctrines of racial superiority and imperialism.

The depiction of Christ and Mary as paler, whiter than everyone else in paintings of the nativity and the crucifixion appears to have begun in the late fifteenth century. The gentilisation of Christ was achieved by the end of the Renaissance, but only in the nineteenth century – the age of high imperialism – was 'the image of him as not just fair-skinned but blond and blue-eyed ... fully in place' (ibid.: 68). While the hair and beard of Christ were given the colour of sunshine, and his eyes the hue of the sky from which he came and to which he returned, his whiteness made him a moral symbol. Not only did white imply innocence, it was the conventional way that martyrs and beautiful young men were rendered in art. It thus lent him an alluring aesthetic quality. In addition, 'Christ and Mary are both human and holy, present and non-existent, which is to say, hue white and uncoloured, skin white and universal' (ibid.: 68).

Dyer is particularly concerned with white's associations with moral and aesthetic superiority. He explores the way this superiority is conceived and expressed, with its implications of purity and cleanliness. He suggests that the establishment of white as superior, and of whites as the purest expression of the human race itself, arose out of a particular dynamic of racial and cultural power which allowed pale-skinned people to associate themselves with values which were then universalised. In addition, it provided elites within northern countries with a way in which they could simultaneously distinguish themselves from the lower classes – who worked under the sun and had access to only very rudimentary cleaning methods – and establish a broader hierarchical relationship with the darker-skinned peoples of the South and the East, who were deemed to be inferior. Because the white man, with Christ as the archetypal example, was the most represented figure in art and, later, other media, he established his generality and allure. Because authority is also maintained though display, this focus was important.

Dyer (ibid.: 48) makes the point that the universality and indivisibility of white has been sustained in particular by the royal, aristocratic and wealthy. If skin whitening and cleansing became so popular, from the nineteenth century especially, it was because of the connotations of class and racial superiority white had assumed: 'to be white is to have expunged all dirt, faecal or otherwise, from oneself: to look white is to look clean' (ibid.: 76). Moreover, 'Gender differentiation is crossed with that of class: lower-class women may be darker than upper-class men; to be a lady is to be as white as it gets' (ibid.: 57).

Alison Lurie relates the fascination that white continues to exercise to the long-range influence of its associations with the gods since pre-Christian times. However, she also locates its place in the language of luxury.

> Because it is so easily soiled physically as well as symbolically, white has always been popular with those who wish to demonstrate wealth and status through the conspicuous consumption of laundry soap or conspicuous freedom from manual labor. It is traditionally worn by participants in the high-status sports of tennis and polo, especially in professional competition. (Lurie 1981: 185)

Even in an age when cleaning is neither difficult nor particularly costly, the rejection of practical considerations that is implicit in any decision to wear white has strong connotations of luxury.[1]

Yet, while combinations of white, silver and gold have a long history of association with ruling groups, they also have defects and weaknesses. This element of fragility and vulnerability has been highlighted by both Lurie and Dyer. For Lurie, all-white clothing, because it is often worn by children and invalids, has connotations of delicacy and even infirmity. Moreover, when it is worn by men, the glow of moral superiority can turn into something eccentric or dandified (ibid.). In the Victorian era, and for many years after, the white suit was seen as the prerogative of the British colonial official. It suggested the moral authority of empire. But it was also appropriated by mavericks and artists. In 1913 Gabriele D'Annunzio and Ida Rubinstein were seen in Paris dressed all in white driving a white car (Valeri 1920). Several decades later the American writer Tom Wolfe adopted the white suit as his trademark. Another writer, Graham Greene, linked it to moral ambiguity, while in *Saturday Night Fever* John Travolta used it to express a personal style founded in the suburban discotheques of New York.

Dyer draws attention to a deeper instability. Whiteness is not merely superiority but also death. Whiteness is a blank, immateriality and absence. 'White people have a colour, but it is a colour that also signifies the absence of colour, itself a characteristic of life and presence' (1997: 207). Vulnerability is part of the seductiveness of white. As Dyer notes, within Western art the dead white body, beginning with the Christ's, has often been 'a sight of veneration, an object of beauty' (ibid.: 208). This reinforced an existing association of white with godliness but also added to it values of transcendence. Ultimately, the location of white within a scheme that embraces sun and moon, life and death, heaven and earth, male and female endows it with universality and irrefutable power.

White stood as an ideal as a skin hue in part because, strictly speaking, it was unattainable. For this reason, the ideal was expressed in the nineteenth century through the marble statues of ancient Greece and artistic representations. In classical antiquity, these had been coloured with paint but they were prized by Victorians precisely for their ethereal purity. In part due to the influence of statues such as the Venus de Milo, the glow of the woman took on particular importance within the construction of white heterosexuality. In numerous paintings and illustrations, white women glowed angelically that were extreme precisely because they were an idealisation. This image, Dyer suggests, reached its apogee towards the end of the nineteenth century and served a purpose in giving allure to whiteness at a time of perceived threats to its hegemony: 'The white woman as angel was in these contexts both the symbol of white virtuousness and the last word in the claim that what made whites special as a race was their non-physical, spiritual, indeed ethereal qualities' (ibid.: 127).

In keeping with his own expertise in film, Dyer focuses on the celebration of the Victorian virgin ideal in the cinema, in stars such as 'America's sweetheart' Mary Pickford and the heroine of De Mille's overtly racist *Birth of a Nation* Lillian Gish. But, significant though these figures are, white in fact remained a largely aristocratic privilege throughout the twentieth century. The white woman was often also a woman *in* white, that is to say a lady, a woman of breeding and leisure. Only occasionally, as in the case of Pope Pius XII, was white fully reappropriated into a spiritual dimension. Contemporary descriptions of the latter referred to him as 'a diaphanous figure, the visage concentrated in inwardness, in his gentle look'. Portrayed by implication as a living saint, the 'Man in White' was the perfect foil for Mussolini's bellicosity (Logan 1998: 244–5).

In her memoir of the 1920s, Barbara Cartland cites Michael Arlen's description of an unnamed Edwardian woman as 'the golden-white beauty of the world's last aristocracy' (1971: 55). A great society beauty, she had in fact been born in relative poverty. In the 1920s and 1930s white and gold tones recurred frequently as a social class that was rapidly losing its social as well as political power struggled to assert its cultural supremacy. Beauty, grace, style and luxury were all arms in silent battle for moral and aesthetic leadership. At this time no one represented better the qualities of aristocracy than the golden-haired, blue-eyed Lady Diana Manners. The radiant glow which Dyer indicates as so important to the maintenance of a certain pattern of power was, in her case, exceptionally bright. 'I am not up to her *glare*,' wrote Cynthia

Asquith after a weekend with the Howard de Waldens at Chirk. 'I prefer more of a mental twilight – her exuberance is too much of the electric light' (quoted in Ziegler 1983: 73). 'Awe-inspiring, shocking, like an avenging angel, there was nothing cosy or seductive about Diana's beauty,' writes her biographer:

> The 'blind, blue stare' owed more to bad eyesight than a challenging disposition, but it was intimidating to those who did not know her. ... Even at the age of eighteen, she could not enter a room without being noticed or leave it without causing a sense of loss. Without this radiance her features would still have been remarkable but she could never have caused the impression she did. (ibid.: 37)

Diana Manners became known to the wider public when she took the part of the Madonna in the mime play *The Miracle*, which ran for several years in the 1920s and toured widely. The Madonna's role was 'one of tranquillity and grace, requiring beauty, dignity and a capacity to stand stock-still for long periods while commanding the attention of the audience'. For the play's producer, Max Reinhardt, no one could have been more suitable than Lady Diana for the part. 'She does not seem to touch the ground when she walks. A more aristocratic, more sympathetic and beautiful woman for the part we could never find,' he exclaimed (ibid.: 152–3). And so, in performance after performance, the theatre-mad aristocrat offered a spectacle of golden-haired, white draped stillness. Photographs show her cloaked in yards of material whose drapes, in keeping with established artistic practice, signified lofty ideals and spirituality. As Anne Hollander has pointed out, drapes had a long history of association with magic, myth and religion. Heavy robes indicated authority or sanctity, while white drapery meant Greece or Rome (Hollander 1992: 80–1). In this sense, the Madonna of *The Miracle* would have recalled, for 1920s audiences, the enduring classical images of late Victorian academic painters such as Alma-Tadema, as well as the draperies of altarpieces and religious sculptures.

The aristocratic associations of white were reinforced in the post-First World War years, when whiteness became bound up symbolically with the resistance to Bolshevism. At times the white aesthetic could be pursued to excessive lengths. In her account of British high society in the 1920s and 1930s, Stella Margetson notes how a mania for all-white decor was popularised by Mrs Syrie Maugham:

> Mrs Maugham started by revamping the interior of her own house. She stripped the dark Georgian panelling in the hall and had it

pickled, and completely redecorated her drawing-room in all white –
white walls, a white rug, white brocaded curtains and upholstery and
a white lacquer screen. Every flower in the house had to be white:
camellias, lilies, gardenias, stocks, lilac and chrysanthemums in
season; and the effect produced, according to Cecil Beaton, 'a strange
and marvellous surprise'. (1974: 97)

Numerous upper-class drawing rooms in Mayfair adopted this
ultra-modern, non-colour scheme, employing white walls, white fur
rugs, white satin couches and white metal and glass furniture. Others
moderated the severity and pristine quality of the white by adding
touches of black, gold or colour. Baba d'Erlanger's rooms, for example,
were all white and gold (Rubinstein 1964: 44). In any event, the lure of
gold retained its appeal in London high society. The American heiress
Laura Corrigan successfully if subtley bribed the aristocracy into attending
her parties by promising guests a cabaret from Paris and a tombola with
prizes. 'The prizes consisted of gold cigarette cases from Cartier, gold
sock suspenders and braces with gold tabs for the men, gold vanity bags
and tortoise-shell combs inlaid with gold for the women,' notes
Margetson (1974: 99).

Throughout the 1930s balls and other social events became ever more
elaborate, in a splendid counterpoint to the economic depression. Fancy
dress parties were greatly in vogue and white or silver themes were
recurrent. In the aftermath of the Wall Street Crash the French dress
designer Jean Patou decided to adopt a silver theme for a magnificent
party that he wanted to be more extravagant than ever. According to the
New Yorker,

To obtain the desired effect, the garden was roofed over, and not only
were the walls and low ceiling lined with silver foil, but also as much
of the trees were left visible, trunks, branches, even the twigs being
wrapped in silver paper: and from the metal boughs hung silver cages
as tall as a man, harboring overstuffed parrots as large as a child.
(Etheringon-Smith 1983: 120)

In Paris in 1932 a white ball was held by Cecil Pecci-Blunt: 'the
American beauty Mrs John Monroe wore a beautiful third Empire dress
designed by Patou for her appearance as the Empress Eugénie. Among
the court ladies who surrounded her in her tableau ... was the Baronne
Albert de Goldschmidt Rothschild, in a full, stiffened, chiffon dress'
(ibid.). The Italian noblewoman Vittoria Colonna di Sermoneta noted in

her memoirs (1938: 52) that leading Indians present in London at a reception given by Lord and Lady Lansdowne wore beautiful, rich costumes 'bordered in gold and silver'.

Society weddings through the 1920s and 1930s also provided opportunities for the deployment of white. Society brides favoured classically simple dresses; the sculptural lines worked as a perfect foil for the individuality of their beauty that was captured in magazines like *Vogue*, where photographers including Beaton and Hoyningen-Huene set them against vaguely classical backgrounds. Beaton, for one, found the excessive use of white-on-white, with the subjects often adopting 'flamboyant Greek-tragedy poses, in ecstatic or highly mystical states, somewhat tasteless (quoted in Etherington-Smith 1983: 120). But the associations proved difficult to overcome. Even in 1960, Lord Mountbatten's designer decreed that for his employer's daughter's wedding 'everything should be white – "all white, all white" – from the mink cuffs on the bridal gown to the bridesmaid's coronets of hyacinth petals' (Kelley 1997: 172).

Not by chance, Truman Capote saw the stylish rich women he idolised and whose confidant he became as elegant swans. Barbara 'Babe' Paley, Gloria Guinness, Slim Keith, C. Z. Guest, Marella Agnelli and other trophy wives were his 'armada of swans', women who had married men so rich that they had the freedom to pursue an aesthetic quality in life. Sophisticated, beautiful and stylish, they inhabited a golden Olympus and set the standards of chic in their time. In Europe and America they were regarded as 'high priestesses of the social arts, avatars with a secret knowledge of beauty, fashion, decorating and entertaining' (Tapert and Edkins 1995: 162). What appealed to Capote about them, beyond their wealth and style, which invoked in him – and many others – feelings of awe and envy, was the fact that 'they all had stories to tell': 'Few of them had been born to wealth or position; they had not always glided on serene and silvery waters; they had struggled, schemed and fought to be where they were. They had created themselves, as he himself had done. Each was an artist, he said, "whose sole creation was her perishable self" ' (Clarke 1993: 274).

The 'swan' Capote loved and admired most was Babe Paley. The daughter of a celebrated American surgeon, Harvey Cushing, and an ambitious mother who had moulded her daughters so that they would catch the richest and most distinguished men in the country, she had, according to the decorator Billy Baldwin, an 'immaculate quality and immense serenity'. Tall, slim and exquisitely beautiful, she featured no less than fourteen times on the list of the world's best dressed women.

Possessed of an icy, enamel-like exterior, it was said that 'her only apparent defect was that she may have been too flawless to be real, more like a goddess than a creature of earth'. Capote observed in one of his notebooks: 'Mrs P. had only one fault: she was perfect; otherwise, she was perfect' (ibid.: 80).

In keeping with the image of the society woman, Paley had 'a sculpted bone structure, luminous pearl-white skin, a ballerina's long neck, and a model's willowy figure' (Tapert ad Edkins 1995: 162). The second wife of William Paley, the phenomenally rich radio pioneer and founder of CBS, she dedicated herself to the invention of a glamorous, picture-perfect world in which the key values were precision and luxury. Regarded by her husband as 'a possession and a showpiece' (ibid.: 164), she created numerous fashion looks. Her trademark was a heavy white piqué blouse topped with multiple gold, silver and pearl bracelets. Like her fellow 'swans', she 'maintained a standard of social excellence that emphasized dignity and discipline and downplayed money and power' (ibid.: 162).

Inevitably there came a time when Babe Paley and the other 'swans' aged and died; before them there had been others and it might have been expected that new wealthy icons of style would have emerged to take their place. However this did not take place. According to Capote's biographer, Gerald Clarke, 'sometime between the fifties, when Truman had scaled the heights of golden Olympus, and the eighties, the chain had been broken. There was a new generation of beautiful women, of course, but none who possessed the style of a Babe or a Gloria or the matchless Mona [Countess of Bismarck]' (1993: 541).

The break in the aristocratic chain cannot be dated accurately because people only became aware of it after it happened. In any case, there was a gradual process whereby actresses offered the public the semblance of aristocratic allure, as publicity took the place of elite glamour. The wedding of Hollywood stars Tyrone Power and Linda Christian in Rome in 1949 was a mock-society event which filled newspapers and magazines. Special attention was reserved for Christian's dress; according to one newspaper, 'pearls were distributed like constellations along the milky way of the silver embroidery; here and there golden touches highlighted the embroidery' (d'S 1949: 3).

The most notable film actress of the aristocratic type was certainly Grace Kelly. With her porcelain complexion and poise, she had the bearing and appearance of an East Coast debutante. When he first met her, Fred Zimmerman 'was astonished and delighted by her demure appearance'. 'She was', he said, 'the first actress I ever interviewed who wore white gloves' (Bradford 1984: 61). Playing leading parts in films like *High Society*, *To Catch a Thief* and *The Swan*, she established the screen type of the cool blonde whose suppressed or controlled sexuality is evident just beneath the surface of her icy exterior (ibid.: 76). This duality of warmth and control mirrored in terms of personality the tasteful restraint of gold and silver. This connection was all the more appropriate since Kelly invariably played society girls.

It is well known that Hitchcock had a particular predilection for this type of woman, who in his films variously was incarnated by Tippi Hedren, Kim Novak, Janet Leigh and especially Grace Kelly. All are blonde, which, according to Camille Paglia, the director treated as 'a beautiful, false colour, symbolising woman's lack of fidelity and trust-worthiness' (1998: 40), and, even where their social station is anything but elitist, dress in refined, elegant pastels. So plausible was the aristo-cratic-type actress that, when Grace Kelly married Prince Rainier of Monaco in 1956, it was widely believed in America that she was marry-ing beneath her. 'He's Not Good Enough for a Kelly', headlined the *Chicago Tribune*, adding boldly: 'She is too well bred a girl to marry the silent partner in a gambling parlour' (Bradford 1984: 128).

The French actress Catherine Deneuve offered a native European equivalent of the aloof *haute bourgeoise* look. Roger Vadim claims that he realised as soon as he saw her that 'her delicate nose, her intense but slightly cold expression, her mouth with the finely drawn lips, so classi-cally perfect that they concealed deep sexuality, were the very image of romantic beauty' (1987: 161–2). In time, she became 'blonde, radiant and sure of herself' and filled French cinema's need for a new face that was 'less earthy than Jeanne Moreau's and Simone Signoret's and with less aggressive sexuality than Brigitte Bardot's' (ibid.: 177, 214).

In the 1960s and 1970s the image of formal, dressed-up elegance that was the sign of aristocratic good taste lost influence, while changing pat-terns of sexuality and gender relations diminished the virginal glow that had distinguished upper-class feminine beauty. Yet still in fashion and commercial culture old images resonated and shaped contemporary ideas of style and taste. Despite the demise of the aristocracy, the world of commerce and publicity continued to accord value to styles and aes-thetic codes of aristocratic origin. The great cosmetics houses, for example, traded on ideas of exclusivity and refinement. Elizabeth Arden rejected her rival Helena Rubinstein's artistic approach to her beauty salons; instead, she 'wanted to capture the aura of the drawing rooms of the great mansions that lined upper Fifth Avenue. Consultations were held in the white-and-gold Oval Room. Treatment rooms were decorated in subdued pastels' (Lewis and Woodworth 1972: 87). When she went on a promotional tour of the United States to launch her seven-shade lipstick kit, girls were introduced wearing costumes matching the different shades of lipstick. To complete the effect, dancers performed to 'The Gold and Silver Waltz' (ibid.: 151). Touches of gold and silver were also regularly used on Arden packaging. Revlon's salons were no less striking: 'Beauty editors could not help being dazzled by the sumptuous elegance, the extravagant gold-and-white Barbara Dorn decor, and the lighting design of Abe Feder' (Tobias 1976: 223).

Estée Lauder also sought to capture the mystery and glamour of elegant society and market it to a wider public. She cultivated the Duchess of Windsor, Princess Grace and the Begum Aga Khan. Her aspiration, she claimed in her memoirs, was to use elegance and class rather than sex appeal to sell her products. The Lauder woman was 'classic', 'a sophisticated woman with charm and *éclat*, as well as beauty' who was 'sensual rather than sexy'. She was 'successful' and 'had that certain, indefinable air known as class' (Lauder 1985: 192–3). In particular she pursued good taste, which meant 'classic design for image and packaging' (ibid.: 191). To this end Lauder even marketed solid perfume in elegant porcelain eggs, trimmed in gold and etched in enamel, which looked in every way like Fabergé eggs. She also incorporated aristocratic resonances into the advice she offered on elegant living. For example, on table decoration: 'I often use a gold or silver lamé cloth *under* magnificent ecru lace cloths; this has a festive, rich look but not a *shining* look because the lace mutes the gold and silver' (ibid.: 255–6). In 1998, the Lauder company launched 'two wonderfully different fragrances, both dazzling': *Dazzling Silver* and *Dazzling Gold*.

In contemporary fashion, the taste for understated elegance symbolised by Giorgio Armani may be seen as being in line with a tradition of restraint that is customarily associated with old wealth. But today elegant restraint is no longer exclusive or aloof; it is not a class attitude but a style option. By the same token, colours and metals associated with aristocracy are not always bound up with tasteful restraint. White and gold were the hallmark colours of fashion rebel Alexander McQueen's first collection at Givenchy; they also appeared in advertisements for the couture house's fragrance Amarige, which featured the Czech model Eva Herzigova. Brilliant white is often used by Laura Biagiotti, but it is also associated with the polished glamour of the Munich fashion company Escada and with the ostentatious leather goods of another German firm, MCM.

8
Magnetic Values

More than any other colour, blue dominates magazine covers, advertisements and product packaging. In fashion spreads and catwalk shows, it is frequent to bathe the models in a blue light and the same procedure is used for the photographs of celebrities which accompany magazine interviews. It is striking that a practice which has become so common still manages to have the consequence of making the subject seem rare and exclusive. Blue always suggests enigma, mystery and absence.

One of the sources of blue's appeal is its unique aesthetic quality. Blue is often seen as the most beautiful colour. For Diana Vreeland, the most beautiful sky was to be found in Bahia and the same sky, she held, existed in China. 'It's a *cold* blue of *hard* enamel, and it's *too* beautiful' (1984: 104). Lapis lazuli was termed by the Romans the 'stone of azure' and is still regarded as 'as blue as it gets'. Its exceptional beauty led the Mesopotamians to believe that it was a gift from the heavens and reserve its use for royal jewellery, crowns and seals. 'There's nothing murky or yellow in lapis lazuli,' Elizabeth Locke has said. 'It's clean, cheerful and vibrant. It really is the essence of blue' (Forrest 1997: 163). Blue is also associated with the quality of smoothness, which Edmund Burke singled out as an essential trait in all beautiful things.

Blue eyes, like blonde hair, were often identified with the beauty of the gods. Lighter shades of blue in particular signify purity, rebirth and the fresh morning. They also imply ease, comfort and escape. Goethe first hinted at the sedative qualities of blue and, as Theroux notes, a blue lagoon, under a blue sky, is a cliché of comfort and escape. Contentment, fulfilment as well as depth are also bound up with blue. While Vasily Kandinsky argued that 'The deeper blue becomes, the more urgently it summons man towards the infinite, the more it arouses in him a longing for purity and, ultimately, for the supersensual' (cited in Theroux 1994: 64), the same might be said of the reverse. The lighter the blue, the purer it is.

Blue also conveys moods and atmospheres. Darker shades carry connotations of depth and the mysteries of nature and the universe; lighter shades imply purity and spirituality. The former are associated with the night, the sea and space; the latter with clear skies, the air and fresh water. Blue can be carefree and optimistic, but it is also melancholic. It also refers to the close of the day and to the enchanting ambiguity of twilight.

Examples of blue as reflective, mournful or melancholic are numerous. The Blues originated in the experience of slavery and deprivation and this legacy shaped the development of jazz. Miles Davis made his name with his groundbreaking album *Kind of Blue*, while Duke Ellington gave many of his jazz compositions 'blue' titles, including 'Azure', 'Lady in Blue', 'Mood Indigo' and the suite 'Diminuendo and Crescendo in Blue'. The writer Hanif Kureshi called his collection of melancholic short stories *Tales of a Blue Time*. The shadowy, half-hidden nature of darker shades of blue make it ideal for association with sex. David Hare's adaptation of Arthur Schnitzler's sexually motifed play *La Ronde* to the 1990s was called *The Blue Room*. In the first German 'talkie', *The Blue Angel*, Marlene Dietrich made a startling screen debut as the 'waterfront tart' Lola. In Jean-Jacques Beneix's cult movie *Betty Blue*, Beatrice Dalle offered a portrait of Betty as wayward heroine, an uncontrolled spirit who eventually descends into madness. The blue of the title refers to this melancholy *dénouement*, but also to the open skies under which much of the film is shot, which match symbolically Betty's pure and wild spirit and perhaps, by allusion, to the film's unusual sexual explicitness. Blue always contains a hint of the 'the marvellous and the inexplicable, of desire, of knowledge' (ibid.: 1).

The oldest of fragrances evoking blue, Guerlain's classic *L'Heure Bleu*, was created in 1912. Unlike other perfumes which refer to some more or less exotic altered state, it suggests a specific time and place associated with twilight. Guerlain publicity states:

> At dusk, when the sun leaves some breathing space before night falls, when the sky has lost its sun but not yet found its stars, the hour when the most subtle flowers offer their fragrance, the elements seem to unite to suspend time. The horizon is bathed with a blue light, silence vibrates and all the exalted scents speak of infinity. This is the suspended hour, silent, romantic ... *L'Heure Bleu*. (Quoted in Burchill 1997: 56)

Joseph Urban, the leading stage designer for the Zeigfeld Follies and the Metropolitan Opera House in the years around the First World War, was a master at constructing dream worlds based on the use of colour. His first design for the Follies in 1915 was called 'Blue Follies' because everything on the stage was tinted a shade of blue. Outside the theatre, Urban placed his mastery of colour at the service of hotels and stores. In 1916, he teamed up with the commercial muralist Raphael Kirchner to redecorate the Paradise Room of Reisenweber's Hotel Restaurant in Manhattan. To make 'Paradise' a place worthy of its name, the two men conceived a blue, green and gold colour scheme which unified the furniture, ceiling, floor and walls. In the fantasy space they created, gold lent opulence and green tropical lushness, while blue added the necessary element of infinity to 'an atmosphere of "perfect" ease and comfort' (ibid.: 145).

The gorgeous skies and sea made the French Riviera an ideal location for the pursuit of dreams and luxury. In 1922 the 'Blue Train', 'the most beautiful and culturally significant train of all time', according to Mary Blume, came into being. The inspiration for a Diaghilev ballet with a story by Cocteau,

> It was technically advanced and morally outrageous, with connecting luxury compartments for eighty first class passengers. Nothing so swift and fine could be known by its official title, the Calais-Méditerranée Express, and from the start it was called the Train Bleu because it was the first train not to be a dull brown: its metal sides (another first) were painted blue, with lines of gold. It was known as the train of paradise. (Blume 1992: 88)

This colour choice was not accidental, for Alida Cresti (1998: 121) notes that blue and gold were the colours of triumphant regality.

'There's never been a blue like the blue of the Duke of Windsor's eyes,' Diana Vreeland recalled, as though he were a deity:

> When I'd walk into the house in Neuilly ... I'd see him standing there, and even in the light of the hall, which was quite dim, I could see that *blue*. It comes from being at sea. Sailors have it. I suppose it's in the family – Queen Mary had it too. But he had an aura of blue around him. I mean what I say – it was an azure aura surrounding the face. Even in a black-and-white picture you can feel it. (Vreeland 1984: 104–5)

It was appropriate that this former monarch should have spent so much of his exile on the Côte d'Azur. The Riviera was a fitting place for a blue-blooded aristocrat. Because of blue's associations with magic and aristocracy, it was a favourite colour of eccentrics. Baron de Meyer, whose graceful and elegant photographs adorned the pages of *Vogue* between the 1900s and 1920s, liked to think of himself as a great artist rather than a photographer. Cecil Beaton described the entrance he made on one occasion:

> De Meyer drove down the precipitous path to my small remote house in the Wiltshire downs in an enormous open racing car which was painted bright blue. At its approach, stones, little lumps of chalk, and rabbits scattered in all directions. Inside the car, driven by a chauffeur in livery to match the motor car, sat the Baron de Meyer, a tall, ageless-looking man in a bright blue suit and beret, with hair dyed to match. (Beaton 1954: 80)

Blue also carries connotations of exclusivity. The allure of Modesty Blaise, the deadly ex-criminal and secret service agent who debuted on the cartoon page of the London *Evening Standard* in 1963, owes something to her midnight-blue eyes. These convey not an ideal but the suggestion of the extraordinary and the inexplicable. Cecil Beaton noted that Greta Garbo's eyes were 'like an eagle's – blue-mauve and brilliant' (cited in Paris 1996: 381). In the DC comics, the hair of Clark Kent/Superman is always dark blue. Probably this is intended to 'crown' the character with an aura of rarity. In *Speaking to Clio*, Albero Savinio writes that, in Greece and Rome, 'Deep blue beards were very common in painted sculpture. All statues, before the spiritualist concept that "art expresses the inexpressible", were painted. The blue beard was probably the "ideal" of black beards, that is hair with deep blue reflections' (cited in Theroux 1994: 4). In ancient Egypt the god Ra had silver bones, gold flesh and blue hair. The Pharoahs used lapis lazuli body make-up and facial ornaments to recall their divine origin. Because blue was the colour of the sacred and the immanent, such things also evoked the continuity of life beyond death (Cresti 1998: 218).

Beneath these uses is a much older set of meanings and associations. The skies were traditionally seen as male, but within them the moon was associated with the feminine. In other versions, the sun was male and the moon female, but the heavens encompassed both and therefore escaped specific gender attributions. They stood for a more general, overarching spiritual principle. The symbolic feminine association with dark, night, earth and moon developed in tandem with the male attribution of light, sun and the sky. In some versions, the Moon goddess was benevolent. For the Incas, she was the goddess of weaving and childbirth and perhaps also of maize; she was the sister or wife of the sun god Inti. Among the Maya, by contrast, the moon and the sun had irregular marital relations. According to Jacquetta Hawkes, the moon goddess 'was an unfaithful wife and she came to be identified with sexual indulgence … . When the two deities left the earth to reign in the sky the moon shone less brightly than the sun because the god had pulled out one of her eyes in a tussle' (1962: 143). Even when the moon goddess was styled as a virgin, she was not chaste but rather was 'true to nature and instinct'. The goddess of fertility, like the moon she could never be possessed (Hall 1980: 11). In Papuan mythology, the sun is sometimes a good force and the moon evil, but the sun can also be an avenging ogre (Beier and Chakravarti 1974: 31). So strong did this legacy prove that, even in the early twentieth century, Jung did not hesitate to identify the feminine principle with the earth, the ocean, darkness and the unconscious.

In many primitive cultures, features of the moon and of the feminine experience were seen as intertwined, the parallels between the menstrual cycle and the lunar cycle usually forming the basis of this. The moon's trek across the night sky is likened to 'the travels and travails of the feminine psyche'. The ages of woman were also symbolised by the moon: the new, silvery moon representing the virgin, the full moon the pregnant woman and mother, the declining moon the old crone (Hall 1980: 2–3). In this sense, the mystery of the moon contained the mystery of death and regeneration. For Demetra George, 'The moon, Queen of the Night in all her silvery splendour, reaches out to us as she glides across the black, moonlit skies. Each night she appears robed in a different garment, which hints at the mysteries surrounding her shadowy and luminous displays' (1992: 3). For the ancients, the changing moon showed that nothing was static, all was flux, either rising and falling, dying or being reborn. The white virgin of the waxing moon was seen as carefree and enchanting, and in classical mythology was equated with the hunter or warrior Artemis or Diana; the full moon goddess was lush and ripe, fertile and magnetic, and was linked with Demeter, Isis and Aphrodite. She stood for procreation and continuity of the species. The black crone who received the dead and prepared for rebirth was the queen of spirits and magic. Her realm was that of water and the underworld. 'She rules over the magical arts, secret knowledge and oracles', George writes. 'Her totem animals are those which live beneath the earth: snakes, serpents, dragons – and animals of the night – owls, ravens, crows, and white and black dogs and horses' (ibid.: 19, 32–3). She was often seen as wrathful and was identified with Lilith, Kali and Hecate.

This last aspect signals the negative associations of the dark with evil, the unknown and the hidden and also fears and prejudices about female sexuality. But it should not be imagined that these divisions were rigid. For Sir James Frazer ([1922] 1993: 141), Artemis and Diana, as goddesses of nature, also stood for fertility and the yellow harvest moon. In Diana's sacred grove at Nemi, 'she was worshipped as a goddess of childbirth, who bestowed offspring on men and women'. Although she was the queen of heaven and the true wife of the sky god, she loved solitude. 'She ... loved the solitude of the woods and the lonely hills, and sailing overhead on clear nights in the likeness of the silver moon looked down with pleasure on her own fair image reflected on the calm, the burnished surface of the lake, Diana's Mirror' (ibid.: 711).

The ceilings of Bronze Age temples (none of which survives) depicted celestial images, as did classical ones. The doors and layout of the Temple of Denderah in Egypt and of the Jewish Synagogue at Beth Sham are related to the zodiac. These patterns were absorbed by Christian cathedrals even though the original celestial significance was forgotten (Chetwynd 1991: 143). Stars offered spiritual indicators to assist travel through the waters of time and, as such, they also featured in rose windows in churches throughout Western Europe.

To interpret the signs in the heavens was to have access to the realm of the spirit and mediate between cosmic forces and mankind. The blue cloak in which the Virgin Mary is traditionally clothed in medieval and Renaissance art signified the absorption within the Western Christian tradition of the celestial principle. A further example appears in the work of Hildegard von Bingen, abbess of a Benedictine convent in twelfth-century Germany and one of the most creative women of her time. Through her reading of St John's Gospel, and understanding of the idea of the light of God, she developed the image of the flashing fire at the centre of which was a man in sapphire blue. In her visionary theology, divine compassion and healing was represented by the figure of the 'blue Christ' (Bobko 1995: 44–6). Thus the cloak of the magician, beginning with Merlin, was typically blue and covered in images of stars and the planets. Some medieval kings, including Henry II, Holy Roman Emperor in the early eleventh century, also adopted this garb, a sign of the fusion of secular and spiritual power at that time.

Even outside the framework of religion or astrology, blue suggested a magical dimension that was linked to both nature and to the very glamorous idea of personal transformation. Launching a fragrance named *Sun Moon Stars* in 1994, the designer Karl Lagerfeld declared that 'perfume is all about creating mystery and space is the only bit of our world with any mystery left' (Iverson 1994: 50). In the postmodern world, the fascination of the irrational, the mystical and the natural is present in the interstices of an ostensibly rational culture. Thus suggestions of the seas and space are often employed to evoke infinity and change.

The appeal of changing forms is culturally very deep-rooted. The transformations of Greek and Roman goddesses were matched by similar characteristics in Celtic goddesses. For example, the Celtic goddess of moon and vegetation could change herself from the most hideous animal-like form to radiant beauty; she was also a guide to the Other World. According to Roger Sherman Loomis, this in turn formed the background to Arthurian legend:

> The mysterious Loathly Damsel of Arthurian romance, who is transformed into a paragon of golden-tressed loveliness, can claim descent from the shape-shifting Demeter and Hecate. The transformation of Demeter into a radiant young goddess may derive its meaning from the fact that the young Kore or Persephone was always regarded as the younger self of Demeter. The metamorphosis of Demeter as related in the *Homeric Hymn* may refer, then, to the power of all green things to renew their life and beauty with the return of spring. (1993: 296)

Irish legends also provided stories of the transformation of a hideous hag that can be interpreted as allegories of the fields and forests becoming bountiful under the kiss of the sun.

In matriarchal cultures, goddesses, and in particular goddesses linked to the moon, were dominant. Water was also an important motif of the feminine principle and formed part of woman's identification with nature. Thus blue was associated with time and the mysteries of Nature and with Woman's symbolic identification with the moon and water. Beneath the surface of commercial slogans and marketing aesthetics, widely deployed in fragrance and cosmetics advertising, it is this set of connections which lends blue its special magnetism and allure.

The image of water as the matrix of being – something which Elaine Morgan has tried to elevate into an alternative, feminine-oriented theory of evolution – was amply represented in Arthurian romance. The orphaned Lancelot was raised by the Lady of the Lake, who held court with her maidens at the bottom of a lake. In this sense the flower of chivalry was a matriarchal hero who emerged from the feminine. At the end of his life, Arthur returns to the feminine. He is transported over water in a barge accompanied by ladies to a sort of paradise named Avalon where he slumbers until he is needed again. Many Celtic other worldly locations include lake settings.

The Christian rite of baptism symbolises spiritual renewal, rejuvenation; the fount of youth has the same function. While night-inspired products are generally associated with dark and medium-tone blue, the colour range from medium to light or sky blue is occupied by fragrances which refer to water. Seawater, lagoons and springs appear frequently in advertisements for beauty products, many of which evoke purity and serenity. Advertisements for *Monsoon* perfumes in the late 1990s featured a mysterious and enchanting scenario. From the deep blue-green waters of a lagoon, a beautiful, vaguely exotic-looking woman (blonde in one advertisement, dark in another) emerges, either holding the *Monsoon* bottle like a magic balm or merely staring out from the page. The woman appears to be primitive and to belong in the watery realm. The pictures have a fairy-tale quality which hints that a drop of the perfume might result in a magical transformation.

From the later Middle Ages, femininity lost some of its positive connotations. After the Black Death, culture became darker and lost its confidence. With the fragmentation of Christendom, there was a loss of the earlier intuitive wholeness. Witch-hunting coincided with the triumph of rationalism, science and hostility to nature. In Arthurian legend, Morgan Le Fay, Arthur's sister, was, in early French verse romances, a powerful and generally benevolent fay, but in the prose romances her reputation declines and she becomes the sinister sorceress. She degenerates into a mortal who must hide her advancing age through magic arts. Her once sought-after favours are condemned as promiscuity and she schemes to destroy others, eventually engineering the downfall of Arthur's kingdom. By the time of the rise of industrial rationalism in the nineteenth century, the forces of the unconscious and of nature were no longer seen as inspiring or rejuvenating. Instead they are repressed or are seen as demonic and threatening.

The link between woman and moon was given scientific backing by Havelock Ellis. In *Man and Woman*, he observed that it had long ago been noticed that a 'curious resemblance' existed between a woman's menstrual cycle and the lunar cycle. In more recent times, Darwin had suggested that this connection was formed at a very early stage of zoological evolution and that it had survived in the female organism until the present. Woman was therefore seen as the natural child of the moon (Dijkstra 1993: 122). 'For the artists', Dijkstra argues, 'the link between the moon and woman – her weakness, her imitative nature, her passivity, and her emotional waxings and wanings – was a subject with far too many attractive symbolic possibilities to ignore' (ibid.: 123). Just as fashionable women stayed out of the sun to cultivate a pasty, unhealthy colouring, so painters sought to lend a waxy, moonlight colouring to their renditions of women's skin. This served to convey the virtuous pliability of women and their dependency.

The ideal fragility of women that was so popular in the Romantic period was reinforced by ballet. The success of *La Sylphide* (first performed in 1827) was such that it established the white muslin dress with underskirt of the same material worn by the dancer Taglioni as the standard ballet costume for the rest of the century. 'Her influence on contemporary dress was no less important', James Laver has argued,

> for she inaugurated a rage for white and flimsy materials – not used, as they had been at the beginning of the century, in order to define and reveal the figure, but to wrap the woman up, as it were, in a haze of moonlight. She powerfully reinforced the other-worldly ideal; she provided a starting-point for a sentimental dream, and when the orgies and excesses of Romanticism were over it was this dream which persisted and gave its colour to the succeeding age. (1937: 37)

In the works of Bouguereau, Henri Martin and Alphonse Osbert, pale women glided through moonlit woods, thereby indicating a simultaneous link to night and earth. They were identified with the moon in all its various stages; rising, setting, waxing, waning. However, there was a problem with these women. They were often too coolly perfect and icily self-contained. The very roundness of the moon, which seemed to match the smooth contours of the feminine figure, served also to indicate the distant, circular self-enclosure of woman. Without direction, women reverted to a sterile, self-reflective identity or, in other accounts, to a state of primitive bisexual self-sufficiency, dominated by the feminine urge to physical self-reproduction (Dijkstra 1982: 127–9).

This self-containment was frequently represented in art by female figures encircled in garlands, wreaths and hoops. Woman's self-reflection and self-absorption was also linked to the idea of a mirror-image. Alone or in groups, Woman stared at pools of water, enraptured by the wonder of her existence. Drawn towards the primal fluid, she became hypnotised by her own Medusa-like gaze. The perverse magnetism of the image of the Gorgon was equivalent to the influence of the moon of the tides and on woman's physiological periodicity. Woman, moon and mirror formed a fatal triangle. Such paintings were intended as admonitions, warnings of the dangers of withdrawal and the perils of vanity. Woman and mirror paintings were frequent around the turn of the century. 'The odds-on favourite tool of the painters for the depiction of feminine self-involvement', writes Dijkstra, 'was the hand-held round or oval mirror. With its hint of the moon, its provocative vulva shape, and the versatility it gave the painters when they wished to depict the dramatic gestures of feminine egotism, it was an irresistible prop' (ibid.: 140–1).

The frequency with which this theme appeared in paintings bears witness to the involvement of many society women with the anti-feminine obsessions of the painters, 'an involvement that caused them to permit – even ask – these painters to portray them as creatures of terminal vanity, goddesses of evil, or symbols of bestial passion' (ibid.: 141). The blue tints which recur in society portraits also reflect the pleasure which well-to-do women derived from cloaking themselves in mystery or eccentricity. Boldini's best-known portrait of Luisa Casati, a dramatic full-length painting in which the Italian marchioness holds a magnificent greyhound by a leash, contains strong tones of blue.

A fictional example of a noblewoman revelling in the identification of woman with water is offered by Proust, who adds his own authorial touches to the image. In a scene dominated by the Princess de Guermantes, the theatre appears as a mysterious aquatic realm. Out of the darkness, he focuses on the box of the princess, who is raised above the ordinary mortals seated below in the stalls. 'Like a mighty goddess', she is seated on a sofa, 'red as a reef of coral'. The mirror behind her casts 'a splash of reflection' like 'the flashing crystal of the sea'. 'At once plume and blossom', she appears, 'like certain subaqueous growths, a great white flower, downy as the wing of a bird ... . Over her hair ... was spread a net upon which those little white shells which are gathered on some shore of the South Seas alternated with pearls, a marine mosaic barely emerging from the waves.' But when the play was about to start, the princess leaned forward in her box, as though she was herself a feature of the performance. The box emerged from 'the watery realm' and the princess came into focus, 'turbanned in white and blue like some marvellous tragic actress' and crowned with 'an immense bird of paradise' (quoted in Steele 1998: 208).

Above all, it was actresses who were assumed to express most unambiguously the deceptive and imitative characteristics of women, as well as their relentless vanity. Zola's Nana, like the heroine of Theodore Dreiser's *Sister Carrie*, is endlessly admiring herself before the mirror (ibid.: 135–6). Showgirls and performers played on the dark sexual power that was attributed to women and turned it into profitable fascination (Stuart 1996: 82). Twilight is a moment of transformation, from day to night, which symbolically coincides with other changes, either desired or actual – for example, from one sex to another, or from one season or species to another. Thus blue tones are readily associated with personalities who are linked in the public mind to ideas of transformation. Nowhere was this more apparent in the way the modern city presented continuous problems and challenges that escaped the cognitive boundaries of planners and political leaders.

If, on the one hand, blue implies melancholy, on the other it suggests restfulness and serenity. The two are not unlinked, for precisely the seamlessness of both sky and sea is associated with emptiness, and the void that implies can take on meaning only in the context of a contemplative spirituality. In Buddhism, for example, blue stands for infinity. For Lama Anagarika Govinda, a leading authority on meditation, blue is the only passive primary colour:

> The passivity of blue, however, is of a very positive nature, a quality of cosmic potentiality, not to be confounded with the vegetative passivity of green. Blue, especially deep blue, is associated with the depth and purity of space, the unity and infinity of the universe, the potential, primordial ground of all that exists. Therefore, it is the symbol of the metaphysical emptiness or plenum-void (sunyata) in Buddhism and of Vishnu and Krishna, the divine embodiments of universal reality, in Hinduism. The significance of blue in Christian symbology is shown in its association with the Madonna, the Universal Mother, whose all-embracing universality is symbolized by the deep blue color of her mantle, in contrast to her inner garment, which reveals a deep red, expressing the warmth of motherly love. (Govinda 1977: 167)

In a secular world, few are likely to fill the void with such spiritual devotion. But the suggestiveness of the void, and the feelings of melancholia it arouses, retain a certain aesthetic appeal. Surely it cannot be accidental that blue is the predominant colour of the packets of both Gitanes and Gaulloises cigarettes, the brands whose images (the gypsy woman and the soldier, respectively) Richard Klein takes as archetypal in *Cigarettes are Sublime*. There is a certain equivalence between the repetitiveness and sameness of cigarettes and the infinity of the heavens and the endlessness of the sea. For Klein, cigarettes are like a kind of modern prayers. 'The indifferent reiteration of pure number belongs to their essential nature; each cigarette is the recapitulation of all identical ones smoked before and after. Taken as an object of reflection, cigarettes invite the return of the same, like smoke rings circling round before vanishing' (Klein 1995: xiii). Cigarettes have a capacity to encourage dreaming, 'to open up space and time so that daydreams may be prolonged'. Klein continues: 'Each puff on a cigarette momentarily opens up a gray-blue balloon above the smoker's head, a beautifully defined space for dreaming, an escape from the harsh constraints of necessity and the cruel menace of death. Each puff is a last puff of freedom and dreams' (ibid.: 138).

Smoking is not primitive, but rather a product of civilisation. 'Cigarettes provide the soldier in the jungle not just physical satisfaction or sensual well-being but the taste of civilised nature, of aesthetic pleasure, to the extent that it is not beastly but civilised to taste and judge, appreciate and discriminate' (ibid.: 114). Yet the woman who smokes carries a different image. Mérimée's Carmen, the first woman in literature who accepts a cigarette, places herself in a special realm: 'the gesture unmistakably identifies her as an outlaw sorceress, a demonic whore, who transcends all limits of feminine propriety,' Klein argues. 'But it is her inhuman, unfeminine femininity that makes her ominously beautiful, demonic because divinely beautiful – just as the goddess Diana assumes the hideous form of Hecate, the witch' (ibid.: 114). Whereas the man who smokes a cigarette is resigned – to life, to fate or to his own death – the woman is dangerous.

In the cinema of the 1930s and 1940s, women who smoke are invariably experienced, worldly or threatening. They may be polished and sophisticated, but they also step outside conventional roles and expectations. To women, cigarettes offered a prop for a range of transgressive gestures:

> that explains why, among women, smoking began with those who got paid for staging their sexuality: the actress, the Gypsy, the whore. Such a woman violates traditional roles by defiantly, actively giving herself pleasure instead of passively receiving it. Lighting a cigarette is a demonstration of mastery that violates the assumptions of feminine *pudeur*, the delicate embarrassment women are supposed to feel, or at least display, in the presence of what their innocence and dignity are supposed to prevent them from desiring. (ibid.: 117)

As Klein observes, the most blue film is also the film in which all the male characters smoke compulsively: *Casablanca*. The film posters were coloured blue and the whole atmosphere was blue. This was appropriate, for Casablanca was a watershed, a place of change, uncertain identities, deception and double-crossing.

Of all Hollywood stars, no one better represented the allure of the smoking woman than Lauren Bacall. Moulded by Howard Hawks, her director in *To Have and Have Not* and *The Big Sleep*, into a woman of mystery, knowledge and worldliness, she is remembered for her tantalising scenes with Humphrey Bogart. In her autobiography, Bacall recalls that the insolent, forward attitude with men that she conveyed in these films was entirely the product of Hawks' instructions (Bacall 1979: 127–8). A 19-year-old *ingénue*, she simply played as she was told the scenes of sex by innuendo that Hawks inserted in the films. Cigarettes and smoky bars were crucial props in the creation of this image. However, Bacall's husky voice and angular physique were essential to her twilight image. Like other stars before her, such as Marlene Dietrich and Barbara Stanwyck, who had projected an image of feminine beauty shot through with strength and sexual ambiguity, she adopted certain masculine traits. All three had an eerie quality and charisma that was attractive to both sexes (Paglia 1992: 413–14). The point needs to be made here that the image of the twilight and swirling rings of smoke slowly rising had a purely aesthetic quality that lent to its suggestiveness and sense of being out of time.

In the 1970s and 1980s, no one better than the pop singer David Bowie represented the transformative impulse. A bisexual whose gaunt androgynous appearance was ethereal and charismatically fascinating, he acted out a series of characters, regularly changing both musical style and dress. In contrast to most stars, who were constrained, sometimes to their intense frustration, to maintain the same image and perform similar parts, Bowie conformed to 'the one type which encourages flagrant changes in image, a jester of sorts' (Fowles 1992: 70). However, as Fowles observes, Bowie took ten years of trial and error to arrive at a stable persona approved by a wide audience. Part of this involved studying press accounts of his shows, to understand better what audiences expected of him (ibid.: 88). The decision to change may well have resulted from a desire to perpetuate the brief cycle of fame normally reserved to musical stars. In any event, it is significant that Bowie's predominant image was that of the alien, *The Man Who Fell to Earth* as a film he starred in was entitled. As his alter-ego, Ziggy Stardust, he frequently referred in lyrics to space and the planets, and his backing band was called The Spiders from Mars.

Madonna is another musical star known for her frequent changes of image. As eclectic in her deployment of star strategies and images of the past and heterogeneous in her musical sources as she is unfailing in her commercial instincts, she courts controversy and renegotiates symbolically the boundaries between male and female, black and white, art and pornography and the religious and the secular. Consequently, it has been claimed that, 'much like Karl Marx's "social hieroglyph," Madonna can be read as a barometer of culture that directs our attention to cultural shifts, struggles, and changes' (Schwichtenberg 1993: 3). It is appropriate, therefore, that the colour most frequently used in her marketing is blue. Her 1986 album *True Blue*, with its optimistic melodies and wholesome ballads, was merely the most obvious example of this. Twelve years later, *Ray of Light* found her still firmly rooted in blue. Following the birth of her first child, she took on an indeterminate spirituality that incorporates elements of the earth mother and the sorceress. This was reinforced by the imagery of the 'Frozen' video, which featured a mysterious Madonna, cloaked in blue, at twilight, surrounded by ravens. It is doubtful that such a skilful manipulator of surface images was unaware of the traditional blue image of her namesake, the Virgin Mary, in religious art.

9
Glittering Media

Nothing glitters like the modern city. In countless films, the opening scenes feature a panoramic view of the city by night, a thousand lights flickering to indicate the enclosed atomised worlds of millions of inhabitants whose lives unfold and intersect without ever meshing in the structured forms of the community. The magic of man-made light also stands for the artificiality of the metropolis and the opportunities it affords for individual self-definition. On the stage that is the city by night, everyone can radiate their own aura and assert their own identity. However, it is the glitter of the rich and the successful that is most enchanting. No one can ignore the dazzle of those who live in the glare of publicity, whose names appear in lights and who give material form to society's dreams.

In the nineteenth century, Paris was the leading city that dazzled and enchanted. Zola, Vallès and other writers offered accounts of the city lights as evoking a magical fairyland. The flickering lights of the shop fronts, creating the illusion of daylight and the blaze of gas lamps on café tables 'recapitulated the myth of the illuminated city' (Prendergast 1992: 40). Urban commercial culture first captured the attention of Baudelaire in the 1840s. The prince of the decadents was the first to investigate the elements that comprised the spectacle of the city. His careful descriptions of the surface splendour of café life bore witness to his own 'dazed enchantment' and revealed 'the dream-machine in action', in so far as they exposed 'the terms on which the city entices into a fantasy of comfort, luxury and gratification' (ibid.: 37).

Christopher Prendergast has pointed out that light, both literal and figurative, played a part in the utopian imaginings of the alternative city as a centre of progress and justice. But 'in terms of urban actuality, the essential preoccupation remained with light in its artificial rather than its natural or symbolic forms'. 'The lights of the city are linked to the lure of the city, the beckoning signs of what is deceptively promised by the new and fast-growing leisure and pleasure culture,' he argues. 'Paris as illuminated "spectacle" is Paris offered for consumption, and nowhere, of course, did gas and electric lighting more directly contribute to the function of the city as dream-machine than in the glitter it conferred on the commodity' (ibid.: 34). This began on a small scale in interiors and subsequently blossomed in large-scale displays, shop windows and exhibitions.

These phenomena were acutely analysed by Benjamin in his study of the Paris arcades. The arcade was seen as a city in miniature, an enclosed, glass-covered world in which the first gas-lighting was installed. Glass and iron were also used extensively for exhibition halls and railway stations, 'buildings which served transitory purposes' (Benjamin 1983: 159). Benjamin saw these new constructions and materials as symbolising the rise of the commodity. Glass and light made possible a range of presentational effects that enabled commodities to be 'theatrically transformed and magically reinterpreted' (Falasca-Zamponi 1997: 140). According to Prendergast, Boucicaut, the inventor of the Bon Marché, quickly grasped the commercial advantages of saturating merchandise with all manner of lighting, subtle or strong.

These innovations affected the city as a whole. Lighting began by transforming department stores and window displays. It culminated with the large-scale employment of electricity through which 'the "phantasmagoria" of the commodity culture came finally to be represented as pure "fairyland" by means of the great *fin-de-siècle* light shows'. 'The "luminous fountains" introduced', Prendergast observes, 'along with the completion of the Tour Eiffel, in the 1889 Exhibition and, at the end of the century, the overwhelmingly impressive productions staged by the Palais de l'Electricité in the 1890 Exposition Universelle' (1992: 34–5).

What Benjamin called 'the enthronement of the commodity and the glitter of distraction around it' resulted in the entrancement of nearly everybody, including critics from the Left (Benjamin 1983: 165; Prendergast 1992: 35). The working class was amused and turned into consumers.

> The world exhibitions glorified the exchange value of commodities. They created a framework in which their use-value receded into the background. They opened up a phantasmagoria into which people entered in order to be distracted. The entertainment industry

made that easier for them by lifting them to the level of the commodity. They yielded to its manipulations while enjoying their alienation from themselves and from others. (Benjamin 1983: 154)

These techniques became part and parcel of retail marketing in the first half of the twentieth century. Gail Reekie (1993: 160) notes that in Sydney, David Jones Market Street store opened in 1938 with interior furnishings in marble, silver-ash woodwork and aluminium, while in the same year another store, Fletcher Jones, opened a 'Modern Manner Overcoat Style Exhibition' which presented male models against 'a futuristic, glittering metallic background'.

In all the great cities, it was the rich, the aristocrats of money, who shone most brightly. For although 'the lustre of a crowd with a motion and a soul of its own' was 'the glitter that had bedazzled the *flâneur*' (Benjamin 1983: 154), in reality the glitter was not democratic. In the new city of the commodity, the crowd was no longer the spectacle that it had been for Baudelaire. Rather 'the poor are excluded, [the] spectacle and the pleasures it promises are a matter of class' (Prendergast 1992: 38). Under new conditions, what Prendergast calls 'one of the great fictions of Second Empire Paris', that is 'that the culture of the boulevard has been fully democratized, and that the city of pleasure is available to all', was undone (ibid.: 39).

The emergence of a new category of plutocrats was an international phenomenon. Edward Spann notes that in New York in the 1840s social observers first began to give their attention to 'a comparatively small number of wealthy men and women who attempted to set the fashions and establish the tone of their society'. At a fancy dress ball held at the beginning of the decade at a new mansion on Fifth Avenue, around 500 people competed with each other to wear the most lavish and spectacular costumes. Although some observers 'had the bad manners to note that the glittering and expensive affair was held during a period of mounting poverty ... sensitivity to social problems was not a conspicuous trait among the fashion-loving rich' (Span 1981: 222–3). Such balls became a means whereby the rich struggled to impress each other and to provoke awe in the wider society. 'What was apparent was that the rich were prepared to spend lavishly in order to embellish their lives ... . In a free and open society, without established classes and ranks, strivings for exclusiveness brought that conspicuous display of wealth which Edward Chapin, minister and reformer, referred to as "a vulgar spirit of social rivalry blossoming in lace, brocade, gilding, and fresco" ' (ibid.: 223–6). Yet by no means all Americans were averse to the emergence of fashionable life. The activities and antics of the trendsetters of the 1840s (dubbed the 'Upper Ten' by Nathaniel Parker Lewis), Spann argues, 'was of as much interest to an awed public as those of the later fabled, fabulous Four Hundred' (ibid.: 224).

What had developed in America was a money-driven version of the life of the *salons* which Stendhal (1959: 92) saw in the Paris of the restoration period. He referred, disparagingly, to 'the titillations of style', 'the lustre of civic dignitaries', 'career[s] of celebrity' and 'all this glitter of success'. Everywhere that commerce flourished and cities expanded in the nineteenth century witnessed forms of competitive display. The rich and the fashionable stood out on account of the opulence of their dress and the splendour of their lavish social life. Richard Bushman notes that, with the decline in America of the genteel culture of the eighteenth century, bright rich colours ceased to be the prerogative of people of high birth. 'Bright colors instantly marked a person of fashion,' he observes. 'Poorer people wore the dull, natural browns, greens, and off-whites of homespun clothing colored with vegetable dyes which blended with the hues of the natural world' (1992: 70). Buckles and buttons became an obsession, although there were still resistances to display in certain formal contexts. 'Brocade rarely appeared in portraits,' Bushman observes, 'and buttons did not usually glitter' (ibid.: 71).

It was above all the fashionable woman covered in jewels and expensive fabrics who attracted attention. Fashion was a competitive terrain, just like business and the professions and, in this special sphere, with its complex paths to influence and success, women asserted their pre-eminence. By definition, a woman of fashion did not work and fashion implied pleasure and indulgence. 'It was an outgrowth of the cosmopolitan milieu of cities, particularly of Paris, already a transatlantic symbol of sophistication and vice,' Lois Banner writes.

> It was emblematic of the way elite life was supposed to be: 'a dainty, bonbon, spun-sugar world,' a setting of 'endless carnival,' where dress was a 'round of disguises.' 'The glitter of fashion,' according to Mabel Cummings in *The Lamplighter*, a best-selling novel of the 1860s, had a 'dazzling, blinding effect.' Its hallmark was glamour – a word grounded in the ancient Scottish culture of magic, witches, and spells and transmogrified into the modern meaning of elusive, sophisticated attraction. (1983: 24)

In *Nana* Zola describes the ball given by the Comtesse de Muffat to celebrate the renovation of her house and simultaneously mark the signing of her daughter's marriage contact. The party was not exclusive; rather, 500 invitations had been issued to all levels of polite society. 'In this smart, permissive society dedicated purely to pleasure, full of people whom a society hostess would pick up in the course of some short-lived intimacy', Zola (1992: 360) wrote, the sanctity of the family was destroyed and the primacy of the fashionable crowd asserted. Dukes mixed with crooks and 'girls in low-cut dresses flaunt[ed] their bare shoulders', while one woman 'was in such a skin-tight skirt that people were following her progress with amused smiles'. The 'decline of the ruling classes brought about by their shameful compromises with the debauchery of modern life' was, however, disguised by the sheer magnificence of the occasion and the setting (ibid.: 358). In one splendid drawing room 'the chandeliers and crystal sconces lit up a luxurious array of mirrors and fine furniture' (ibid.: 353), providing an ideal frame for such a 'dazzling, crowded evening'. As the dancing began, 'Women in light-coloured dresses were going past, mingling with the dark patches of the men's tail-coats, while the large chandelier gleamed down over the surging heads below with their sparkling jewels and the rustle of white feathers, a whole flower garden of lilacs and roses' (ibid.: 355–6).

The sparkle of the fashionable woman was captured in *belle époque* Paris by painters like John Singer Sargent and Giovanni Boldini. Boldini in particular, with his trademark dramatic brushstrokes and unique ability to convey both edgy modernity and the beauty of fashion, became the preferred portraitist of the cosmopolitan elite. By the 1910s one or two photographers could also capture the surface elegance of a fashionable woman and make the image conform to an idea of grace and distinction. Baron De Meyer was one of these. 'His was the triumph of mind over the matter of mechanism,' Cecil Beaton observed.

> By using a soft focus lens of particular subtlety he brought out the delicacy of attractive detail and ignored the blemishes that were unacceptable. Utilizing ladies in tiaras and silver lamé as his subject matter, he produced Whistlerian impressions of sunlight on water, of dappled light through trees. As in the instance of many true artists, De Meyer managed to convey his enjoyment of a subject, and he never conveyed too much: he was not afraid of producing an almost empty photograph. (Beaton 1954: 79)

There was also something more. 'Photography', said Kafka, 'concentrates one's eyes on the superficial. For that reason it obscures the hidden life which glimmers through the outlines on things like a play of light and shade' (Brayfield 1985: 76). This could not be caught with a lens unless it formed part of the effect sought by a photographer, like De Meyer, who allowed for it.

People were impressed by opulence and grace, but what they also saw in the shimmer of the city and the blaze of fashionable life was the glimmer of perfection, and possibly a hint of the divine. When Homer described the appearance of the gods, he referred to their glittering beauty and bright eyes. Athena, the goddess of war 'of the flashing eyes', equipped Achilles for battle by shedding 'a golden mist around his head' and causing 'his body to emit a blaze of light' (quoted in Warnwe 1985: 106–7). In his short story 'Useless Beauty', Guy de Maupassant refers to the eyes of the Comtesse de Mascaret as being 'grey as a frosty sky'. 'In her night-black hair', he continued, 'the diamond coronet scintillated like a milky way' (1997: 184). In the Paris arcade, David Frisby suggests that the sense of space was enhanced by 'its wealth of mirrors which extended spaces as if magically and made more difficult orientation, whilst at the same time giving them the ambiguous twinkle of nirvana' (1989: 241).

Although the glitter and opulence of the *belle époque* would, as Benjamin observed, be drowned in the mud of the First World War, the media of advertising and cinema showed no hesitation in the 1920s and 1930s in portraying the wealthy as a separate, gilded elite. Even more than before, America's wealthiest families acted as 'a mirror of the social fantasies of the public'. According to Ronald Marchand, 'The "smart set" was still a highly visible and relatively cohesive group. Whether or not the pre-1929 rich truly "glittered as they walked," as Caroline Bird later recalled, advertising writers and artists strongly encouraged American consumers to think of them that way. Advertising not only reflected but exaggerated and embellished the steeper social pyramid of the late 1920s' (1985: 198).

In the early twentieth century, the most glittering city was New York.[1] As skyscrapers became the dominant form of urban architecture, so money and ambition dwarfed the city inhabitant and his or her concerns. Many initial observers of the phenomenon were perplexed. Frank Lloyd Wright, the pioneer in low-lying architectural design, acknowledged the skyline's night-time beauty – 'a shimmering verticality, a gossamer veil, a festive scene-drop hanging against the black sky to dazzle, entertain and amaze' – but he could not forget, he wrote in *The Disappearing City* (1932), that the skyscrapers were 'volcanic crater[s] of blind, confused human forces ... forcing anxiety upon all life' (quoted in Douglas 1996: 438–9).

Nevertheless, many enthused about the energy of New York, and in particular of Manhattan – 'the electric town' Wallace Stevens called it in the early years of the century. It was the spectacle of the city, especially at night, that most stimulated its muses. Although Stevens soon moved to Connecticut, New York lived on in his poetry as 'an aesthetic principle and an ideal'. 'Like Fitzgerald', Ann Douglas writes, 'Stevens favored verbs like "bloom," "gust," "flash," "glitter," "enlarge," "flock," "buoy," "blow," and "flutter," – all suggesting matter effacing its boundaries, extending its promise, rearranging its relationship with gravity, matter in a state of translation' (ibid.: 439–40). Skyscrapers were associated directly with energy and communication. They hosted radio antennae and provided publicity for the industries that commissioned them. 'The self-promoted "frankly spectacular" RCA Victor Building culminated in a series of clustered Victrola-needle-like points. The Chrysler Building sported hubcaps amid its decoration, and the Radiator Building was lit at night to glow softly in the dark like an incandescent radiator' (ibid.: 439).

New York was enveloped in an overwhelming opulence. It had a glitter that was likened to that of Constantinople or Baghdad. The city had never been tasteful. Although prominent citizens in the middle of the nineteenth century founded many cultural institutions including libraries, academies and theatres, money always dazzled. According to Edward Spann,

> Wealth and culture combined – thus was raised the prospect of a metropolitan culture which would call the talents of the nation to it and fuse them into a gleaming model of beauty and grace that would raise the tastes and so improve the collective life of all of America. It was a nice dream, but the realities of the metropolitan marketplace indicated that the glitter of the new wealth was not necessarily cultural gold. (1981: 220–1)

The popular fiction of the period is full of depictions of the rich and fashionable set against cityscapes. In *Glitter and Glamour*, a novel by Ameryl Clyde, a dowdy 25-year-old schoolteacher, is contrasted with a London actress who has caught the attention of the former's fiancé. The latter, Daryl, was fascinated by 'the other woman [who] dazzled him by her personality and by the atmosphere with which she contrived to surround herself. There was a certain magnetism about her. She was part of the London life which fascinated him' (1935: 25). At the theatre, the alluring Aurea Harding was 'beautifully dressed in a wonderful amber gown, with an elusive glitter about it' (ibid.: 55).

It was appropriate that it should have been an actress who sparkled, for in the twentieth century it was the professional performer who took on the fascinating glitter of the appearance of wealth. This occurred for a set of interlocking reasons: the rise of mass entertainments and electronic communication, the development of highly profitable cultural industries, the reproducibility of the appearance of wealth, and the social and political risks involved in flaunting riches. This meant that the relationship between performer and audience changed. The large auditoria which housed the theatres of the Baroque period were half-audience, half-stage. 'It was not, however, the case of a dull, undifferentiated throng watching a glittering show: both halves were in balance,' notes Anne Hollander. Both were gorgeously decorated, well-lit and magnificently dressed. The glamour, therefore, was shared between all parties within an enclosed environment. Candles and reflectors contributed to ingenious stage lighting, but there were also 'thousands of candles in chandeliers and sconces illuminating the glittering house' (Hollander 1978: 274). In the modern context, the glamour was concentrated entirely on the performer, while the audience, whether of the theatre or the cinema, was swathed in the anonymity of darkness.

This did not mean that performers ceased to be receptive to the tastes and aspirations of audiences; but it did result in a rupture between the stage and ordinary life. 'There is a recurring motif on the stages of the music halls,' writes Andrea Stuart, 'that of a shimmering showgirl, emerging from an egg, or a birdlike creature with wings about to take off. With its connotations of birth and flight, transformation and new beginnings, this was a striking image for mesmerised early twentieth-century audiences at the Folies Bergère and the Moulin Rouge. As they watched the revelation of this ravishing creature rising from her restrictive shell, it must have seemed as if the modern woman was performing herself into being before their very eyes' (1996: 71). The prototype of this figure was none other than Zola's Nana, whose final public appearance was at the Gaietés as Blanche in *Mésuline*: 'The grotto round her, made up entirely of mirrors, was glittering with cascades of diamonds, streams of white pearl necklaces amongst the stalactites of the vaulted roof, and in this sparkling mountain spring, gleaming in a broad beam of electric light, with her skin and fiery hair she seemed like the sun. Paris would always see her like that,' Zola concluded, 'blazing with light in the middle of all that crystal, floating in the air like an image of the good Lord' (1992: 415).

This type of visual objectification of the showgirl, her enclosure within pure artifice of the spectacle, allowed her to reinvent herself and, paradoxically, secure a measure of autonomy from social expectations and restrictions. Colette wrote that the showgirl was not only observed but observer. Finding the power to look back at the audience from the other side of the spotlight, what she saw was

> thousands and thousands of faces, simultaneously hidden and revealed by the light. It was almost as if, refracted back to herself in such a wide variety of eyes, the showgirl was finally liberated from those very special scrutinisers – husbands, parents, children – who proscribed most women's lives. Simultaneously diffuse and intensified, the nature of being looked at changed, and she was finally liberated from their gaze. (cited Stuart 1996: 71)

There was no more striking showgirl than Mae West. Whereas a rich young woman like Jay Gatsby's adored Daisy in Scott Fitzgerald's *The Great Gatsby* had a voice 'full of money' (with a 'jingle' and a 'cymbals' song' to it) and a porch that 'was bright with the bought luxury of star-shine' (Fitzgerald 1991: 113, 139), Mae West created a persona which required her to be covered from head to foot in glitter and gold-dust. Even the new rich were tasteful when compared with the professional gold-digger. In her greatest stage success, West played Diamond Lil, 'a provocative, dazzling entertainer' who had 'risen from a shady past to a position of power' (Hamilton 1995: 90). West was known for her tart one-liners: her response to the remark, 'Goodness, what beautiful diamonds!' was simple: 'Goodness had nothing to do with it, dearie' (ibid.: 160). According to Mary Beth Hamilton, 'In a decade [the 1930s] short on material luxuries she showed girls the wealth that was theirs for the taking should they only make use of their bodies to follow her character's lead' (ibid.: 182–3). West created an unreal, ironical, teasing figure that coated in humour the suggestion of sex being exchanged for money. In her Hollywood films, the latter was confined to her celebrated *double-entendres* and her lavish, sparkling costumes. The Paramount Studio fashion chief, Edith Head, drew attention in her memoirs to the importance of this:

> I designed thirty of forty pounds of jewellery for Mae to wear as 'Diamond Lil'. I first found pictures of period jewellery to show her. 'Fine, honey', she said, 'just make the stones *bigger*'. The period of the picture was one of the most beautiful in the world fashion-wise, and she was the one woman of the modern world who could offer the figure needed to round those fashions out. There was a walking

costume of lace and ostrich feathers with a lace parasol to match ... .
There was a white costume of satin embroidered in diamonds and
trimmed with ostrich feathers and a dust ruffle of tulle. Her very
favourite was a jewelled black satin worn with an ostrich feather boa.
(1959: 59)

Many other stars were similarly decked out in the 1920s and 1930s.
For the tango sequence with Rudolph Valentino in *Beyond the Rocks*,
Gloria Swanson wore 'a gold-beaded and embroidered lace evening
gown so shimmering and beautiful that moviegoers talked about it for a
year'. 'I also wore a king's ransom in velvet, silk ruffles, sable and
chinchilla', she later wrote, 'all dripping from shoulders to the floor
with over a million dollars' worth of jewels' (Swanson 1982: 173). Jean
Harlow was habitually attired in a lavish fashion; 'a totally *outré* appearance, Harlow's glittering Christmas-tree image enchanted audiences and
helped guide them through the gray Depression years' (LaVine 1981:
54). Greta Garbo often wore quite simple attire, but in *Mata Hari* she
appeared in some of the most extravagant costumes ever made. 'Garbo's
Byzantine-looking bugle-headed skull cap, designed by Adrian, was
hung with glittering disks,' LaVine writes (ibid.: 58–9). According to
Barry Paris (1995: 191), she too looked like a Christmas tree in the film
as she 'shimmies around a huge Polynesian idol, balancing a triple-
tiered hat ... on her head'. The glitter effect was deliberately cultivated
by 'chiaroscuro lighting and Adrian's dazzling costumes – a backless
lamé gown with metallic leggings, for example, and a host of other
furbelows' (ibid.: 193).

Vulgar, extravagant costumes were the stock-in-trade of many
Hollywood films of the 1930s. Bracelets, jewellery, diamonds embroidered
on satin, sequins and paillettes, gold and silver lamé all sparkled and glittered and contributed much to cinema glamour (see Bailey 1988: 24–39).
Beads and sequins on a dress could add a swirl of glitter or act as a design
accent that could be subtle, but was more frequently stunning. Gleam,
glitter and shine were the epitome of Hollywood glamour. They were a
crucial part of the make-believe; by constructing a fairyland appearance,
Hollywood invited its audiences to dream, to escape their troubles and
revel in the pleasure of excess. In historical films, a considerable effort was
made to ensure the accuracy of costumes and the magnificent jewellery
items were almost always genuine (see Prodow et al.: 1992). Whereas
Chanel was a little too restrained for Hollywood tastes, Schiaparelli was
'tough and brash, offering sensational effects in bright and bold colours'.
According to Palmer White, 'this hard, highly individual femininity was

personified by Tallulah Bankhead, bolt upright, prancing to a brass band on parade in the circus' (White 1995: 94).

The studios did everything possible to promote the stars and the fabulous image of their lives. In the mid-1930s major stars were typically living in white-pillared plantation or Regency-style mansions fitted out with a projection room, tennis courts, swimming pools, three-car garages and fully equipped beauty salon and gymnasium (LaVine 1981: 42). Seeing these magnificent dwellings in magazines, the public believed that its favourites were a new aristocracy, chosen by the fans themselves. But although stars were often depicted in the company of nobility, they knew the difference. At the end of the day, Hollywood was 'tinsel town', a showy façade in which the glitter was the substance and the glamour was not backed up by education, culture or breeding.

The surface appearance of wealth, and the sentiments of greed that were always aroused by the sparkle of gems and metals, formed part of a broader aesthetic in capitalist society. If the shimmer always contained an element of innocence, in so far as it hinted at perfection, it also contained a promise. This was the promise that, in theory, wealth and elegance was within everyone's grasp. All that was required was luck, uncompromising determination and the right look. Not surprisingly, therefore, Las Vegas is the glitter capital of the world. Brash, tacky and seductive, it is a hymn to greed and inelegance, an oasis of dreams in the Nevada desert. The nearest European equivalent was Monte Carlo, 'a dazzling center for chance and caprice ... with its casino ("a place of enchantment," Liégeard said, "where night descends in a robe of light")' (Blue 1994: 58). But whereas the Monte Carlo casino was a place where kings, millionaires and crooks expected to lose, Las Vegas drew those who deluded themselves that they could win. The gamblers were spivs, gangsters, high-rollers and low-lifers, prostitutes and obsessives.

Nevertheless, the appeal of glitz is enduring. Estée Lauder even aimed to incorporate it into the perfume to which she gave her first name.

> Once at a party after *Youth Dew* came out, I saw the light from two crystal chandeliers shimmering in a glass of champagne. Imagine if I could capture that image in a fragrance, I immediately thought. For years I worked on that incredible light. I mixed hundreds of precious essences in every possible combination until, one day, I had what I searched for – the light in the champagne. (Lauder 1985: 109)

Ultimately, it was the nightclub that was the setting where glitzy irony meshed with accessibility. As Edith Head wrote (1959: 122), 'Nightclubs have become the "theatre" of our day in terms of glamour, while pictures have become concerned with realism'. The disco boom of the late 1970s thrived on physical heat, drugs and sexual tension. For the wild-eyed patrons of Studio 54, the *ne plus ultra* New York nightclub of the 1970s, 'it was a hallucinatory vision: a surreal, arousing kaleidoscope of light, sound and sensuality' (Margulies 1999: 11). As the glitterball cast its random beams across the pulsating crowd, so the illusion of escape and exclusivity was renewed.

In the late 1990s, 1970s disco chic returned to the fashion pages, although in a cooler, less garish form. Sequins were used sparingly and appeared in unexpected places such as on bikinis. Metallic dresses by Donna Karan and Katherine Hamnett aimed to combine the sparkle factor with a sense of elegance (Murray Greenway 1997: 99; Richardson 1997: 173). 'Glitz is back, with a touch of class', *The Times Weekend* shopping supplement headlined in August 1998. But, in the final analysis, the combination of class and glitz could work only if a dose of irony was added. Even then, the uncompromising embrace of the tackier aspects of glitter was ultimately more honest and convincing. 'Dazzling Irresistible Supersexy Couture Outrageous (DISCO)' ran one *Vogue* title in 1994; 'It's about star-spangled glamour, blazing colour, high energy extravagance. It's mad, bad and dangerous to know'. Glitter no longer carried any meaningful connotations of exclusivity, but its shimmer was at least sexy, daring and fun.

10
Thrilling Graphics

Black-and-white designs recall Op Art, the Space Age and the Swinging Sixties. In 1965 two fashion innovations were launched simultaneously in Paris. On the one hand Op Art fashion grew out of an artistic current associated with Bridget Riley which explored graphic solutions and *trompe-l'œil* visual effects. Within a short space of time black-and-white graphic effects spread through the garments and accessories that had already distinguished British youth culture: mini-skirts, caps, plastic costume jewellery and so on. On the other hand, Courrèges brought to the world of *haute couture* geometric effects and ample use of white. According to Enrica Morini, the designer did not have a purely decorative aim, rather his intention was structural; he wanted to invent a new vestimentary ideal for women who were apparently tending towards a rejection of past models in favour of acceptance of technocracy and futuristic scenarios. Influenced by the advent of space travel, Courrèges substituted the stiff formality of 1950s couture with straight, simple lines, flat shoes and trousers cut in a rather masculine way (Morini 1991: 74–8). In particular he made use of white, a 'non-colour' which lent itself to architectural and geometric constructions, especially when supported by other colours or materials. Using artistic inspiration, he sought to introduce fundamental changes to chic dressing. To some extent Courrèges succeeded. Although some of his ideas remained marginal, white became highly popular with the fashionable women of the early 1960s. The look of Audrey Hepburn or of Jacqueline Kennedy (who wore Courrèges at the inauguration of a monument to John F. Kennedy in England in 1967) owed much to white modernism. Geometric cuts, minimalist clothes, white sunglasses and hats, and micro-jackets gave them a pure, essential style. They also adopted 'a two-tone look with black for a positive-negative contrast'. Far from being unfeminine, this style showed a desire for 'class and refinement, formal perfection and absolute charm' (Rotta 1995). Emanuel Ungaro and Pierre Cardin were also considered space age designers. In the early 1960s the latter abandoned his trademark pale wool and scalloped skirt suits in favour of what were known as 'crazy furs'. 1962's 'crazy fur' was 'a white fox hat and coat hand-printed with big, ugly black polka-dots' (Morais 1991: 111). In the mid-1960s he started his 'shocking stocking' look: candy-striped body suits plastered with cut-out vinyl necklaces and skirts made of white vinyl strips.

The broader influence of Op Art ensured that black-and-white designs and geometry spread through interiors, retailing and popular culture. Vinyl, plastic and patent leather were often employed to underline the modernist impulse. While the appearance of Jane Fonda in *Barbarella* in a brief black-and-white costume accompanied by matching vinyl thigh boots, and the regular monochrome costumes of Diana Rigg in the British television series *The Avengers*, were briefly modish, Fornasetti and other designers carried on their research with graphic monochrome effects for many years. In 1994–95 a revival of this style spread through furniture design and fashion.

In order to trace the development of geometry and monochrome in twentieth-century art and design, it is necessary to refer to technical and political changes as well as to the broader cultural impact of modernism. According to one interpretation, the birth of photography had a significant influence even on nineteenth-century couturiers. This new technical invention opened up awareness of the potential of contrasting the two 'non-colours', creating an unusually pure decorative effect. Photographic magazines explored the significance of black and white as well as of the infinite range of greys that stood between them. Before long, textile manufacturers responded by developing precise new designs and couturiers experimented with *trompe-l'œil* motifs. In 1865 Charles Frederick Worth created a refined black-and-white costume that was decorated along the border of the skirt with black vertical stripes which resembled piano keys (Bellezza Rosina and Morina 1991: 70–1).

What distinguished these early designs from later ones was their largely static character. Movement tended to spoil the effect, which was best appreciated on large expanses of material, such as crinolines. By the early twentieth century, the development of cinematic photography and machine civilisation produced an engagement with the effects of movement. The experiments of the artistic avant-gardes with abstraction and optical effects led to the employment of geometric lines to convey speed and dynamism. At one level this opened up possibilities for purely aesthetic experiments, such as those later conducted by Balenciaga and Paquin. At another, it led to opportunities for convergence and collaboration with revolutionary political vanguards. In Italy the Futurists' celebration of machines, war, virility and destruction of the heritage of the past produced an alignment with Fascism. In Russia Constructivism threw its weight behind the Bolsheviks, producing artworks and clothing designs that reflected the ideological urge towards simplicity, progress and development. In both cases geometric lines and ample use of black and white signified rationality and rejection of the elaborate aesthetics of the past.

The 1925 exhibition of decorative arts in Paris, which was intended to reaffirm France's place at the forefront of developments in the applied arts, saw the triumph of abstract design and the Art Deco style. The curves and elaborations of Art Nouveau were replaced by a modernist and functional aesthetic which favoured straight lines, simplicity and what, with reference to Le Corbusier, was termed 'architectural nudism'. Not all fashion designers understood the change; Poiret, for example, 'totally missed the art deco turn that made *easy* and *practical* the key words of fashion seduction'. Chanel, however, grasped it immediately. 'She, too, had long scarves, whiffs of the Orient in her 1925 collection, and her models were made up with kohl eyes, but she knew how to mold the liberated feminine body in pliant jersey and how to make skirts shorter,' Alex Madsen writes. 'She introduced the Chanel suit, which, with its collarless, braid-trimmed cardigan jacket with long, tight-fitting sleeves, and its graceful skirt, would be more copied, in all price ranges, than any other single garment designed by a couturier' (1990: 163).

Geometry signified rationality and modernity, although the opportunities for optical effects always ensured that there could be a certain playfulness that escaped the control of the forces of order. This dichotomy can be seen in relation to the opposition between order and disorder that lay at the heart of modern culture. 'The primary ethos of all the urban moderns was accuracy, precision, and perfect pitch and timing,' writes Ann Douglas (1997: 8) in her study of New York in the 1920s. But on the other hand, she also draws attention to the modern hostility to conventionally-minded restraints and moralising. 'Going public with one's animal nature became a popular pastime in the 1920s' (ibid.: 48), she argues, pointing out that many of the voguish dances of the period bore names like the Grizzly Bear, the Turkey Trot and the Monkey Glide. Modern experience was not always 'rational'; it involved confusion, impulsiveness, an engagement with the profane and the unrespectable.

This gave rise not infrequently to complaints about an alleged loss of dignity or morality that was also sometimes cast in terms of racial anxiety. 'Great astonishment and not a little indignation is being expressed over the revelation that in the early hours of yesterday morning a large number of Society women danced in bathing dresses to the music of a negro band at a "swim and dance" gathering organized by some of Mayfair's Bright Young People,' wrote the London *Sunday Chronicle*. The principal objection of a 'well-known Society hostess' was the Negro band. 'It seems to me to be wholly wrong', the hostess said, 'to introduce a coloured element to a scene where white men and women, though they may be thoroughly enjoying themselves, are not appearing in the most dignified role' (quoted in Balfour 1933: 171).

It is only against the background of such views, and the assumptions on which they were based, that the furore caused by Josephine Baker's stage debut in Paris be understood. Reviewers struggled to make sense of the contradictions and threat she represented. Her lips were painted black, her short hair was plastered to her head, her voice was shrill, and her body moved in a perpetual trembling and twisting: 'She grimaced, she tied herself in knots, she limped, she did the splits and finally she left the stage on all fours with her legs stiff and her bottom higher than her head, like a giraffe in old age. Was she horrible, delicious, black, white? She moved so quickly nobody could decide ... . Her finale was a barbaric dance ... a triumph of lewdness, a return to prehistoric morality' (quoted in Stuart 1996: 76–7).

Baker was seen as 'the sexiest woman alive' and at the same time as 'a danger to civilisation'. While she gave rise to expressions of wild admiration, reviewers also implied that she constituted a menace to decent society, its morality, order and racial balance.

Nevertheless, one of the most strikingly novel features of the 1920s was what Douglas calls 'the Negroization of American culture' (ibid.: 77). In the theatre, popular music and entertainment generally, black culture exercised for the first time a recognised role. However, the background of slavery and racial discrimination meant that this role was rarely simple and straightforward. Often white entertainers stole or parodied back forms, although there were also many examples of blacks paying back this unlicensed appropriation in kind. Minstrelsy, which for Douglas was 'racism in action: the expropriation and distortion of black culture for white purposes and profits', involved mainly white minstrels in blackface touring the country and gaining access where black entertainers would be barred. However, there was some mixing. Flo Ziegfeld pioneered black and white entertainment by staging a mixed minstrel show number in 1919, after which 'blacks imitating and fooling whites, whites imitating and stealing from blacks, blacks reappropriating and transforming what has been stolen, whites making yet another foray on black styles, and on and on' (ibid.: 76–7) came to be a staple element of American popular culture.

Many actors and musicians crossed the colour barrier stylistically or symbolically. In particular, white stars flirted with aspects of Negritude. Elvis Presley made his name as a white boy who sounded black, while Chuck Berry succeeded by using white diction and enunciation for black music (ibid.: 76). Earlier, Rudolph Valentino undertook 'a titillating journey into the world of blacking up' in his biggest hit, *The Sheik* (ibid.: 78). An Italian whose dark skin lent him to southern and even Arab roles, he played in this film an 'Arab' who ultimately turns out to be of English and Spanish parentage. He kidnaps a young Englishwoman who is then kidnapped again, this time by darker and more savage Arabs who take her to a stronghold filled with fierce coal-black African henchmen. The movie offers an intriguing set of moral and chromatic contrasts between the purity and whiteness of the woman, the light tan of Valentino and the evil darkness of the wicked captors.

Douglas cites Cary Grant as a further interesting example of an actor who oscillated between the poles of black and white, sometimes layering his personality so as to combine tantalisingly elements of both (ibid.: 78–9). The black elements in Grant's case stood on the one hand for his rumoured secret identities (with varying degrees of accuracy, it was claimed that he was a Jew, of Middle Eastern descent and homosexual), all of which were hidden beneath the white, heterosexual mask of the matinée idol. Graham McCann (1996: 130) also alludes to this in his biography of Grant; a still of *Suspicion* picturing the actor climbing a shadowed staircase with a beverage for the wife who believes he is poisoning her is accompanied by the caption, 'Grant as the man who lied too much, blending light and dark in a single look'. On the other hand, Grant often immersed himself in black culture; like minstrel George Thatcher, who discovered a hidden side to himself when blacked up, he wore a perennial suntan from the early 1930s. This, it has been claimed, was nothing other than light blackface (wearing light blackface on stage at this time was known in fact as 'tanning up'). At a Hollywood party held to celebrate his thirty-eighth birthday, Louis Armstrong played the music while the guests, Grant included, wore blackface. Finally, at the costume ball in *To Catch a Thief*, Grant's character arrives disguised as a Moor.

In Europe in the late nineteenth and early twentieth centuries, it was widely believed that blacks shared with women a primitiveness that the white man was called upon to resist. Thus it was not uncommon to find a black figure and a white female figure paired in paintings. Sander Gilman has argued that if a black woman was paired with a white female in nineteenth-century representation – as, for example, in Edouard Manet's extraordinarily controversial portrayal of a prostitute, 'Olympia' – 'the black figure's emblematic role was to suggest her white counterpart's primitive concupiscence and sexual degeneracy … . The link was all the easier to make given Olympia's identity as a prostitute, the prostitute's deviant sexuality being associated popularly with an atavistic return to unbridled eroticism' (quoted in Bernheimer 1989: 120–2). Thus, for Charles Bernheimer, 'the black maid is not … simply a dark-coloured counterpart to Olympia's whiteness. In 1865 she may well have aroused in many viewers their fantasy of a dark, threatening, anomalous sexuality lurking just underneath Olympia's hand' (ibid.: 122–3). The point was made explicit by the artist Thomas Theodor Heine in 1896 in a painting which showed a black man as 'the motivating force behind a white woman's desire to pluck the sterile flower of sensuality'. In order to make the link with the thought of Baudelaire absolutely unambiguous, he entitled the work 'The Flowers of Evil' (Dijkstra 1986: 240–1). The pairing of a black man and a white-skinned woman against a stylised background is still used occasionally in commercial art today, as in a series of advertisements for the designer Thierry Mugler. It may be assumed that this is done in innocence of the racist and sexist assumptions that underpinned the first uses of this combination in European art.

Richard Dyer offers a further perspective on this question. He points out that in the representation of the white heterosexual couple, 'the bearers of the race', there is 'a persistent differentiation between men and women in terms of light'. 'In painting, in shots of love scenes in films, in, perhaps supremely, film stills', he argues, 'the man is darker: his clothes are more sombre, his fair body is more covered, what is visible of his flesh is darker, light falls less fully on him. There is almost never any departure from this – it is as true of art cinema and pornography as of mainstream movies' (Dyer 1997: 132–3). The difference may on many occasions be subtle but there is a persistent convention according to which the man is illuminated by the woman. In classical Hollywood cinema virtually all celebrated couples were represented in this way: Valentino and Nazimova in *Camille*, Garbo and Gilbert in *The Flesh and the Devil*, Robert Taylor and Jean Harlow in *Personal Property* and so on. Dyer argues that the practice is still current and cites the example of Isabelle Adjani and Vincent Perez in *La Reine Margot*.

Several possible explanations may be advanced. First, it may be suggested that the lighter tone of the woman reflects her desirability according to the assertion that cinema is dominated by a 'male gaze'. Second, Dyer suggests that white male heroes occupy a flexible place within the extremes of male darkness and female lightness. Tarzan, for example, is lighter than the natives, but darker than other white men and especially white women. 'The hero is never equated with racial blackness: when even good, and physically spectacular, black men are present, the films are at great pains to stress the hero's superiority to them. White male heroism is thus constructed as both unmistakably yet not particularistically white,' Dyer concludes. 'The muscle hero is an everyman: his tan bespeaks his right to intervene anywhere' (ibid.: 162–3). Third, purely aesthetic considerations should not be overlooked, at least as a supplementary explanation. Black, white and grey contrasts in tone and light were the stuff of the filmmaker's art in the pre-colour era. This did not apply only to the way that actors were photographed or to the conventions of gender representation, but also to costume and set design. 'Since black-and-white film lacks the opportunity for fantasy that color film has, with its "pastel potential," one way to maintain a look of fantasy was with fabric texture and pattern,' Sybil DelGaudio has written. 'Excessive stripes, plaids and polka dots, as well as shiny taffetas and satins, provide a sparkle that compensates for lack of color' (1993: 91). They serve to 'musicalise' the general look of a film.

It cannot be casual that the aesthetic of geometric lines, black-and-white surfaces, checkerboard flooring and optical effects developed at just the time when popular culture was undergoing an unprecedented 'mongrelisation'. Between rationalism, Deco style and the multiracial rhythm of modernity, there was a series of secret linkages and oppositions. Mondrian is an interesting case here. The Dutch artist who created paintings out of nothing more than vertical and horizontal lines in black, white, grey and the three primary colours, Mondrian loved jazz and detested nature. His aim was to pare down art, to strip away rhetoric and explore purely visual effects. 'The compositions are anything but decorative or bland,' Frank Whitford has observed. 'The black verticals and horizontals, and the colours and volumes of the areas between them, suggest rhythmic movement and constantly shifting space ... . There is balance but it is precarious; to imagine any part of an image shifted by as little as a hair's breadth is to feel the fragile unity shatter into fragments' (1997: 9).

In the seventeenth and eighteenth centuries French colour and luxury triumphed as a model of aristocratic distinction. Black and white was left to 'retrograde Spanish noblemen, Dutch burghers, and English puritans' (Steele 1988: 23). By the nineteenth century black and white had achieved the connotation of elegance it still retains. In the ball-rooms, 'those sumptuous festivities of social brokerage and symbolism where the two genders massed to confront each other *as* genders and *as* sexes – the men in black, the women mostly in white – with the inten-tion of dancing in pairs', an antithesis was created that was immensely suggestive (Harvey 1995: 16). According to some interpretations, the white of the women can be seen as a coding of the idea of femininity as absence while black masculinity stood for negation, negation primarily of the feminine. Whether or not this line of thought is accepted, mono-chromatic gender coding allowed for standardisation, in other words for the members of each sex to present themselves as simply that, without stressing individual qualities. Coding was in a sense a leveller and at the same time a factor of differentiation. As John Harvey concludes, 'though one may find various expressions of the complementarity of men and women, still the century's black/white gender-coding does seem to reflect an exacerbated sense of sexual difference, a magnified sense of sexual distance' (ibid.: 220). This is confirmed by the use of black and white to mark other oppositions, such as that between the 'black' papal aristocracy and the 'whites' loyal to the throne in post-unification Italy.

Perhaps the best-known example of Victorian and Edwardian gen-dered black and white appears in *My Fair Lady*, the 1964 film version of George Bernard Shaw's play *Pygmalion*. Following his Academy Award for best costume design on *Gigi*, Cecil Beaton was put in charge of costumes and given the task of art director. For his efforts he won two further Oscars. His designs for Audrey Hepburn were a striking, romantic evocation of the Edwardian era, while 'the famed Ascot black-and-white ensemble brought gasps from movie-goers everywhere' (LaVine 1981: 183).

Beaton spent a great deal of time researching the costumes. He spent hours leafing through old fashion periodicals and visiting the Los Angeles Museum. Diana Cooper sent him descriptions of what her mother wore at Ascot before the First World War and Aubrey Ensor, his old schoolmaster, sent him postcards of early actresses. The Warner Brothers costume department worked to exacting professional standards to turn Beaton's drawings into reality. No fewer than 100 women extras filled the Ascot sequences and all required lavish costumes. According to his biographer, 'Cecil converted upturned buckets, black straw hats and chauffeur's caps into extraordinary Ascot visions. Audrey Hepburn's Ascot hat was a masterpiece of architectural construction' (Vickers 1985: 463). Some costumes were adaptations of Poiret and Lucile originals.

Hepburn's gown was intended to overpower her, so for inspiration Beaton turned to his favourite embodiment of Edwardian glamour, Gaby Deslys. The successor to the great Parisian *cocottes* of the 1890s, she was also, according to Beaton, 'the precursor of a whole school of glamour that was to be exemplified twenty years later by the Marlene Dietrich of the Cinema screen' (Beaton 1954: 38).

'The abstract beauty of the black-and-white combination for clothing has been exploited over and over, even by certain societies in Tierra del Fuego that create the effect with stripes of body paint,' writes Anne Hollander (1993: 369). 'Black and white used together have a dramatic beauty ... . They mean both the same thing and opposite things, and any costume combining them in equal areas has a certain symbolic neutrality'. This was certainly true of Hepburn's gown for, even though it was predominantly white, denoting her femininity, the addition of striped black-and-white ribbons lent it an abstract quality. It took it firmly into the realm of the movie tradition of stylised reality.

In 1966 Truman Capote decided to hold a ball in New York that would long be remembered as one of the most splendid ever held in the city. 'Unlike fabled gatherings from New York's past, in which champagne spurted from fountains, live swans floated on artificial lakes, or gilded trees were hung with golden fruit, his would be a model of good taste and simplicity,' writes Capote's biographer: 'Inspired by the Ascot scene in *My Fair Lady* ... he decided to call his party the Black and White Ball and require his guests – the characters in his own play – to dress in nothing else' (Clarke 1993: 370). At the time Capote was at the height of his celebrity and his connections spread through the worlds of entertainment, politics, high society and letters. His guest list of 500 was rigorously drawn up to resemble what the *Washington Post* called 'a Who's Who of the World', a ploy which 'escalated his party to a social "happening" of history-making proportions', the *Post* continued: 'the New York newspapers are calling it variously the party of the year, the decade or the century' (ibid.: 376).

Capote wanted to choreograph the whole event, refusing to let single guests bring companions and staging pre-party dinners. By insisting on black and white, he hoped to bring 'at least visual unity to a convocation of people as different', says former *Harper's Bazaar* fashion editor D. D. Ryan, as 'chalk and cheese'. Capote explained that he wanted the party to be united in the way you make a painting. Furthermore, all guests would be required to wear masks, and the ladies to carry fans. 'I haven't been to a masked ball since I was a child,' he said. 'That's why I wanted to give one.' The masks, according to his scenario, would free guests to dance and mingle as they pleased. At midnight the disguises would be removed. 'It was complete autocratic hosting,' recalls Ryan (*Vanity Fair* July 1966: 112–31).

The costumes, masks and make-up were spectacular. Isabel Eberstadt arrived in an astonishing construction created by the milliner Bill Cunningham – two interlocking swans, one of which was white, the other black. Amanda Burden rented one of Beaton's original costumes from *My Fair Lady* for the evening. According to *Vanity Fair*'s commemoration, Denise Bouché wore the party's most extraordinary coiffure. Hairdresser of the moment Kenneth parted her hair in the centre, dying one side black and powdering the other half white (ibid.: 125). The same look would be conferred on Glenn Close in Disney's non-animated remake of *101 Dalmations*. As Cruella De Vil, she wore her hair like her clothes: black and white in equal parts.

According to the French historian Michel Pastoreau (1991: 10), stripes have been accorded a wide variety of symbolic meanings over the centuries. Possibly due, he argues, to the Biblical injunction against the wearing of clothing of two textiles (or, according to some translations, colours), stripes became a feature of the costumes of marginals and reprobates: criminals, fools, prostitutes, executioners, lepers, Jews and the figure of Judas. In some measure, all of these were perceived to have something to do with the devil. As long ago as the thirteenth century, Wolfram von Eschenbach had written, in his romance *Parzival*, of a liaison between his hero's father and an African queen, which had producing a son whose skin and hair are likened to the black-and-white plumage of a magpie. The medieval conception of stripes declined markedly in the seventeenth century; zoologists no longer saw the zebra as an imperfect and dangerous creature, but rather as one of the more harmonious and elegant animals. In the eighteenth century stripes came to be associated with romanticism and revolution; both the American and French revolutions made ample use of striped flags, clothes and symbols. Robespierre's striped coat acquired symbolic importance from 1792.

Having acquired one positive connotation, stripes were accorded another in the late nineteenth century. They came to be used as a symbol of hygiene or in association with healthy activities. In reality, it is white that signifies most strongly purity and hygiene, but, as Pastoreau points out, everywhere that was concerned with health, hygiene or the body – kitchen and bathroom walls, hospital rooms, swimming pools, toiletries and kitchen utensils – saw 'the passage of white ... through the mediation of pastel tints or striped surfaces' (ibid.: 71). By means of stripes, white was enlivened and colour simultaneously purified.

Pastoreau suggests that stripes came to be seen as chic as long as they were narrow, when sea-bathing, swimming and other physical activities became fashionable during the *belle époque*. The stripes of bathing costumes, deckchairs, awnings and parasols adapted the stripes of sea-farers to leisure and land use, and at the same time satisfied moralists who wanted to be sure that health, and not pleasure, was the purpose of these pursuits. The high point of the fashionable stripe was between 1900 and 1920, but although beachwear, like the seaside itself, ceased to be an aristocratic preserve, 'stripes never became proletarianised ... . As a general rule, to appear on the beach in striped wear has remained more or less constantly "chic" ' (ibid.: 78). The chic quality of stripes is limited to those involving white and another colour; white seems to confer an unalterable quality of freshness and cleanliness. Thus it is often employed by shopkeepers selling fresh goods; striped blinds or canopies add an elegant, youthful, holiday air. 'All this is possible', concludes Pastoreau, 'because, over the decades, the stripes of beachwear, which became a symbol of holidays and the summer, have not only been employed in connection with the clothes of sailors or the hygiene of bathers, but came to be part of the world of leisure, of games and sport, of childhood and youth. Once maritime, healthy and worldly, stripes became playful, sporting and fun' (ibid.: 78).

In fact, it may be argued that the role of stripes in ideas of elegance is rather older and more universal than Pastoreau suggests. In the Regency period, in early nineteenth-century Britain, pastel and white-striped women's clothes, furniture coverings and interior decorations all acquired fashionable qualities that carried over into the later period. It is also possible to find examples of stripes being used as signs of aristocratic distinction or elegance from as early as the fifteenth century. This may have something to do with the possibilities that stripes offer for expressing precision, equilibrium and taste. It is significant that the Japanese aristocrat Kuki Shuzo (1992), in his investigation of the traditional concept of *iki* (roughly, 'chic'), should also have drawn attention to the importance of stripes. *Iki* was a quality manifested by geishas; it was an expression of the refinement and grace with which they rehearsed their skills of seduction. Everything about the geisha had to be harmonious, understated and cultivated; her appeal was the product of 'an ethical ideal founded on Unreality' (ibid.: 88). Her facial expression was to be melancholic and her smiles low key, her composure glacial; in other words, 'an *iki* facial expression presupposes a detachment from Western-type vulgarities such as winking, pouting and cheeks that "jump to a jazz rhythm" ' (ibid.: 90).

At the root of this idea was a concept of seduction as duality. 'It is necessary', wrote Suzo,

> that such duality is expressed with precise characteristics, in other words as objectivisation of 'spiritual energy' and 'renunciation'. No geometric form expresses duality better than parallel lines. Proceeding eternally without ever meeting, they represent the pure visual objectivisation of duality. It is not by chance that stripes, as a decorative motif, are considered *iki*. (ibid.: 99)

Vertical stripes were particularly *iki*, he argued, because their duality was more immediately apparent and because they emanated a sense of sublime spirituality which horizontal stripes lacked. Colours were also significant.

> The task of conferring a particular emotive suggestion on the duality is entrusted either to the different gradations of a colour or to a colour at a precise degree of saturation. And if anyone were to ask which colour should be used, I would reply that, to express *iki*, a brash colour absolutely must not be used. Colour as an expression of *iki* must affirm the duality in an understated way. (ibid.: 108–9)

Although there is no reason to suggest that the Japanese idea of *iki* had any currency in the West, it would seem that a similar concept of retrained seduction underlies the frequent use of pastel and white stripes in the confection of fragrances, hat boxes and so on.

Black and white are, of course, the purest expression of duality, although the extremes of good and evil that, in the final analysis, they express may not lend them to a graceful symbolisation of *iki*. However, the more muted tones of grey that are the reality of black-and-white cinematography transport us into a world of light and shade that is at once restrained and dramatic. To contemporary eyes, black-and-white photography either conveys poverty and hardship or has the elitist connotations of a status symbol. Either way, it is a minoritarian counterpoint in a world that is hyperbolically colourful (Ortoleva 1995: 13–14). But it may be argued that it is not only 'an indelible period attribute', but also 'a socio-cultural state of mind'. 'Would anyone understand what I meant if I proposed, for example, that Auden's verse and the thirties

novels of Isherwood and Orwell were somehow "in black-and-white"?'
Gilbert Adair has asked. 'Was it entirely incidental that Picasso, when
painting *Guernica*, elected to resist the temptation of those brasher, more
ingratiating hues at whose manipulation he was so brilliantly adept?
Or ... that the thirties and forties witnessed the ascendancy of *film
noir* thrillers in America and France and of the so-called *telefono bianco*
comedies in Italy?' (Adair 1992: 79).

The answer is that it was not. The moral issues, racial contrasts,
aesthetic harmonies and graphic intertextualities that can be explored
in monochrome find no ready equivalent in colour. But also, geometric
designs suggest a simplification and have a surface appeal that immediately aestheticises and renders abstract any specific subject. This is also a
reason why iconic photographic portraits are very rarely in colour.
David Bailey, Patrick Demarchalier, Bruce Weber and many other photographers prefer to work in black and white. It has the advantage of
being frivolous and pure surface, in an elitist way. It thus retains the
fascination it acquired in the early decades of the twentieth century.

11
Alluring Plastics

In *Plastic: The Making of a Synthetic Century*, Stephen Fenichell argues that plastic has become the defining medium of our time because 'it combines the ultimate twentieth-century characteristics – artificiality, disposability, and synthesis – all rolled into one. The ultimate triumph of plastic has been the victory of package over product, of style over substance, of surface over essence' (1996: 5). By virtue of its ubiquity in Western households, and its associations with the cheap and the chintzy, it may be thought that plastic long ago lost any qualities of glamour that it might conceivably have once had. But precisely its intrinsically artificial nature and its enduring contribution to the veneer of gloss that is an essential part of the attraction of so many products mean that plastic retains a central place in the material culture of glamour. While 'plastic' may have become a term of derision, particularly applied to processed cheese, airline food, shopping malls, Disneyland and American popular culture in general, the very falseness of such products ensures that they can be appropriated and appreciated by the connoisseur of kitsch. Moreover, because plastic represents the quintessence of pop, both Pop Art and pop music, it is perennially associated with youth, hedonism and utopia. Plastic's inauthenticity constitutes both the core of its appeal and versatility and the reason for its frequent rejection.

Plastic's cultural associations are numerous. To understand these, it is necessary first to investigate its origins and explore its place in the culture of artificiality of industrial society. Then its gender connotations and its contribution to consumer culture can be considered. Finally, some reflections will be advanced, first on the relationship between plastics and transparency and, second, on the rainbow of synthetic colours with which plastic later became associated, with particular importance being given to pink.

The plastics of the late nineteenth and early twentieth centuries first took shape as substitutes capable of imitating natural materials. Celluloid, Bakelite and other varieties were created from artificial substances which were limitless in supply and cheaper than ivory, pearl, wood and the other materials they replaced. In time plastics became the source of a more autonomous aesthetic of their own, often not connected at all to the natural, which opened up a new world of the visual imagination. Unlike the natural plastics of the 1850s and 1860s, made from vegetable fibres, and early artificial plastics (Celluloid was patented in 1870), later plastics became associated with 'bright, uniform, solid colours intended to look like nothing other than plastic' (Friedel 1983: 88). This connected in a variety of ways with the values, lifestyles, and aesthetic sensibilities of industrial and post-industrial society.

Plastic products have always had miraculous associations; created by scientific alchemy, they have given rise to promises of multiple uses and of images of freedom from drudgery and disorder.[1] New, man-made materials have been given a wide variety of brand names. From Parkesine, first launched at the Great Exhibition of 1852, to Celluloid, Cellophane, Bakelite, Nylon, Vinyl, Viscose and Formica, these names have acquired meanings and feelings that have gone beyond the often extraordinary contributions the products made to everyday life. Celluloid, for example, conjures up in one word the whole history of cinema, while nylon, much more than silk, is synonymous with lingerie. Bakelite, a defunct product owing to its inflexibility and resistance to colour, is the object of nostalgia on the part of cultivators of objects of the 1930s and 1940s.

Plastic's synthetic allure owes much to modern aesthetic and ethical systems. The rise of mechanical productivity and the abundance of capitalism displaced symbolically the fecundity of nature. It was no longer the land and woman that were the source of creativity and plenty, but man and the industrial process. Thomas Malthus was among the first, at the beginning of the nineteenth century, to note that the logic of technical progress implied the elimination of fertility. However, many others made similar observations. 'The high point of a technical arrangement of the world lies in the liquidation of fecundity. The ideal beauty of *Jugendstil* is represented by the frigid woman. *Jugendstil* sees in every woman not Helena but Olympia,' wrote Walter Benjamin (quoted in Buck-Morss 1990: 99).

How can this be reconciled with Bram Dijkstra's view that 'the eroticised body of woman became the late nineteenth century male's universal symbol of nature and of all natural phenomena'? (1986: 87).

In innumerable Victorian paintings women are depicted, naked or in loose gowns, tripping through the woods, wandering among undergrowth and in the company of animals. In fact, the connection is not so difficult to establish. In both instances woman was objectified and deprived of subjective expression. Nature in late nineteenth-century art is not innocent; it is rather idyllic 'nature'. It has been looked over and appropriated for consumption by the very society in which mechanical productivity had become central. It is re-created nature, no less false than the heritage centres of the late twentieth century. It is an image which is more interesting for its ideology than for its figurative content. Moreover, as Dijkstra powerfully argues, the anonymous young women who filled the work of Charles Curran, William Bouguereau and other artists were often weightless, floating and insubstantial. In short, they were submissive. This ethereal insubstantiality was anti-maternal and vaguely autoerotic, and consequently the depiction was usually situated in the twilight hours, the period of the day most linked to the pleasures of the flesh (ibid.: 91).

For Dijkstra, more individualised pictures of women often featured weak-shouldered, dead-eyed subjects whose attitudes were listless. Women were indolent, useless and vacant. He quotes Maurice Hamel's 1890 comment on Edgar Degas' attitude towards women. In the latter's work, Hamel stated, woman 'is transformed into an illogical creature, almost a dragonfly, almost a doll'. This occurred 'by means of a transliteration of human feelings which remains somehow beyond what is real as a result of the fixed stupor of expression' given by the artist to his subjects. 'Degas has pushed to its limits an artistic formula which, in the last analysis, depends upon sentiments of hatred, of aristocratic distaste, and perhaps on a kind of tenderness mixed with revulsion,' he concluded (cited in Dijkstra 1986: 161).

The attitude of a single artist, even one as prominent as Degas, would not be of particular interest were it not for the fact that this attitude was generalised. In the August 1891 issue of the *Mercure de France*, the critic Albert Aurier noted Pierre Renoir's 'propensity to depict women whose extinguished eyes seem to float like thimbles on lakes of plump, fruity flesh. Aurier described these women enthusiastically as "playthings" with the "beautiful, deep, azure, enameled eyes of dolls, of adorable dolls, with flesh molded of roseate porcelain" ' (ibid.). Men overcame their fear of women either by revelling in depictions of them either as weightless matter or sleeping (or dead) beauties or by reconstructing them in ways that were acceptable and unthreatening to the male ego.[2]

The emergence as an ideal of the frigid woman, also depicted as a vampire figure, threatening in her predatory paleness, coincided with

precisely the rise of the 'sex appeal of the inorganic'. Reduced, in the
male imagination, to acceptable dead matter, women could be reinvented and rendered alluring by being decked out with attractive
clothes and commodities which were divorced from nature. The
essence of this shift was represented by fashion. In the modern city, the
natural cycle which led from birth to death to birth of the new was displaced by fashion, which supplied a more rapid dynamic of renewal. In
such a context, where the pressure to be current and newsworthy was
strongest, fashion offered the means whereby the value hierarchy of
nature could be substituted with a cycle of innovation that denied
reproduction, ageing and death. This resulted in a significant shift in
the nature of sexual appeal. 'In the process of displacing nature's tran-
siency onto commodities, the life force of sexuality is displaced there as
well,' Susan Buck-Morss argued in her exegesis of Walter Benjamin's
Arcades project. 'For what is it that is desired? No longer the human
being: sex appeal emanates from the clothes that one wears' (ibid.:
100). According to Benjamin, clothes mimicked organic nature, while
the human body was obliged to mimic the inorganic world: skin strove
through cosmetics to attain the colour of rose taffeta, crinolines turned
women into triangles or walking bells (ibid.: 101). Thus birth and death
ceased to be 'natural' and became 'social'. Fashion transcended nature
by making the inorganic commodity itself the object of human desire.
It became the medium that 'lures [sex] ever deeper into the inorganic
world' – the 'realm of dead things'. It is 'the dialectical switching
station between woman and commodity – desire and dead body.' With
its power to direct libidinal desire on to inorganic nature, fashion
connected commodity fetishism with the sexual fetishism characteristic of modern eroticism, which 'lowers the barriers between the organic
and the inorganic world'. For this reason, Benjamin continued, the
modern woman who allies herself with fashion's newness in a struggle
against natural decay represses her own productive power, mimics the
mannequin and enters history as a dead object, a 'gaily decked-out
corpse'. Fashion prostituted the living body to the inorganic world at
the moment when prostitutes themselves were beginning to rely on the
commodity appeal of fashionable dress, selling their living bodies as a
thing, he argued (ibid. 101). This observation was not entirely new.
In 1910 Marcel Prevost spoke of the 'failure of beauty' and its displacement in favour of elegance, defined by the latest fashions. A year later,
an Italian commentator suggested that elegance had been replaced by
luxury. In order to conquer the admiration of men, a society woman
had to *waste*, spending vast sums on jewels, dresses, hats, beneath

which her individuality disappeared (Anon., *La Tribuna illustrate* June 1911: 362).

Fashionable women participated in the elaboration of the male fantasy of the dead woman. The emaciated, elongated, snow-white look was fashioned after the real-life example of Ida Rubinstein, the actress of Russian origin whose wasted figure, thin to the point of anorexia, set a trend in the Paris of the 1910s (Dijkstra 1986: 348: see also de Cossart 1987: chapter 4). Like other show business women (Sarah Bernhardt, for example, kept a skeleton and made a pet of a vampire bat, which resided in a black satin-hung room containing a white coffin, in which she occasionally reclined), she gleefully played on the fears and phobias of bourgeois men and did her best to make her life and appearance conform to the image of alluring, objectified femininity. The prevalence of the 'vamp', from Theda Bara (a name which itself conjured up death) to Pina Menichelli, gave a further twist to this. Not by chance, the screen vamps were generously draped in costumes, jewels and make-up. These images had nothing to do with women as agents of reproduction, as healthy bearers of the future of the nation; instead, they posited the triumph of artifice and art over biology.

There may be many explanations for the obsession with death in the late nineteenth and early twentieth centuries, but the ascendance of inorganic over organic, of alienated labour over productive labour, in addition to the reification process whereby everything was turned into a thing, the expropriation of nature by industry, and the downgrading of the feminine were all crucial. These stood at the basis of the triumph of an aesthetic of artifice. As Elizabeth Wilson (1987: 9) has argued, fashion reduced humanity 'into the distilled moment of glassy sophistication'; it did not negate emotion, but displaced it into the realm of aesthetics.

The desire literally to substitute women with some sort of automated doll became a recurrent fantasy theme of masculine fiction – from the robots of Villiers de l'Isle-Adam's *Eve Future* and Fritz Lang's *Metropolis* to John Updike's somnambulant *Stepford Wives*. Although such a dream remained unfulfilled (at least until the invention in the 1950s of the inflatable doll 'molded of sturdy flesh-like vinyl with lovely soft-skin finish') (Dorfles 1969: 189), there was none the less a significant displacement of organic femininity by an expanding object world. In the late nineteenth and early twentieth centuries, the new technologies of light, glass, photography and synthetic materials offered opportunities for manufacturing desirable femininity. An important aspect of this was the taste for the translucent. Translucency carried within it an ancient fascination, a semi-spiritual appeal and the mystery of veiling; but it also acquired a new impetus deriving from more recent associations with the luxury of thinness and subtlety, and from a modern aesthetics of packaging and display.

It is important to grasp this in order to understand the allure of the first translucent plastic products. Cellophane was invented in France immediately prior to the First World War. Its inventor, Jacques Brandenburger, saw it as an upmarket rival to tinfoil. His first sale was to the fragrance company Coty, which won the exclusive right to a variety of cellophane embossed with a silk-like surface. Further sales followed to producers of luxury toothpaste, gingerbread and chocolates. 'Cellophane was defining itself as a carriage-trade product, a shimmering jewel in sheet form, the epitome of elegance and glamour in the new commercial art form called packaging,' Fenichell (1996: 126) writes. After the First World War, Du Pont bought out Brandenburger and took cellophane to America, where it was first used by R. J. Reynolds Tobacco Company to provide Camel cigarettes with 'Lock-in Freshness'. It was subsequently employed to sell many other products, including top-of-the-range tyres, bath towels and even grand pianos. Such was its glamour that Helena Rubinstein seized on it to wrap her combination of face powder and rouge. 'America was getting all wrapped up in cellophane. A new humor magazine, *Ballyhoo*, produced a first issue covered in it, as its droll editor, Norman Anthony, showed up at a news conference wearing a cellophane suit. A cellophane bathing suit garnered a predictable amount of publicity, though it was only semitransparent' (ibid.: 110).

By the end of 1932, the yen for transparency had become a popular passion in America. 'Even when no protective value was needed, when mere visibility was of no obvious material benefit', Fenichell continues, 'cellophane's shimmering presence conferred on the most mundane of products a strong dose of sex appeal – though retailers coyly called it "eye appeal" ' (ibid.: 112). Part of its appeal derived from the visibility of goods and the removal of handling, and therefore a guarantee of cleanliness. However, there was something else.

> There was something dramatic, even cinematic, about cellophane. In the frothy manner of those escapist musicals of the thirties, cellophane succeeded in wrapping everyday reality in a shiny new coat and tying it off with a glittering bow. Cellophane lent a touch of glamour and gloss to the most mundane objects, enhancing their appeal and allure not by changing their essence but enhancing the context in which they were sold. (ibid.: 113)

There was never any doubt that cellophane was feminine. As far as the image of woman was concerned, diaphanousness worked in two directions, creating a paradoxical allure. Both of these involved a negation of the flesh. On the one hand, transparency suggested an insubstantiality which referred back to the weightlessness and passivity of Victorian painting. On the other, the plastic film had something in common with the mystique of the veil and its sexual connotations. In Turkish tradition the veil signified harem; it offered a concealment that served simultaneously to render the wearer anonymous and to arouse interest in her (Blanch 1983: 275–6). This effect was magnified and ritualised in striptease, which, according to Roland Barthes, achieved its effect by constantly making the unveiled body more remote. The performer manufactured sex-appeal through the construction of a magical decor comprised of luxury objects: 'Feathers, furs and gloves go on pervading the woman with their magical virtue even once removed, and give her something like the enveloping memory of a luxurious shell.' The professionals of striptease, he continued, 'wrap themselves in the miraculous ease which constantly clothes them, makes them remote, gives them the icy indifference of skilful practitioners, haughtily taking refuge in the sureness of their technique' (Barthes 1973: 85–6).

The continuing appeal of the sheer, transparent look could also be seen in its return to favour in the fashions of the 1997–98 season. For fashion designers the diaphanous primarily signified femininity. Floaty chiffon dresses and transparency in blouses and dresses suggested a dream-like state like that mentioned above. 'I love chiffon because it's languid, dreamy, dainty, and delicate. I'd say it's swoony,' said Isaac Mizrahi to *Harper's Bazaar*, while Miuccia Prada confirmed that 'this isn't a season when I wanted to be intellectual or think too hard. I just wanted to create pretty, feminine clothes' (in *Harper's Bazaar* January 1997). First experimented by Yves Saint Laurent in 1968, transparent dresses had the peek-a-boo effect of semi-nudity, but also had the semi-miraculous appeal of the lightest, sheerest, most difficult fabrics. They had the lightness and effortlessness of chic, but also a mixture of spirituality, romance and precision. The appeal lay in part in the contradictions. In a further throwback to the past, transparency was taken to suggest spiritual purity. Its ethereality stood as a metaphor for life. Chiffon, organza and Perspex all conveyed a sense of space and light (Armstrong 1998: 72–5).

The glamour photography of the Hollywood golden age provides the most striking modern example of the fascination of translucency. The stills photographers of the 1920s and 1930s were unknown to the public and enjoyed no professional prestige in their time. Their role was a circumscribed one; it was to create portraits that reflected the allure, luxury of the Hollywood stars; in short, to sell the dream. As John Kobal wrote in the introduction to a collection of such portraits:

> Don't look for or expect to find the faces of real people. These beings have no warts; their lines, if any, are not the wrinkles of age, or of myopia – they are furrows of experience such as mere mortals rarely have. They have neither scars nor imperfection of any kind. They don't even possess pores in their skin through which to breathe. After all, gods are immortal. Their skin, like marble, like alabaster, has a translucent sheen in which, as in a mirror, one can see reflected the fantasies of the beholder. The ideal only remains. When they made good in pictures, they didn't just change, they shed that coarse cocoon and emerged translucent, transformed. (Kobal 1976: v)

Stars were artificial in several ways. Not only were they obviously manufactured, they were part of the new royalty of Hollywood. Thus they were ideally aligned with plastic which, according to Barthes (1973: 97), was less a substance than 'the very idea of its infinite trans-formation; as its everyday name indicates, it is ubiquity made visible'. Screen actors were associated in the public mind with new fibres and sub-stances because they were new and were *ersatz* just like the viscose which substituted for silk. Viscose had shine and lustre but also came in a de-lustred form. It was especially popular for form-fitting evening gowns, which it endowed with a slinky film star allure. Sales of rayon under-wear, sleek like silk but cheaper, shot up in the 1920s, largely due to the popular association of seductive synthetics with Hollywood vamps.

The most striking example of such an icon in the 1930s was Jean Harlow, the star of *Hell's Angels, Red Dust* and *Platinum Blonde*. Harlow was unequivocally an American star, of lower-class extraction. She was 'any girl', the 'slut next door' (Shulman 1992: 35), whose distinctive traits could be copied by anyone. More than any other star of the time, she was invented, a product of studio alchemy. In particular her trademark platinum blonde hair and white clothing lent her the translucency of marble. In still portraits, she appears truly as a corpse or a doll. Although on screen she was loud, blousy, funny and sexy, the standardised aspects of her image were always more important than her individuality. Artificial hair colour, drawn eyebrows, false eyelashes, deep mascara and lipstick, white satin dress and mask-like retouched skin were the compo-nents of 'Jean Harlow'. It is difficult to think of her in any other shade than monochrome since photographers' lights appeared to cut through her like an X-ray, creating a diffused, milky white radiance.

Given plastic's absolute 'quick-change artistry', and ability to transform itself into 'buckets as well as jewels' (ibid.), it could take on both exclusive and accessible forms. Cellophane moved both up- and downmarket, becoming a wrapper for cigarettes and mass-market chocolates and also a material for experimentation, for example by the fashion designer Elsa Schiaparelli, whose use of cellophane, rayon and viscose contributed to the emergence of a new, sleeker feminine silhouette. Reactions to plastics in the 1930s differed widely. While Aldous Huxley saw plastics and syn-thetic colours as a fearsome feature of his homogenising dystopia *Brave New World* (his test-tube heroine Lenina wears a jacket 'made of bottle green acetate with green viscose fur at the cuffs and collar' and carries a 'perfumed acetate handkerchief'; Huxley [1932] 1963: 50, 117), Schiaparelli rejoiced in the creative possibilities that they offered. A designer who enjoyed a creative relationship with the avant-garde, she pioneered the development of chemical colours and the use of artificial fibres in high fashion. In 1936, for example, she promoted the remarkable fluorescent Rhodia satin. Artificial colours appealed because they suggested a fantasy world of escape that was entirely man-made.

Although the monochrome celluloid aesthetic would retain a certain nostalgic appeal, the inorganic allure of plastics came to be associated more and more with colour. Colour first became part of everyday experience with the development of consumer culture and the growth of packaging in the late nineteenth century. Colourful boxes and brand names replaced loose goods and colour-printed advertisements for food, drink and other products appeared on billboards and roadsides. The colouring of celluloid prints of silent films was part of an attempt to capture something of the allure of the burgeoning commercial culture.

After Schiaparelli launched ice blue in 1932, startling, zany colours became a trademark of the House of Schiaparelli. Scarlets, violets and the bright colours of the Futurists and the Surrealists were employed for the first time in haute couture. With the aid of Jean Clément, who used an air-brush to project droplets of tinted cellulose varnish, usually used for the bodies of motorcars, on to white paper, she selected the particular mixture of ingredients which gave her the shade she wanted. In this way, she 'rein-vented' many colours from black to orange. However, it is her Shocking Pink that is best remembered. Produced one day in 1936 when Clément added magenta to pink, creating an iridescent cyclamen tint, Schiaparelli immediately labelled it 'Shocking' and proceeded to dress a whole collec-tion in it. Shortly thereafter it became her signature colour: 'The colour became one of Schiaparelli's most famous trademarks and the predomi-nating colour in the world of fashion, no matter how many other names its copies and variations assumed .... A shocking pink sheath worn with a shocking pink skull cap was "Schiaparelli's loveliest dinner dress", according to *Harper's Bazaar* in October 1940' (White 1995: 154).

The explosion of synthetic colour and pinks in the 1950s was bound up with technological development and the emergence of new plastics and the extension of consumer society to wider sections of the population. 'In the decade that America came into its own', Richard Horn wrote, 'its citizens went mad for bright, bold colors, using whichever ones they pleased in every room they lived in' (1985: 118). 'The new plastics, many of which had been developed during the war years, made an enormous contribution to the domestic landscape. In the form of small kitchen accessories, and, increasingly, as the 1950s progressed, items of tableware, they performed the role of units of pure colour which could be arranged in the interior like paint marks on a canvas' (Sparke 1995: 201). In this way they added a fantasy dimension to daily life.

Tupperware was the emblematic plastic of the 1950s. Unlike the hard, monochrome and masculine Bakelite, it was tough, but soft and sensual; it was mouldable and frosted translucent. It was available in a wide range of pastel hues. It was eminently practical and efficient as containers for the preservation of foodstuffs. Through the innovative selling device of the Tupperware house parties, it became a central part of domestic feminine culture. 'At its peak, the Tupperware world was a secret society without men (with the notable exception of Tupper)', Fenichell writes,

> a place where women of skill and ambition could be hard-headed and practical – while, like the products they sold, maintaining a placid, pliant, pious exterior. Like his contemporary Hugh Hefner – who enjoyed playing the consummate host at Playboy house parties – Earl Tupper's world oozed with sexuality, though in Tupper's case it was a repressed kitchen kinkiness, an object-fetishism gratified by lavish gifts of girlish goodies – pink Cadillacs, mink stoles, diamond bracelets – bestowed on the best Tupperware Ladies by Big Daddy. (1996: 234)

The triumph of plastic coincided with the ubiquity of pink, which was the most obviously feminine colour of all those that appeared in the 1950s domestic interior. This confirmed the way in which plastic symbolised objectified femininity. It made an appearance in a wide range of shades – from rose pink to salmon pink to 'shocking' pink – on automobiles, radios, refrigerators. Yet not all shades meant the same thing and sometimes the meanings went beyond the solely feminine. In broad terms, there were two, quite different pinks. The first of these was an elegant, ultra-feminine pastel pink, often combined with decorative touches of gold. This evoked the historical decorative idiom so beloved of the decorator Elsie de Wolfe: the eighteenth-century 'French taste' of Madame de Pompadour and Louis XV. Reappearing in the 1950s interior on the surfaces of radios and refrigerators, these evocative colours recalled the feminine taste, craftsmanship and luxury that were part of that historical moment. As Penny Sparke points out, pink and gold subsequently became linked with what was seen as the vulgarity of 1950s consumerism and of the exaggerated image of feminine sexuality, epitomised in the appearances, homes and possessions of the Hollywood film stars of that period (Sparke 1995: 197–8). This image was best captured by Jayne Mansfield, the Hollywood star who represented the same opulently synthetic aesthetic that produced the monstrously kitsch 1959 Cadillac coup de ville. Excessive in every respect, she once held a press conference in a pink swimming pool filled with pink champagne.

Appropriately, this aesthetic lives on in Barbie doll, the key icon of plastic pink femininity. A product of the late 1950s, Barbie offered an image of perfect, constructed femininity in moulded plastic form. As a toy, it provided girls with a consumption ideal; as an exaggerated, inorganic feminine image, devoted to waste and self-fashioning, it also offered a new version of the artificial model of the late nineteenth century. Like a film star, Barbie offers 'a face full of nothing that demands we make it into something' (Birkett 1998: 15). Although Barbie was the ultimate conformist, a truly malleable woman, her willingness to please led her to adopt every new style. The fact that 'she stares blankly into our eyes whoever we are, whatever age, whatever sex, whatever sexuality' led Dea Birkett to conclude that 'No whore could be more accommodating. No girl could give us more than Barbie' (ibid.: 21). Her 'availability' was intrinsically linked to her being made of plastic.

The second variety of pink was tied no less explicitly to the world of synthetics and artificiality; yet it was much more brash and subversive. Karal Ann Marling has argued that a 'sassy pink' was the hottest colour of the 1950s. While Mamie Eisenhower was turning the White House pastel pink, Elvis Presley turned up to his high school in Memphis wearing brilliant pink trousers. He wore pink suits at his first singing dates, bought his parents a pink Ford with his first large cheque and slept in a mock-erotic pink bedroom (Marling 1994: 40). In addition to lady-like pink, she argues, there was 'the aggressively hot pink of the teenagers'. While the former was 'a visual code of receptivity to new styles and products', the latter was 'a mark of rebellion against social conventions, including the rigid sexual coding of blues and pinks' (ibid.: 41). Both, however, 'seemed to signify a culture in love with novelty, change, and visual stimulation. Rock 'n' roll singles justly celebrated the joys of acquiring "Pink Pedal Pushers" (1958), "Pink Shoe Laces" (1959), and a "White Sport Coat [with a Pink Carnation]" (1957)' (ibid.).

The ultimate victory of brash pink was due not only to the rise of youth culture but also to the triumph of a broader plastic aesthetic, of which the former was a part. Colour mania was ultimately the sign of a definitive cultural shift away from the natural. Barthes noted that the spread of 'chemical-looking' colours derived from plastic's inability to retain any other type; 'of yellow, red and green', he wrote, 'it keeps only the aggressive quality and names, being able to display only concepts of colours' (Barthes 1973: 98). Sparke also highlights plastic product's historical origins in the world of simulation, and their ability to adopt, chameleon-like, either a modernist or a traditional aesthetic. 'Lacking craft roots, they could have no essential "truth". In contrast, their essential "dishonesty" cast them into a world without values, the world of the marketplace where anything was possible' (Sparke 1995: 201). Thus there was nothing exclusive about chemical colours, since plastic was the first imitation material that did not aim only to reproduce cheaply precious materials.

It was precisely this quality of commonness that appealed to Andy Warhol, who saw positive qualities in the banality of plastic. The disposable world of artificial fibres, television advertisements, space travel, instant celebrity and pop music appealed to him because it was transient and insubstantial. After the film *Vinyl*, Warhol's Factory made *Kitchen*, which indulged in the pleasures of white worktops and surfaces. The shop Paraphernalia, which was said to resemble transparent candy, sold clothes made by designers in the Warhol circle which fastened with Velcro or glowed in the dark (Wollen 1998). Slightly later, the designers Courrèges and Paco Rabanne turned shiny plastic clothes into high fashion. Warhol pushed the plastic aesthetic in new directions, inventing his own superstars and turning himself into a plastic icon.

Following Warhol, the master of surface glamour and repetition, the plastic world of pop culture became one of the main idioms of postmodern art. In the 1980s one example was Jeff Koons' kitsch plastic sculptures, notably of himself and his then wife, the blue-movie actress Cicciolina (herself a devotee of infantile pink) enjoined in carnal congress. Pierre et Gilles offered a similar plastic utopia. Devoid of the breath of life, their world is the kitsch one of snow domes, religious trinkets and holographs. Like Koons, they displayed a certain camp body fetishism, where the body is shiny and air-brushed; it is ageless, flexible and inorganic.

The fashion photographer David LaChappelle also developed a distinctive new artificial aesthetic with his hyper-coloured, super-kitsch portrait compositions. Following Guy Bourdin, the photographer who, in the 1960s, first brought sex and colour into the icy cool world of the fashion shoot, he mined a rich field of ephemeral culture to produce a highly personal trash aesthetic filled with pinks, turquoises and plastics. 'It is as if Alice in Wonderland, under the influence of a line of cocaine, had landed in Disneyland,' commented François Jonquet (1998: 53). By locating celebrities such as David Bowie, Elton John, Madonna or Faye Dunaway amid plastic flowers, leopard skin pianos and circus acts, he created a slightly disquieting parallel world mixing the familiar 'non-places' of McDonald's and shopping malls with a drug-inspired imagination and a certain sexual menace. An *habitué* of the legendary 1970s New York discotheque, Studio 54, LaChappelle was influenced by the surface glamour of a place where everything was beautiful, the people, the music, the make-up (ibid.: 54). The plastic, disposable quality that is the most striking aspect of his photographs derives from the fact that it is wholly bound up with surfaces, second-hand impressions, images working off images, the inorganic reworking of the already inorganic. It is a cloned or virtual reality that celebrates its own artificiality and lack of depth.

'Plastic is wholly swallowed up in the fact of being used: ultimately, objects will be invented for the sole pleasure of using them,' Barthes (1973: 99) predicted in 1957. 'The hierarchy of substances is abolished: a single one replaces them all: the whole world *can* be plasticized, and even life itself since, we are told, they are beginning to make plastic aortas'. What Barthes underestimated was that, more than science, it would be culture that would fuel the drive towards plasticisation. 'We have seen the fantasy to look like Barbie enacted by film stars such as Cher, who has undegone radical surgery to "resculpt" her body to fit the ideal upheld by Barbie,' one author has argued. 'The back-and-forth shuttle of influence is clear: while many models and actresses strain to attain Barbie-like figures, there is no doubt that young girls look to actresses and models for role models' (O'Sickey 1994: 36). The widespread use of silicone breast implants meant that, for the first time, the physical barrier between the organic and the inorganic was eroded and the latter penetrated the former. *Baywatch* star Pamela Anderson and Hefner creation Anne Nicole Smith offered the most striking examples of plasticised icons of the 1990s. However, supermodel Claudia Schiffer and Hollywood actress Cameron Diaz are also 'plastic' in the sense that they are no more than substitutes; they are reminiscent of something else, they are shallow, objectified and passive, pure features of a derivative culture of imitation. Yet, far from undermining their allure, this repetitive quality was intrinsic to it, a proof of the power of the modern alchemy of plastic.

Conclusion

This book has sought to examine the origins and development of glamour. It has outlined the way in which the aura of the aristocracy was turned, in burgeoning commercial metropolises, into a commodified aura capable of adoption by or conferment on a range of people, places and things. It has explored how seductive techniques were forged that blended upper-class allure, popular spectacle and street culture. Attention has also been paid to the way glamour evolved as a series of distinct visual effects which are still in wide use in advertising, the press, fashion and fashion promotion, and film. This striking continuity suggests that glamour became wholly detached from class-related situations and rituals and acquired an autonomous dignity as a dynamic of seduction and enchantment. This was so because the alignment of class and glamour was only ever conjunctural. It is a persistent misunderstanding of glamour to see it as a property of the well-born or well-bred (see McKibbin 1998: 43). In fact, the social elite became glamorous in a meaningful way for the first time as they acquired the mannerisms and styles of a modern consumption elite. It was the dreams of commercial mass society that sustained glamour, not the persistence of aristocratic social influence.

What, then, is contemporary glamour? Is it possible to distinguish specific hallmarks relative to the theoretical and historical observations made in this book? In so far as the consumer culture that was the primary factor in creating the conditions for glamour is more dominant today than at any previous time, there is every reason to suppose considerable continuity. Dreaming is still a feature of individual sensibility and products are still cloaked in an imaginative aura. Enticing images, staged and constructed pictures of people, places or things that invite consumption are thus integral features of the economic and cultural system. The subjects of glamour continue to seduce by association with the qualities of beauty, sexuality, theatricality, wealth, dynamism, notoriety and leisure. In addition, the complex material culture of glamour reinforces these values by lending each of them a vividness that derives from their associations with specific colours and visual effects. Yet, the core values that compose glamour do not have the same connotations today as in the past. In particular, the detachment of contemporary glamour from social referents and its tendency to become pure image gives it a repetitive, even claustrophobic quality. This reifying trend was inscribed within glamour from the beginning, but the redesigning of society on the basis of the practices and values of consumerism, as well as the growing emphasis on image and visual spectacle over more than a century, have given it a particular impulse.

Glamour has evolved from an invisible allure that bathed the fortunate and the fashionable into a structure, a product and, above all, a culture with its own history of moments, places, objects and people. It is above all fashion practitioners, make-up artists, photographers, publicists, image-makers and models who today provide for consumer society's need for fantasies of wealth, style, notoriety, beauty and sex. The press and the broadcast media furnish the raw material of glamour. Their unique capacity to provide a stage on which the famous and the not-yet-famous can parade before the greedy eyes of public opinion connects them directly with the dreams and aspirations of the masses who are their readers and viewers. However, in order to work as a desirable dream, as an enchantment for the masses combining elements of exclusivity as well accessibility, it must include elements of mystery and distance. Yet the structures of contemporary glamour, taken as a whole, tend to undermine these qualities. The demise of formalised inequalities, established hierarchies and patterns of deference set the scene for a situation in which an attention-grabbing presence is not seen as a privilege or an accompaniment of talent and beauty, but rather as a right for all.

The diminished capacity today to manufacture glamour in a way that retains something of the exclusive and the unattainable leads to certain effects. In particular, it can be said that glamour is heavily influenced by its own history and that backward-looking elements are strong. If glamour sometimes acquires a dull and repetitive feel, it is because the weight of the past is heavy. Although no longer recent, the signs of the glamour manufacture of the major Hollywood studios of the past remain available to be imitated, appropriated and reconfigured. Contemporary cinema offers only a small place to glamour, but other industries make ample recourse to it. Cosmetics, lingerie, fashion, photography, television and popular spectacle all base part of their appeal on the special allure of Hollywood. The frequency with which contemporary film and television actors are photographed in the manner of George Hurrell or Clarence Sinclair Bell's stills of Clark Gable, Joan Crawford and Jean Harlow suggests that such portraits are unequalled in their allure. Volumes such as Len Prince's *About Glamour* or Serge Normant's *Femme Fatale*, which feature contemporary stars photographed in the manner of the old, cover their subjects in an aura of shadows, light, glistening surfaces and seductive materials (Prince 1997; Normant 2001). Today, at a time when celebrity is widely thought to have become irredeemably cheapened, the images of the handful of stars who enjoyed almost universal admiration stand as a paradigm or at least as a possible cloak for the hundreds of television and film actors who seek to hold the attention of the public for more than the bat of an eye. There are important differences, though, between the use of photographic techniques in the 1930s and in the 1990s and today. What, then, was innovative and novel, while also being seductive and even vulgar in its desire to please, now takes on the air of the classic and the artistic. The Hollywood past is still to some extent popular culture, but it is also high culture and this gives it a wide-ranging resonance.

Even more striking than the ubiquity of Hollywood imagery is the recurrent reference to the courtesans of the Second Empire and after. There are few aspects of the style, behaviour, culture or values of that period or that category that can be transferred meaningfully to the present. Moreover use of images and attitudes from that time in con-temporary fashion, publishing and photography is relatively infrequent. But they are sufficiently prominent to warrant mention. No less a figure than Diana Vreeland celebrated the great figures of the *demi-monde* in her autobiography (Vreeland 1984: 119). She also confirmed the contin-uing role of low culture. An appreciation of vulgarity, she said, was particularly American. 'Vulgarity is a very important ingredient in life. I'm a great believer in vulgarity – if it's got vitality. A little bad taste is like a nice splash of paprika. We all need a splash of bad taste – it's hearty, it's healthy, it's physical' (ibid.: 122). Debora Silverman (1986: 11) has shown how Vreeland put this credo to use in the 1980s as one of the creators of the cultural style of the Reagan era. As the curator of a series of exhibitions dedicated to Chinese emperors, French aristocrats and English noblemen, she championed 'a style of unabashed opulence'. This dovetailed with the 'fully-fledged cult of visible luxury and unre-strained flaunting of wealth' that Reagan and his associates promoted. Silverman offers an indictment of these practices. 'Reagan's politics and the aristocratic fashion culture share a fundamental inauthenticity, a reliance on fabrication, and a glaring disparity between symbolism and reality,' she argued. But what is striking from the point of view of glamour is the great continuity with the fabrications and theatricality of the past in Vreeland's work. As Silverman herself points out, Vreeland had little formal education, trained briefly with the Ziegfeld Follies and regarded the world as a stage (ibid.: 46). The ahistorical arrangements chosen for her exhibitions at New York's Metropolitan Museum and consequent emphasis on surface reflected a deracinated cult of display. The courtesans fascinated her. She saw the *demi-monde* as a world of glamour 'full of laughter and fun, marked by lots of noise, lots of romance, and *great* style' (ibid.: 74). The exhibition she organised on the '*La Belle Epoque*', Silverman notes, 'effected a fundamental contextual levelling; historical meaning and substance were eliminated in a narcissistic project of identity'.

The courtesans represent the oldest distinctive image of glamour that still exercises a continuous influence. Even the high fashion models who so captivated public attention at the start of the twenty-first century owe a debt to them. As the catwalk shows became more public and spectacular and the fashion show became theatre on a grand scale, the models 'approximated their behavior to that of the chorus girls and prostitutes whose history paralleled their own' (Evans 2001: 300). In this respect, the distance between Cora Pearl and La Païva on the one hand, and Claudia Schiffer and Linda Evangelista on the other, was short. What these women shared was a capacity to enchant that relied not merely on their beauty or their fame, but on a careful manipulation of material goods and visual effects.

Notes

Introduction

1 This applies also to J. Rosa (ed.). *Glamour: Fashion + Industrial Design + Architecture* (San Francisco: San Francisco Museum of Art, 2004). The essays in this catalogue survey glamour, mostly in the post-1945 period, but no theory is offered.

2 This definition of glamour was first set out in R. C. V. Buckley and S. Gundle, 'Fashion and Glamour', in Nicola White and Ian Griffiths (eds.), *The Fashion Business: Theory, Practice, Image* (Oxford: Berg, 2000), p. 42.

3 On the democratisation of desire, see W. Leach, *Land of Desire: Merchants, Power and the Rise of a New American Culture* (New York: Pantheon, 1993).

4 L. Mulvey, 'Visual Pleasure and Narrative Cinema', in *Visual and Other Pleasures* (Basingstoke: Macmillan, 1989), p. 19. L. Irigaray, *Speaking of the Other Woman* (Ithaca, NY: Cornell University Press, 1985).

2 The Gender of Glamour

1 Lillie Bart is depicted as a woman whose beauty appeared to be glazed. She was a figure whose 'impenetrable surface suggested a process of crystallization which had fused her whole being into one hard, brilliant substance' (see Bronner, *Consuming Visions*, p. 149). This sort of commodity appeal was an example of how fashion directed libidinal desire onto the inorganic. Benjamin argued that fashion was the medium that that 'lures [sex] ever deeper into the inorganic world – the realm of dead things' (see Buck-Morss 1990: 101).

2 For a fuller discussion of Boldini and Sargent, see Gundle 1999.

3 The role of beauty, fashion and seduction in the development of luxury is considered by Sombart 1967.

4 Richardson 1971: 71. It is worthy of note that the chief providers of funds for the courtesans were newly rich bourgeois. For reasons of image, these figures were eclipsed in the public imagination, and indeed in the memoirs of courtesans themselves, by the various princes and aristocrats who also enjoyed their favours.

5 On La Goulue and the Moulin Rouge, see Jarrett 1997: Chapter 2.

3 Hollywood Lifestyles

1 For example, the Austrian designer Ernst Dryden worked for stores and advertising agencies in Berlin and Paris before placing his talent at the service of Paramount studios. See Lipman 1989.

2 For a long-range perspective, see Meyrowitz 1986.

3 Charles and Watts 2000: 254. This element of unreality was more powerful in the media age than the more grounded attempts of Paris in the 1920s to turn itself into an illusory city based on imagination. See Gronenberg 1998.

4   This practice was still in operation in the 1950s. In his analysis of the publicity campaigns used to build up Grace Kelly and Marilyn Monroe, Thomas Harris found that actual biographical material was used to an extraordinary degree. Kelly's wealthy, genteel background was used to cultivate her image as 'elegant', 'lady-like', 'patrician', while Monroe's youthful waywardness and early marriage were used to bolster a more sexually connoted image. See Harris 1991: 41.

5   The perplexity derived from the novelty of sexuality being displayed without sexual favours apparently being granted (notwithstanding the casting couch). For a discussion of this transition, see Marwick 1988: 245–9.

6   Glyn's impact is chronicled in Gloria Swanson's memoirs; Swanson 1981: 159–73.

7   On the 1925 Paris exhibition, see Gronenberg 1998.

8   On the history of the fashion show, see C. Evans, 'The Enchanted Spectacle', *Fashion Theory*, 5:3 (2001), 271–310.

9   See Fitzgerald 1966: 223. The issue permeates the whole of Fitzgerald's *The Great Gatsby*.

10 This theme is recurrent in Desser and Jowett 2000.

11 See, for example, Swanson 1981: 508–9. On p. 223 Swanson says that, on her trip to France, 'snobbish Parisians' were not above asking her discreetly 'what people did at parties at Pickfair and what kind of pomade Rudolph Valentino wore on his gorgeous hair'.

12 Even in the more prosperous 1950s, the sexuality and luxury of the stars appealed to a conformist middle class. See Baritz, 1989: 94.

6   Clamorous Chroma

1   In folk culture, however, red often carry positive connotations of fertility. In the peasant costume of the Black Forest, for example, the pompoms on the hats of unmarried girls are red, while those of married women are black. In China, wedding dresses are red.

7   Captivating Metals

1   See, for example, the photographic service 'White Heat', in *Maxim*, April 1999. The introductory text reads: 'Who wants to be a millionaire playboy? We do. And with this summer's great white clothes you're halfway there' (p. 134).

9   Glittering Media

1   See, however, the case that is made for the glittering surfaces of pre-Nazi Berlin in Ward 2001.

11   Alluring Plastics

1   The 'miraculous' aspects of plastic's appeal are stressed by Barthes 1973.

2   Very similar points are made in Theweleit 1987, an investigation of the fantasy life of the *Freikorps* officers who roamed Germany repressing internal enemies after the First World War. He shows that, in the dreams of these pathologically misogynistic men, women were often turned into something cold and dead.

References

Adair, G. 'Black and White in Colour', in G. Adair, *The Postmodernist Always Rings Twice* (London: Fourth Estate, 1992).

Albrecht, D. 'Images et merchandises', in A. Masson, *Hollywood 1927–1941* (Paris: Autrement, 1991).

Alexander, S. 'Becoming a Woman in London in the 1920s and 1930s', in D. Feldman and G. S. Jones (eds.) *Metropolis London: Histories and Representations since 1800* (London: Routledge, 1989).

Amory, C. *Who Killed Society?* (New York: Harper and Brothers 1960).

Anon. 'Il fallimento della bellezza', *Tribuna illustrata*, 4 June 1911.

Anon. 'Metro-Goldwyn-Mayer', *Fortune*, December 1932, reproduced in T. Balio (ed.), *The American Film Industry* (Madison: University of Wisconsin Press, 1976).

Anon. *The Age of Innocence: The Paintings of John Singer Sargent* (London: Phaidon, undated [1996?]).

Anon. 'A Matter of Gold', *Italia*, November 1998.

Aretz, G. *The Elegant Woman* (London: Harrap, 1932).

Armstrong, L. 'The Irresistible Lightness of Being', *Vogue*, March 1998.

Auerbach, N. *Woman and Demon: The Life of a Victorian Myth* (Cambridge, Mass.: Harvard University Press, 1982).

Bacall, L. *By Myself* (London: Coronet, 1979; first published 1978).

Bailey, M. J. *Those Glorious Glamour Years: Classic Hollywood Design of the 1930s* (London: Columbus, 1988).

Bailey, P. 'Parasexuality and Glamour: The Victorian Barmaid as Cultural Prototype', *Gender and History*, 2:5 (1990).

Balfour, P. *Society Racket* (London: Lang, 1933).

Banner, L.W. *American Beauty* (New York: Knopf, 1983).

Baritz, L. *The Good Life: The Meaning of Success for the American Middle Class* (New York: Knopf, 1989).

Barthes, R. *Mythologies* (London: Paladin, 1972, first published 1957).

Bartley, L. 'Show Us Your Metal', *Frank*, November 1998.

Basinger, J. *A Woman's View: How Hollywood Spoke to Women 1930–1960* (London: Chatto and Windus, 1993).

Baudrillard, J. *Revenge of the Crystal* (London: Pluto, 1990), p. 92. The chapter, entitled 'Mass Media Culture', originally appeared in *La Societé de consommation* (Paris: Donoël, 1970).

Beaton, C. *The Glass of Fashion* (London: Weidenfeld and Nicolson, 1954).

Beatty, L. *Lillie Langtry: Manners, Masks and Morals* (London: Chatto & Windus, 1999).

Becker, C. Preface to E. Zola, *Au Bonheur des Dames*, in *Les Rougon-Macquart* (Paris: Robert Laffont, 1992).

Beier, U. and P. Chakravati (eds.). Sun *and Moon in Papua New Guinea Folklore* (Port Moresby: Institute for Papua New Guinea Studies, 1974).

Bellezza Rosina, M. and Morini, E. 'Bianco e nero: tessuto e moda', in M. Carmigiano (ed.) *Bianco e Nero* (Novaro: De Agostini, 1991).

Benjamin, W. 'The Work of Art in the Age of Mechanical Reproduction', in W. Benjamin, *Illuminations* (London: Fontana, 1969).

Benjamin, W. *Charles Baudelaire: A Lyric Poet in the Era of High Capitalism* (London: Verso, 1983).

Benjamin, W. *The Arcades Project* (Cambridge, Mass.: Harvard University Press, 1999).

Bernheimer, C. *Figures of Ill-Repute: Representing Prostitution in Nineteenth-Century France* (Cambridge, Mass.: Harvard University Press, 1989).

Berry, S. *Screen Style: Fashion and Femininity in 1930s Hollywood* (Minneapolis: University of Minnesota Press, 2000).

Bertelli, S. *Il corpo del re* (Florence: Ponte alle Grazie, 1990).

Binder, P. *The Truth about Cora Pearl* (London: Weidenfeld and Nicolson, 1986).

Birkett, D. 'I'm Barbie. Buy Me', *The Guardian Weekend* (28 November 1998).

Blanch, L. *Pierre Loti: Portrait of an Escapist* (London: Collins, 1983).

Blume, M. *Côte d'Azur: Inventing the French Riviera* (London: Thames and Hudson, 1992).

Bobko, J. (ed.). *Vision: The Life and Music of Hildegard von Bingen* (New York: Penguin, 1995).

Boorstin, D.J. *The Image* (London: Weidenfeld and Nicolson, 1962).

Booth, M. R. 'Ellen Terry', in J. Stokes *et al. Bernhardt, Terry, Duse: The Actress in Her Time* (Cambridge: Cambridge University Press, 1988).

Bowles. H. 'Flights of Fancy', *Vogue USA* (December 1994).

Bracalini, R. *La Regina Margherita* (Milan: Rizzoli, 1983).

Bradford, S. *Princess Grace* (New York: Stein and Day, 1984).

Brayfield, C. *Glitter: The Truth about Fame* (London: Chatto and Windus, 1985).

Bronner, Simon J. *Consuming Visions: Accumulation and Display of Goods in America, 1880–1920* (New York: Norton, 1989).

Bruzzi, S. *Undressing Cinema: Clothing and Identity in the Movies* (London: Routledge, 1998).

Buck-Morss, S. *Dialectics of Seeing: Walter Benjamin and the Arcades Project* (Cambridge, Mass: MIT Press, 1990).

Buckley, R. C. V. and Gundle, S. 'Fashion and Glamour', in N. White and I. Griffiths (eds.) *The Fashion Business: Theory, Practice, Image* (Oxford: Berg, 2000).

Buckley, R. C. V. and Gundle, S. 'Flash Trash: Gianni Versace and the Theory and Practice of Glamour', in S. Bruzzi and P. Church Gibson (eds.) *Fashion Cultures: Theories, Explorations and Analysis* (London: Routledge, 2000).

Burchill, J. 'The Blue Hour', *The Modern Review*, October 1997.

Burkhardt, T. *Alchemy: Science of the Cosmos, Science of the Soul* (Shaftesbury: Element Books, 1967; first edition 1960).

Burns, E. *Theatricality: A Study of Convention in the Theatre and in Social Life* (London: Longman, 1972).

Bushman, R. L. *The Refinement of America: Persons, Houses, Cities* (New York: Vintage, 1992).

Butazzi, G. 'La sera della festa: ragionamenti sul nero', in M. Carmigiani *et al. Bianco e Nero* (Novara: Dr Agostini, 1991).

Campbell, C. *The Romantic Ethic and the Spirit of Modern Consumerism* (Oxford: Blackwell, 1987).

Cannadine, D. *The Decline and Fall of the British Aristocracy* (New Haven, Conn.: Yale University Press, 1990).

Carlyle, T. *On Heroes, Hero-Worship and the Heroic in History* (Boston: Ginn and Co, 1901).

Carmigiani, M. (ed.). *Bianco e Nero* (Novara: De Agostini, 1991).
Carter, E. *How German is She? Postwar West German Reconstruction and the Consuming Woman* (Ann Arbor, Mich.: University of Michigan Press, 1997).
Cartland, B. *We Danced All Night* (London: Hutchinson, 1971).
Castelbajac, K. de. *The Face of the Century* (London: Thames and Hudson, 1995).
Cecchi, D. *Giovanni Boldini* (Turin: UTET, 1962).
Cendrars, B. *Hollywood: la mecque du cinéma* (Paris: Grasset, 1936).
Charles, J. and Watts, J. '(Un)Real Estate: Marketing Hollywood in the 1910s and 1920s', in D. Desser and G. S. Jowett (eds.) *Hollywood Goes Shopping* (Minneapolis: University of Minnesota Press, 2000).
Chetwynd, T. *The Age of Myth* (London: Mandala/HarperCollins, 1991).
Christiansen, R. *Tales of the New Babylon: Paris 1869–1875* (London: Sinclair-Stevenson, 1994).
Clark, T. J. *The Painting of Modern Life* (London: Thames and Hudson, 1985)
Clarke, G. *Capote* (London: Abacus 1993; first published 1988).
Clyde, A. *Glitter and Glamour* (London: Stevens, 1935).
Collodi. *Le avventure di Pinocchio* (Milan: Rizzoli, 1998; first published 1882).
Colonna di Sermoneta, V. *Memorie* (Milan: Treves, 1938).
Cook, P. *Fashioning the Nation* (London: BFI, 1996).
Corbin, A. *Women for Hire: Prostitution and Sexuality in France after 1850* (Cambridge, Mass.: Harvard University Press, 1990).
Coslovi, M. 'Il Glamour ci viene da Hollywood: l'immagine dell'America in una rivista femminile del dopoguerra', unpublished paper, undated.
Cresti, A. *Nell'immaginario cromatico:symbol e colore* (Milan: Medical Books, 1995).
d'S, G. 'Lynda e Tyrone hanno ditto "si" ', *Il Messaggero* (24 January 1949).
Davis, R. *The Glamour Factory: Inside Hollywood's Big Studio System* (Dallas: Southern Methodist University Press, 1993).
de Beauvoir, S. *The Second Sex* (Harmondworth: Penguin, 1964).
Debord, G. *The Society of the Spectacle* (New York: Zone Books, 1995; first published 1967).
de Castelbajac, K. *The Face of the Century* (London: Thames and Hudson, 1995).
de Cossart, M. *Ida Rubinstein (1995–1960)* (Liverpool: Liverpool University Press, 1987).
DelGaudio, S. *Dressing the Part: Sternberg, Dietrich and Costume* (London and Toronto: Associated University Press, 1993).
de Marly, D. *Worth: Father of Haute Couture* (London: Elm Tree, 1980).
De Maupassant, G. *The Best Short Stories* (Ware: Wordsworth edition, 1997).
Desser, D. and Jowett, G. (eds.). *Hollywood Goes Shopping* (Minneapolis: University of Minnesota Press, 2000).
Dewald, J. *The European Nobility, 1400–1800* (Cambridge: Cambridge University Press, 1996).
Dickens, C. *Sketches by Boz: Illustrative of Every-Day Life and Every-Day People* (London: Oxford University Press, 1957; first published 1839).
Dijkstra, B. *Idols of Perversity: Fantasies of Feminine Evil in Fin-de-Siècle Culture* (New York: Oxford University Press, 1986).
Dorfler, G. *Kitsch: The World of Bad Taste* (New York: Universe, 1969).
Douglas, A. *Terrible Honesty: Mongrel Manhattan in the 1920s* (London: Picador, 1996).
Dyer, R. *Stars* (London: BFI, 1979).
Dyer, R. *Heavenly Bodies: Film Stars and Society* (London: Routledge, 1987).
Dyer, R. 'Monroe and Sexuality', in Janet Todd (ed.) *Women and Film* (New York: Holmes and Meier, 1988).

Dyer, R. *White* (London: Routledge, 1997).

Eckert, C. 'The Carol Lombard in Macy's Window', in C. Gledhill (ed.) *Stardom: Industry of Desire* (London: Routledge, 1991).

Edwards, A. *Throne of Gold: The Lives of the Aga Khans* (London: HarperCollins, 1996; first published 1995).

Elias, N. *Court Society* (Oxford: Blackwell, 1983).

Emberley, J. V. *Venus and Furs: The Cultural Politics of Fur* (London: I. B. Tauris, 1997).

Engstead, J. *Star Shots: Fifty Years of Pictures and Stories by One of Hollywood's Greatest Photographers* (New York: Dutton, 1978).

'Esotico charme', *Vogue Italia* (December 1995).

Etherington-Scott, M. *Patou* (London: Hutchinson, 1983).

Evans, C. 'The Enchanted Spectacle', *Fashion Theory*, 5:3 (2001).

Ewen, R. *All Consuming Images: the Politics of Style in Contemporary Culture* (New York: Basic Books, 1988).

Falasca-Zamponi, S. *Fascist Spectacle: The Aesthetics of Power in Mussolini's Italy* (Berkeley: University of California Press, 1997).

Felski, R. *The Gender of Modernity* (Cambridge, Mass.: Harvard University Press, 1995).

Fenichel, S. *Plastic: The Making of a Synthetic Century* (London: HarperBusiness, 1996).

Findlater, R. *The Player Queens* (London: Weidenfeld and Nicolson, 1976).

Fine Collins, A. 'A Night to Remember', *Vanity Fair* (July 1996).

Fitzgerald, F. S. *The Beautiful and Damned* (Harmondsworth: Penguin edition 1966; first published 1922).

Fitzgerald, F. S. *The Great Gatsby* (London: Abacus edition, 1991).

Forrest, K. 'Blue Notes', *W* (April 1997).

Fowles, J. *Starstruck: Celebrity Performers and the American Public* (Washington: Smithsonian, 1992).

Fox, P. *Star Style: Hollywood Legends as Fashion Icons* (Santa Monica, Cal.: Angel City Press, 1995).

Frazer, Sir J. *The Golden Bough* (Ware: Wadsworth edition, 1993).

Freud, S. 'On Narcissism: An Introduction' (1914), in S. Freud, *On Metapsychology*, Penguin Freud Library, vol. 11 (Harmondsworth: Penguin, 1991).

Friedel, R. *Pioneer Plastic: The Making and Selling of Celluloid* (Madison: University of Wisconsin Press, 1983).

Frisby, D. *Fragments of Modernity* (Cambridge: Polity, 1988).

Gabler, N. *An Empire of Their Own: How the Jews Invented Hollywood* (New York: Anchor, 1985).

Gaines J. and C. Herzog (eds.). *Fabrications: Costume and the Female Body* (New York: Routledge, 1990).

Gamson, J. *Claims to Fame: Celebrity in Contemporary America* (Berkeley: University of California Press, 1994).

George, D. *Mysteries of the Dark Moon* (San Francisco: Harper, 1992).

Girouard, M. *The Return to Camelot: Chivalry and the English Gentleman* (New York: Yale University Press, 1981).

Glenn, S. A. *Female Spectacle: The Theatrical Roots of Modern Feminism* (Cambridge, Mass.: Harvard University Press, 2000).

Gomery, D. *The Hollywood Studio System* (London: BFI, 1986).

Gomery, D. *Shared Pleasures: A History of Movie Presentation in the United States* (London: BFI, 1992).

Govinda, Lama A. *Creative Meditation and Multidimensional Consciousness* (London: Mandala/Unwin, 1977).

Gronenberg, T. *Designing Modernity: Exhibiting the City in 1920s Paris* (Manchester: Manchester University Press, 1998).

Guerrand, R.-H. *Moeurs citadines* (Paris: Quai Voltaire, 1992).

Guiles, F. L. *Loner at the Ball: The Life of Andy Warhol* (London: Bantam Press, 1989).

Gundle, S. 'Mapping the Origins of Glamour: Giovanni Boldini, Paris and the Belle Epoque', *Journal of European Studies*, 29 (1999).

Hall, N. *The Moon and the Virgin: Reflections on the Archetypal Feminine* (London: The Women's Press, 1980).

Halttunen, K. *Confidence Men and Painted Women: A Study of Middle-Class Culture in America, 1830–1870* (New Haven, Conn.: Yale University Press, 1982).

Hamilton, M. *The Queen of Camp: Mae West, Sex and Popular Culture* (London: HarperCollins, 1995).

Hanák, P. *The Garden and the Workshop: Essays on the Cultural History of Vienna and Budapest* (Princeton, NJ: Princeton University Press, 1998).

Hansen, M. *Babel and Babylon: Spectatorship in American Silent Film* (Cambridge, Mass.: Harvard University Press, 1991).

Harris, T. 'The Building of Popular Images: Grace Kelly and Marilyn Monroe', in C. Gledhill, *Stardom: Industry of Desire 1991* (London: Routledge, 1991).

Harvey, J. *Men in Black* (London: Reaktion, 1995).

Hawkes, J. *Man and the Sun* (London: Cresset, 1962).

Hayden, I. *Symbol and Privilege: The Ritual Context of British Royalty* (Tucson: University of Arizona Press, 1987).

Head, E. *The Dress Doctor* (Kingswood: World's Work, 1959).

Herford, C. H. 'Gabriele D'Annunzio', *Bulletin of the John Rylands Library*, 5 (1919), cited in J. Woodhouse, *Gabriele D'Annunzio: Defiant Archangel* (Oxford: Oxford University Press, 1998).

Higonnet, M. 'Real Fashion: Clothes Unmake the Working Woman', in M. Cohen and C. Prendergast (eds.) *Spectacles of Realism: Body, Gender, Genre* (Minneapolis: University of Minnesota Press, 1995).

Higonnet, P. *Paris: Capital of the World* (Cambridge, Mass.: Harvard University Press, 2002).

Hillier, B. *The Style of the Century 1900–80* (New York: Dutton, 1983).

Hobsbawm, E. *TheAge of Empire 1875–1914* (London: Weidenfeld and Nicolson, 1987).

Hollander, A. *Seeing Through Clothes* (Berkeley: University of California Press, 1993; first published 1978).

Horn, R. *Fifties Style: Then and Now* (London: Columbus, 1985).

Huxley, A. *Brave New World* (Harmondsworth: Penguin edition; first published 1932).

Irigaray, L. *Speaking of the Other Woman* (Ithaca, NY: Cornell University Press, 1985).

Iverson, A. 'Man in the Moon', *Harpers Bazaar* (August 1994).

Jackson, R. *Victorian Theatre* (London: Black, 1989).

Jacobs, L. *The Wages of Sin: Censorship and the Fallen Woman Film 1928–1942* (Madison: University of Wisconsin Press, 1991).

Jarrett, L. *Stripping in Time: A History of Erotic Dancing* (London: HarperCollins, 1997).

Jhally, S. *The Codes of Advertising: Fetishism and te Political Economy of Meaning in the Consumer Society* (London: Routledge, 1987).

Jonquet, F. 'Direction LaChappelle', *L'Evennement du jeudi* (2–8 July 1998).

Kelleher, D. L. *Paris: Its Glamour and its Life* (London: Lunn's, 1914).

Kelley, K. *The Royals* (New York: Warner Books, 1997).

Kindem, G. 'Hollywood's Movie Star System: A Historical Overview', in G. Kindem (ed.) *The American Movie Industry* (Carbondale, Ill.: Southern Illinois University Press, 1982).

Klein, R. *Cigarettes are Sublime* (London: Picador, 1995; first published 1993).

Kobal, J. (ed.). *Hollywood Glamor Portraits* (New York: Dover, 1976).

Kobal, J. (ed.). *George Hurrell: Hollywood Glamour Portraits* (London: Scirmer, 1993).

Kracauer, S. *Offenbach and the Paris of His Time* (London: Constable, 1937).

Kracauer, S. *The Mass Ornament: Weimar Essays* (Cambridge, Mass.: Harvard University Press, 1995).

Lameyre, G. *Haussman 'Préfet de Paris'* (Paris: Flammarion, 1958).

Lancaster, B. *The Department Store: A Social History* (Leicester: Leicester University Press, 1995).

Lauder, E. *Estée: A Success Story* (New York: Ballantine, 1985).

Laver, J. *Taste and Fashion: from the French Revolution to the Present Day* (London: Harrap, 1937).

LaVine, W. R. *In a Glamorous Fashion: the Fabulous Years of Hollywood Costume Design* (London: Allen and Unwin, 1981).

Leach, W. 'Strategies of Display and Production of Desire' in S. J. Bonner (ed.) *Consuming Visions: Accumulation and Display of Goods in America, 1880–1920* (New York: W. W. Norton, 1989).

Leach, W. *Land of Desire: Merchants, Power and the Rise of a New American Culture* (New York: Pantheon, 1993).

Lears, J. *Fables of Abundance: A Cultural History of Advertising in America* (New York: Basic, 1994).

Lepschy, A. L. and Lepschy, G. 'La Grammatica', in G. Barbieri Squarotti and others, *L'italianistica: introduzione allo studio della letteratura e della lingua italiana* (Turin: UTET, 1992).

Lerner, L. *La vita d'Ingrid Bergman* (Milan: Sperling and Kupfer, 1987; first edition, 1986).

Lewis, A. A. and Woodworth C. *Miss Elizabeth Arden* (New York: Coward, McCann and Goeghegan, 1972).

Lipman, A. *Divinely Elegant: The World of Ernst Dryden* (London: Pavilion, 1989).

Logan, O. 'Pius XII: Romanità, Prophesy and Charisma', *Modern Italy* 3:2 (1998).

Lovatelli, W. *Roma di ieri: cronache e fasti* (Roma: Ruffolo, 1948).

Lowenthal, L. 'The Triumph of Mass Idols', in *Literature, Popular Culture, and Society* (Englewood Cliffs, NJ: Prentice Hall, 1961).

Lurie, A. *The Language of Clothes* (London: Bloomsbury, 1981).

Lyle, J. *Body Language* (London: BCA, 1990).

Madsen, A. *Coco Chanel: A Biography* (London: Bloomsbury, 1990).

Marchand, R. *Advertising the American Dream: Making Way for Modernity, 1920–1940* (Berkeley: University of California Press, 1985).

Marchand, B. *Paris, histoire d'ine ville XIX–XX siècle* (Paris: Seuil, 1993).

Margetson, S. *The Long Party: High Society in the Twenties and Thirties* (Farnborough: Saxon House, 1974).

Margulies, E. 'All that Glitters', *The Guide* (23–29 January 1999).

Marling, K. A. *As Seen on TV: The Visual Culture of Everyday Life* (Cambridge, Mass.: Harvard University Press, 1994).

Marwick, A. *Beauty in History: Society, Politics and Personal Appearance c. 1500 to the Present* (London: Thames and Hudson, 1988).

Massey, A. *Hollywood beyond the Screen: Design and Material Culture* (Oxford: Berg, 2000).

Mayer, A. *The Persistence of the Old Regime: Europe to the Great War* (New York: Pantheon, 1981).

McCann, G. *Marilyn Monroe* (Cambridge: Polity, 1988).

McCann, G. *Cary Grant: A Class Apart* (London: Fourth Estate, 1996).

McDowell, C. *Dressed to Kill: Sex, Power and Clothes* (London: Hutchinson, 1992).

McKibbin, R. *Classes and Cultures: England 1918–1951* (Oxford: Oxford University Press, 1998)

Meyrowitz, J. *No Sense of Place: The Impact of Electronic Media on Social Behaviour* (New York: Oxford University Press, 1986).

Middleton, W. 'Prince Val', *W* (April 1997).

Miller, M. *The Bon Marché: Bourgeois Culture and the Department Store 1869–1920* (Princeton, NJ: Princeton University Press, 1981).

Mizejewski, L. *Ziegfeld Girl: Image and Icon in Culture and Cinema* (Durham, NC: Duke University Press, 1999).

Montgomery, M. E. *Displaying Women: Spectacles of Leisure in Edith Wharton's New York* (New York: Routledge, 1998).

Morais, R. *Pierre Cardin: The Man Who Became a Label* (London: Bantam, 1991).

Morin, E. *The Stars* (New York: Grove Press, 1960).

Morin, E. *Les Stars* (Paris: Seuil, 1972; first published 1957).

Morin, C. *Dead Glamorous: An Autobiography of Seduction and Self-Destruction* (London: Gollancz, 1996).

Morini, E. 'Bianco e nero di moda', in M. Carmigiani *et al. Bianco e Nero* (Novara: Dr Agostini, 1991).

Mosse, G. L. *The Nationalization of the Masses* (New York: Fertig, 1975).

Mulvey, L. 'Visual Pleasure and Narrative Cinema', in *Visual and Other Pleasures* (Basingstoke: Macmillan, 1989).

Murray Greenway, S. 'Time to Shine', *Vogue* (May 1997), p. 173.

Need, L. *Victorian Babylon* (New Haven, Conn.: Yale University Press, 2000).

Nicefero, A. *Parigi: una città rinnovata* (Turin: Bocca, 1911).

Normant, S. *Femme Fatale* (New York: Viking, 2001).

O'Shea Borrelli, L. 'Dressing up and Talking about it: Fashion Writing in *Vogue* from 1968 to 1993', *Fashion Theory* 3 (1997), pp. 247–59.

O'Sickey, L. '*Barbie Magazine* and the Aesthetic Commodification of Girls' Bodies', in S. Benstock and S. Ferriss (eds.) *On Fashion* (New Brunswick: Rutgers University Press, 1994).

Olson, S. *John Singer Sargent: His Portrait* (London: Barrie and Jenkins, 1986).

Ortoleva, P. *Un ventennio e colori* (Firenze: Giunti, 1995).

Paglia, C. *Sexual Personae: Art and Decadence from Nefertiti to Emily Dickinson* (Harmondsworth: Penguin, 1992).

Paglia, C. *The Birds* (London: BFI, 1998).

Paris, B. *Garbo* (London: Pan, 1996; first published 1995).

Pastoreau, J. *La stoffa del diavolo* (Genova: Il Melansolo, 1991).

Peiss, K. 'Making up, Making over: Cosmetics, Consumer Culture and Women's Identity', in V. de Grazia and E. Furlough (eds.) *The Sex of Things: Gender and Consumption in Historical Perspective* (Berkeley: University of California Press, 1996).

Peiss, K. *Hope in a Jar: The Making of America's Beauty Culture* (New York: Metropolitan/Holt, 1998).

Pemble, J. *Venice Rediscovered* (Oxford: Oxford University Press, 1995).

Powdermaker, H. *Hollywood: The Dream Factory* (Boston: Little, Brown, 1950).

Praz, M. *La carne, la morte e il diavolo nella letteratura romantica* (Firenze: Sanzoni, 1986, first edition 1948).

Prendergast, C. *Paris and the Nineteenth Century* (Oxford: Blackwell, 1992).

Prettejohn, E. 'Sargent and the End of High Society', *Tate: The Art Magazine*, 16 (Winter 1998).

Prince, L. *About Glamour* (New York: Simon and Schuster, 1997).

Prodow, P. *et al. Hollywood Jewels: Movies, Jewelry, Stars* (New York: Abrams, 1992).

Rappaport, E. D. *Shopping for Pleasure: Women and the Making of London's West End* (Princeton, NJ: Princeton University Press, 2000).

Rearick, C. *Pleasures of the Belle Epoque* (New Haven, Conn.: Yale University Press, 2002).

Reekie, G. *Temptations: Sex, Selling and the Department Store* (St Leonards, NSW: Allen and Unwin, 1993).

Reisman, D. *The Lonely Crowd: A Study of the Changing American Character* (New Haven, Conn.: Yale University Press, 1950).

Rémaury, B. 'L'illusion et l'apparence', in A. Masson (ed.) *Hollywood 1927–1941* (Paris: Editions Autremont, 1991).

Richards, J. *The Age of the Dream Palace: Cinema and Society in Britain 1930–1939* (London: Routledge, 1984).

Richardson, J. *The Courtesans* (London: Weidenfeld and Nicolson, 1967).

Richardson, J. *La Vie parisienne 1852–1870* (London: Hamish Hamilton, 1971).

Richardson, S. 'The Shining', *Vogue* (British edition) (December 1997).

Rosa, J. (ed.). *Glamour: Fashion + Industrial Design + Architecture* (San Francisco: San Francisco Museum of Art, 2004).

Rosen, M. *Popcorn Venus: Women, Movies and the American Dream* (London: Owen, 1973).

Ross, K. Introduction to E. Zola, *The Ladies' Paradise* (Berkeley: University of California Press, 1992).

Rotta, R. 'Sixties in Vogue', *Vogue Italia* (March 1995).

Rubinstein, H. *My Life for Beauty* (London: Bodley Head, 1964).

Ryan, D. D. 'A Night to Remember', *Vanity Fair* (July 1996), pp. 112–31.

Said, E. W. *Orientalism: Western Perceptions of the Orient* (Harmondsworth: Penguin 1995; first edition 1978).

Schickel, R. *Douglas Fairbanks: The First Celebrity* (London: Elm Tree Books, 1976).

Schwichtenberg, C. 'Introduction', in C. Schwichtenberg (ed.) *The Madonna Connection: Representational Politics, Subcultural Identities and Cultural Theory* (Boulder, Col.: Westview, 1993).

Seebohm, C. *The Man Who Was Vogue: The Life and Times of Condé Nast* (London: Weidenfeld and Nicolson, 1982).

Seidner, D. 'Still Dance', in D. Seidner (ed.) *Lisa Fonssagrives: Three Decades of Classic Fashion Photography* (London: Thames and Hudson, 1997).

Sherman Loomis, R. *Celtic Myth and Arthurian Romance* (London: Constable, 1993).

Showalter, E. *Sexual Anarchy* (New York: W. W. Norton, 1990).

Shulman, I. *Jean Harlow: An Intimate Biography* (London: Warner, 1992).

Shuzo, K. *La struttura dell'iki* (Milan: Adelphi, 1992).

Silverman, D. *Selling Culture: Bloomingdale's Diana Vreeland and the New Aristocracy of Taste in Reagan's America* (New York: Pantheon, 1986).

Sklar, R. *Movie-made America* (New York: Random House, 1975).

Solomon-Godeau, A. 'The Other Side of Venus: The Visual Economy of Feminine Display', in V. de Grazia and E. Furlough (eds.) *The Sex of Things: Gender and Consumption in Historical Perspective* (Berkeley: University of California Press, 1996).

Sombart, W. *Luxury and Capitalism* (Ann Arbor: University of Michigan Press, 1967).

Spadini, P. 'La "civilisation de piacere" ', in L. Chiavarelli *et al., La Belle Epoque* (Rome: Casini, 1966).

Spann, E. K. *The New Metropolis: New York City, 1840–1857* (New York: Columbia University Press, 1981).

Sparke, P. *As Long as It's Pink: The Sexual Politics of Taste* (London: Pandora, 1995).

Stacey, J. *Star Gazing: Hollywood Cinema and Female Spectatorship* (London: Routledge, 1994).

Steegman, V. *Victorian Taste* (London: Century, 1987; first published 1950).

Steele, V. *Fashion and Eroticism: Ideals of Feminine Beauty from the Victorian Era to the Jazz Age* (New York: Oxford University Press, 1985).

Steele, V. *Paris Fashion* (New York: Oxford University Press, 1988).

Stendhal. *Rome, Naples, Florence* (London: Calder, 1959).

Stokes, J., Booth, M. R. and Bassnett, S. 'Introduction', *Bernhardt, Terry, Duse: The Actress in her Time* (Cambridge: Cambridge University Press, 1988).

Stuart, A. *Showgirls* (London: Cape, 1996).

Swanson, G. *Swanson on Swanson* (London: Joseph, 1981).

Sweet, M. *Inventing the Victorians* (London: Faber, 2001).

Tapert, A. *The Power of Glamour* (London: Aurum, 1998).

Tapert, A. and Edkins, D. *The Power of Style* (London: Aurum Press, 1995).

Theroux, A. *The Primary Colours* (London: Picador, 1996).

Theweleit, F. *Male Fantasies* (Cambridge: Polity, 1987).

Thorp, M. F. *America at the Movies* (London: Faber and Faber, 1945; first published 1939).

Tobias, A. *Fire and Ice: The Story of Charles Revson – The Man Who Built the Revlon Empire* (New York: Morrow, 1976).

Tolstoy, N. *The Quest for Merlin* (London: Hamish Hamilton, 1985).

Tynan, K. 'Garbo', *Sight and Sound* (April–June 1954).

Vadim, R. *Bardot, Deneuve and Fonda* (London: NEL, 1987; first published 1983).

Valeri, D. *Parigi, 1912–1913 nelle impressioni di un giovane 'boursier'* (Milan: Treves, 1920).

Veblen, T. *Theory of the Leisure Class* (Boston: Houghton Mifflin, 1973; first published 1899).

Vickers, H. *Cecil Beaton* (London: Weidenfeld, 1985).

Vreeland, D. *DV: An Autobiography of Diana Vreeland* (New York: Knopf, 1984).

Walker, A. *Sex in the Movies* (Harmondsworth: Penguin, 1968).

Ward, J. *Weimar Surfaces: Urban Visual Culture in the 1920s Germany* (Berkeley: University of California Press, 2001).

Warner, M. *Monuments and Maidens* (London: Weidenfeld and Nicolson, 1985).

Warner, M. *From the Beast to the Blonde* (London: Chatto and Windus, 1994).

Weber, M. *On Charisma and Institution Building*, ed. S. N. Eisenstadt (Chicago: University of Chicago Press, 1968).

Weil, A. *The Marriage of the Sun and Moon* (Boston: Houghton Mifflin, 1980).

White, P. *Elsa Schiaparelli: Empress of Paris Fashion* (London: Aurum, 1995).

Whitford, F. 'A Man Driven to Distraction', *The Sunday Times*, culture section (3 August 1997).

Williams, R. *Dream Worlds: Mass Consumption in Late Nineteenth-Century France* (Berkeley: University of California Press, 1982).

Wilson, E. *Adorned in Dreams: Fashion and Modernity* (London: Virago, 1987).

Wilson, E. and Taylor, L. *Through the Looking Glass: A History of Dress from 1860 to the Present Day* (London: BBC Books, 1989).

Wolf, N. *The Beauty Myth* (London: Chatto and Windus, 1990).

Wollen, P. 'Plastics: The Magical and the Prosaic', in M. Francis and M. King (eds.) *The Warhol Look: Glamour, Style, Fashion* (New York: Little, Brown, 1998).

Ziegler, P. *Diana Cooper* (London: Penguin 1983; first published 1981).

Zola, E. *Nana* (Oxford: Oxford University Press edition, 1992).

Zola, E. *Au Bonheur des Dames* (Paris: Fasquelle, 1998; first published 1883).

Index